micro-PROLOG:

PROGRAMMING IN LOGIC

Prentice-Hall International
Series in Computer Science
C. A. R. Hoare, Series Editor

Published

micro-PROLOG:
PROGRAMMING IN LOGIC

K.L. Clark
and
F.G. McCabe

with contributions by:

M.H. van Emden
J.R. Ennals
P. Hammond
R.A. Kowalski
F. Kriwaczek
M.J. Sergot

Prentice/Hall **PHI** International

Englewood Cliffs, New Jersey · London · New Delhi
Rio de Janeiro · Singapore · Sydney · Tokyo · Toronto · Wellington

Library of Congress Cataloging in Publication Data
Clark, K. L. (Keith L.)
  micro-PROLOG: programming in logic.

  Bibliography: p.
  Includes index.
  1. micro-PROLOG (Computer program language) I. McCabe,
Frank, 1953–   .   II. Title.
QA76.73.M5C55 1983   001.64'2   83–16066
ISBN 0–13–581264–X (pbk.)

British Library Cataloging in Publication Data
Clark, Keith L.
  micro-PROLOG.
  1. PROLOG (Computer program language)
  2. Microprocessors
  I. Title   II. McCabe, Frank G.
  001.64'24   QA76.73.P/
  ISBN 0–13–581264–X

© 1984 by Logic Programming Associates, Ltd.

ISBN 0–13–581264–X

PRENTICE-HALL INTERNATIONAL, INC., *London*
PRENTICE-HALL OF AUSTRALIA PTY. LTD., *Sydney*
PRENTICE-HALL CANADA, INC., *Toronto*
PRENTICE-HALL OF INDIA PRIVATE LIMITED, *New Delhi*
PRENTICE-HALL OF JAPAN, INC., *Tokyo*
PRENTICE-HALL OF SOUTHEAST ASIA PTE. LTD., *Singapore*
PRENTICE-HALL INC., *Englewood Cliffs, New Jersey*
PRENTICE-HALL DO BRASIL LTDA., *Rio de Janeiro*
WHITEHALL BOOKS LIMITED, *Wellington, N.Z.*

Printed in the United States of America

10 9 8 7 6 5 4 3 2

Contents

Part II Logic programming using micro-PROLOG   121
K.L. Clark & F.G. McCabe

Preface

This book is a self instruction tutorial on logic programming using micro-PROLOG (version 3.1 or later) for someone unfamiliar with PROLOG logic programming. The concepts of logic programming and the corresponding features of micro-PROLOG are introduced step by step through the development of a series of example programs.

Exercises, with answers given at the back of this book, reinforce and elaborate on the example programs. Ideally, the examples and exercises should be followed using a computer, but this is not essential.

micro-PROLOG is currently available for Z80 machines under CP/M80 and for 8088/86 machines under MSDOS. It is also available for the Sinclair Spectrum, the Acorn BBC micro and other computers which have the UNIX operating system.

Since micro-PROLOG is one of the PROLOG family of logic programming languages (PROLOG stands for **PRO**gramming in **LOG**ic), each of which is a derivative of the version of the language as first implemented in 1972/73 in Marseilles, the book also serves as an introduction to logic programming using any version of PROLOG. The differences between micro-PROLOG and the other PROLOGs are mostly in the syntax of programs and in the allowed forms of query.

Structure of the book

The book is divided into four parts. Part I introduces the basic concepts of logic programming emphasising the use of logic and of micro-PROLOG as a data description and data query language. Part II deals with more advanced concepts and the corresponding features of micro-PROLOG. The emphasis is more on the list processing uses of logic. Part III introduces the standard syntax of micro-PROLOG, the syntax into which the programs of Parts I and II are compiled. It also describes features of the language that enable other logic programming systems to be implemented on top of micro-PROLOG. Finally, Part IV has four guest Chapters dealing with applications of micro-PROLOG. They introduce the use of logic programming in the areas of game playing, problem solving, expert systems and critical path analysis.

The Chapters in each section are more fully described in the introductory Chapter 0 that precedes Part I. This Chapter also gives a flavour of the style of programming that is logic programming.

System note - using this book in conjunction with a computer - if you have access to a computer with micro-PROLOG on it, you may want to follow the examples and exercises in this book on the computer. To allow this we have included a number of *System notes* (such as this one) on using micro-PROLOG on a real computer. Usually System notes refer to non-logic programming activities such as interrupting program execution.

If a computer is used you may sometimes need to consult a micro-PROLOG Reference Manual for the implemention being used. This is because the book only describes the features of the language that are available in every implementation and it does not describe the machine specific features such as the use of the line editor.

Acknowledgements

The approach to programming using logic which underlies many of the ideas presented in this book was supported by the British Science & Engineering Research Council in a series of research grants held by R.A.Kowalski and K.L.Clark at Imperial College. Of particular relevance is the "Logic as a Computer Language for Children" project which is concerned with teaching the principles of logic programming to school children. This project uses micro-PROLOG. The extension to the standard micro-PROLOG, which is the SIMPLE program development system described and used in this book, is an enhancement of the program development system that was used on the school's project. We are also grateful to the groups of people in various parts of the world who have acted as hosts for demonstrations and talks on logic programming using micro-PROLOG. These provided excellent opportunities for testing different methods of explanation to interested non-specialists.

Finally, the authors would like to thank Diane Reeve and Sandra Evans whose patient 'slaving over a hot word processor' during the preparation of the early drafts made this book possible.

0.   Introduction

0.1   Why program in micro-PROLOG

Ever since von Neumann first described the form of the stored program computer they have been programmed in essentially the same way. The first programming language was the binary language of the machine itself: machine code; then came assembler, which is symbolic machine code; then the so-called high level languages like FORTRAN, COBOL and BASIC, followed by today's more modern variants ADA and Pascal. All of these programming languages share a common characteristic: the programmer must describe quite precisely *how* a result is to be computed, rather than *what* it is that must be computed.

A computer program in one of these programming languages consists of a script of instructions each of which describes an action to be performed by the computer. For example, the *meaning* of the BASIC statement:

10 LET X = 105*X + 10

is that the memory location whose name is X should have its contents updated to 10 plus 105 times the old value in the location.

Languages like BASIC are primarily *imperative* programming languages. Programs in these languages mostly comprise commands which specify actions to be performed. They are geared to the description of the *behaviour* needed to achieve the desired result.

While undoubtedly we sometimes *think* behaviourally, most often we do not. For example, the first question we ask someone about a particular computer program is:

1

"What does it do?"

not:

"How does it do it?"

Certainly the answer to the first question will not be:

```
1 INPUT X,Y
2 IF X>Y THEN 5
3 PRINT Y
4 GOTO 6
5 PRINT X
6 END
```

We shall *not* list the program. What we are more likely to do is to describe the *relation* between the input and output of the program. We might say, for example, "it prints the greater of the two numbers read-in". If our enquirer did not understand what "greater of two numbers" meant we would give a descriptive definition of the relation, perhaps defining the "greater-of" input/output relation in terms of the ">" order relation on numbers.

Even imperative programming languages have descriptive components. For example, the expression $105*X+10$ in the above example assignment is a description of the value to be assigned. It is not the sequence of actions that the computer must perform in order to compute its value. Arithmetic expressions are small descriptive programs - they describe the value to be computed and only indirectly do they prescribe the way it should be computed. Indeed, in some programming languages the order of evaluation of expressions is explicitly left undefined.

The high-level imperative languages are easier to use than assembler language precisely because *they are more descriptive.* Generally, the more descriptive the language the easier it is to develop a correct program, and the closer the program to a specification of what it computes.

Descriptive versus imperative languages

The alternative to an imperative programming language with a descriptive component is a descriptive language with an imperative component: a language in which programs are primarily *descriptive definitions* of a set of relations or functions to be computed.

The *execution* of a descriptive program is then a use of the definitions to find an output corresponding to a given input. The way in which the definitions are used in order to compute the output value gives each definition an alternative imperative or control reading. By taking into account the control reading we might prefer one set of definitions to another, and we might improve the efficiency of the evaluation by adding extra control conditions to the definition which are ignored in the descriptive reading. This is the *pragmatics* of programming in a descriptive language. However, it is still the case that the program is primarily a description of *what* it is supposed to compute, rather than a description of *how* to compute it.

micro-PROLOG is an example of a descriptive language. It is based on predicate logic, a language developed by logicians as a formal language of description. "PROLOG" stands for **PRO**gramming in **LOG**ic. The "micro" means that it is implemented on micro-computers.

A micro-PROLOG program is essentially a set of logical definitions of relations. An execution of the program is a use of these definitions to compute instances of the relations.

The following micro-PROLOG program:

```
x greater-of (x x)
y greater-of (x y) if x LESS y
x greater-of (x y) if y LESS x
```

is a definition of the input/output relation of the above BASIC program. It is a program comprising three rules expressed as sentences of predicate logic. The x and y are variables representing any numbers. Each rule is a true statement about the "greater-of" relation. To use it to find the greater of two numbers 3.45 and 67.34 we pose the query:

```
which(x : x greater-of (3.45 67.34))
```

The answer 67.34 is returned by an evaluation which computes a value of x that satisfies the condition "x greater-of (3.45 67.34)" using the definition of the relation.

Multi-use definitions

This single definition of the relation is a program for *finding* or *checking* the greater of a pair of numbers. This ability to use definitions of relations for both finding and checking is a distinctive feature of logic programming and micro-PROLOG. Indeed, it is often the case that a single definition of some input/output relation can be used in the inverse mode. It can be used to find an input that will give rise to a particular output! This invertibility of use is onle possibly because the program is descriptive. In an imperative language programs have only one use because they directly encode the sequence of evaluation steps of that use.

An example of an invertible program is the program for the pre-defined relation **TIMES** (it is part of the micro-PROLOG language).

TIMES(x y z)

is satisfied if and only if $z = x*y$. This relation can be used both to multiply and divide. To multiply we use a query such as:

which(x : TIMES(34 2.4 x))

To divide we use a query such as:

which(x : TIMES(23 x 106))

Data base programs

Logically viewed, a data base is a set of facts defining one or more relations. micro-PROLOG treats data base relations in the same way that it treats input/output relations of programs. Data base relations are defined by a sequence of facts such as:

(Smith D) salary 1800
(Jones K L) salary 1850

To retrieve Smith's salary we use the query:

which(x : (Smith D) salary x)

To find all the employees with a salary less than 1800 the query:

which(x : x salary y & y LESS 1800)

is used. **LESS** is another pre-defined relation of micro-PROLOG.

We can also include rules in the definition of a data base relation. For example, we might have the rule:

x salary 1600 if x job-is junior-clerk

expressing the company 'rule' that all junior clerks have a fixed salary. By mixing facts and rules we get *deductive data bases*. Retrieving information from a deductive data base is a computational inference using the facts and the rules.

Pattern directed rule based programming

micro-PROLOG computes by trying to find values for the variables of a query such that every condition of the query is a consequence of the definitions of the program.

It does this by searching through all the sentences for each condition matching the condition with the conclusion of the sentence. When it finds a match, the pre-conditions of the matched sentence represent a new query which must be solved to give a solution to the matched condition.

This use of a matched rule to reduce a condition to a new query is pattern directed rule based programming. It is a style of programming that is increasingly being used in Artificial Intelligence, particularly for Expert Systems.

List Processing

Using special list patterns, relations can be defined over lists. As an example

x belongs-to (x|z)
x belongs-to (y|z) if x belongs-to z

defines the list membership relation. The pattern "(x|z)" is read: the list which is the element x followed by the list z. This definition can be used for checking membership or as a *non-deterministic* program for generating elements of a list. It is used in both roles in the query:

all(x : x belongs-to (1 2 3 4) & x belongs-to (3 4 5 6))

which has the answers 3,4. all is a synonym for which. Non-deterministic pattern directed list processing is a unique feature of PROLOG and logic programming.

Imperative features

micro-PROLOG does have imperative features. For example, it has commands to add and delete sentences in programs, to edit sentences, and to read or write to the terminal or a file. Commands can be used in programs and program defined relations can be used as commands. Thus, micro-PROLOG programs can be written which define new commands in terms of the primitive commands of the system. In this way the knowledgeable programmer can tailor the system to a specific application, or build up his own programming environment of special commands.

0.2   Chapter descriptions

The rest of the book is divided into four parts. We briefly describe the contents of each chapter.

Part I Basic Concepts

Chapter 1 introduces micro-PROLOG by using it to develop and query a data base of facts. The ease with which one can construct and query such a data base is one of the prime features of the language. The chapter also introduces the built-in arithmetic facilities of micro-PROLOG. These are quite different from those of a conventional programming language. We add *and* subtract by querying an (implicit) data base of facts about the addition relation, likewise we multiply and divide by querying a data base of 'times tables'.

Chapter 2 describes how the data base can be augmented by rules. Rules can be used to abbreviate queries. They can also be used to give a recursive definition of a relation.

Chapter 3 introduces lists and describes how they can be

used to structure information, often compressing many statements into one. The elements of a list are accessed using special list patterns. This pattern processing of lists is a major feature of micro-PROLOG. The chapter ends by introducing the "isall" condition. This can be used to wrap up the *set* of answers to a query as a *list*. It provides the interface between the use of micro-PROLOG as a data base language and its use as a list manipulation language.

Part II Logic Programming using micro-PROLOG

Chapter 4 describes new forms of condition that can be used in queries and rules. These involve the use of: "not", "forall .. then .." and "either .. or ..". The use of these conditions significantly enhances the power of micro-PROLOG for data base applications and for the development of 'executable' specifications. Expressions are also introduced: these are compiled into conditions for the arithmetic primitives described in Chapter 1.

Chapter 4 also describes the relation **is-told** which can be used to make micro-PROLOG query us whilst it is answering one of our queries. This relation can be used to facilitate the top-down development of programs and to write simple query the user expert systems.

Chapter 5 describes several programs for more complex list processing tasks. In particular it examines the "append" program that defines the appending relation over lists. We shall see that it has very many uses. It can be used not only to append two lists but to find all splittings of a list, even to define the membership relation for a list. The Chapter ends with the development of three list sorting programs, one of which is a specification of the sort relation.

Chapter 6 is an introduction to the use of micro-PROLOG for parsing - the mapping of lists of words into lists of lists that reflect the grammatical structure of the sentence. Parsing and natural language understanding are major applications of logic programming, applications for which it is highly suited.

Chapter 7 deals with some issues concerned with the pragmatics of programming in micro-PROLOG. It describes various features of the language that can be used to reduce the space used or the time taken during a query evaluation.

In Chapter 8 the imperatives of micro-PROLOG are introduced. These are built-in relations that have a side-effect when they are evaluated. An example is the built-in relation that reads data from the terminal. Its logical reading is: something that can be read at the terminal. Its control reading is: read the *next thing to be typed*.

The imperatives of micro-PROLOG detract somewhat from its descriptive nature, a program that uses them is not a purely descriptive program. However, as we shall see, the use of the imperatives can often be restricted to the definition of one or two auxiliary relations, the rest of the program being entirely descriptive.

More positively, the availability of such imperatives as primitives of the language enables the programmer to tailor the system to his own needs by developing his own program development system. This is illustrated by the development of a simplified version of the is-told relation introduced in Chapter 4.

Part III Core micro-PROLOG

In Chapter 9 we describe the standard syntax of a micro-PROLOG program. This is the form in which the facts and rules are accessed and evaluated by the micro-PROLOG interpreter. It is also the form in which programs are saved on backing store. The user friendly sentence syntax, the syntax used in Chapters 1 to 8, is translated into the standard syntax by the SIMPLE program development system used to develop the programs of Parts I and II. SIMPLE is itself a micro-PROLOG program written in the standard syntax.

All micro-PROLOG programs are just lists of a special form. It is therefore very easy to write micro-PROLOG programs that manipulate lists that are other micro-PROLOG programs. In Chapter 9 we show how this is done by the SIMPLE program and we introduce one or two features of micro-PROLOG that can only be used by programs written in the standard syntax. We also give micro-PROLOG definitions of the various forms of query that have been used in Parts I and II and show how alternative query evaluators can be defined as micro-PROLOG programs.

Part IV Applications of micro-PROLOG

There are four chapters in Part IV in which various guest authors illustrate some of the applications of micro-PROLOG.

Frank Kriwaczek in Chapter 10 looks at project management using critical path analysis techniques. This is an everyday application of graph searching: the activities which make up a complex project form a loop free graph, and the critical path analysis program searches this graph for various kinds of paths.

In Chapter 11 Peter Hammond introduces some of the methods needed for today's Expert Systems. An Expert System is a collection of 'rules of thumb' which an expert uses in solving problems in his area of expertise. An Expert System is built by formalising the expert's rules of thumb and allowing micro-PROLOG to use them to solve problems itself.

Maarten van Emdem and Keith Clark develop in Chapter 12 some of the classical algorithms used in game playing programs such as chess. The game of Nim is used as a simple example though the techniques have been the basis of many computer chess programs.

Finally in Chapter 13 Marek Sergot and Bob Kowalski give a taste of general purpose problem solving methods. By looking at some simple examples, the farmer, goat, wolf and cabbage problem and the water containers problem, a number of important issues in problem solving are tackled.

Part I
Basic Concepts

1.   Facts and queries

1.1   Developing a data base of facts

In this chapter we introduce some of the basic ideas of logic programming by giving an example of the setting up and querying of a data base in micro-PROLOG.

System note - using micro-PROLOG on a computer - If you have access to a computer which has micro-PROLOG we recommend that you follow through the examples and exercises using the computer. **You need to load the SIMPLE front-end system along with micro-PROLOG.** SIMPLE is a program supplied on the micro-PROLOG distribution tape or disk. Consult the micro-PROLOG documentation for the computer you are using for details of how to start up micro-PROLOG and LOAD SIMPLE.

Adding facts

Let us suppose that we want to set up a data base describing the family relationships of some group of people. We will do this by making statements about these relationships, adding them one at a time to the data base.

The statements are expressed as sentences of symbolic logic. There are two kinds of sentences: *simple* and *conditional*. To begin with we shall only need simple sentences which express facts.

In any family there are a number of facts about the relationships between individuals. Let us suppose that for our group of people two such facts are:

Henry Snr is the father of Henry	(1)
Henry Snr is the father of Mary	(2)

There are many such facts, each of which describes an instance of one of the family relationships. Now these English sentences are almost sentences of micro-PROLOG! One form of micro-PROLOG sentence has three components:

name-of-individual name-of-relationship name-of-individual

In sentences (1) and (2) above the name-of-relationship is "is the father of". In micro-PROLOG we have to make this into one word by hyphenating, so we must use: "is-the-father-of" or "father-of" for brevity. Similarly, we must name individuals by a single word. Again we can do this by hyphenating, writing "Henry-Snr" instead of "Henry Snr". Rewriting (1) and (2) in this way transforms them into sentences of micro-PROLOG.

Henry-Snr father-of Henry
Henry father-of Mary

These two sentences in a micro-PROLOG data base are a direct representation of the two facts (1) and (2). We enter them into the data base using a special **add** command.

&.add (Henry-Snr father-of Henry)
&.add (Henry father-of Mary)

Notice that the sentence to be added is surrounded by brackets. The brackets are essential: they tell micro-PROLOG where the sequence of words in the sentence to be added begins and ends. For micro-PROLOG a sentence is a bracketed list of words of a certain form.

System note - errors and prompts - The "&." is not typed, it is the prompt printed out by micro-PROLOG to tell us it is ready to accept a command. Moreover, each add command must be terminated by hitting the **RETURN** or **ENTER** key on the keyboard. Before you hit this key you can correct typing mistakes using the **RUBOUT**, **BACKSPACE** or **DELETE** key to delete back to before the mistake. Which one you use depends on the computer.

Alternatively, you can use the line editor for the version of micro-PROLOG that you are using: this will enable you to correct mistakes without the need to retype every thing after the mistake. The line editor is described in the micro-PROLOG documentation that is specific to your computer (it is different for different machines).

When you are satisfied that what you have typed needs no more correction, hit the **RETURN** or **ENTER** key. micro-PROLOG will then obey the command. If there is a mistake in the syntax of the sentence, for example if you forget to put the hyphen in "father-of", you will get an error message telling you that the sentence is not a valid simple sentence form. If you misspell the "add", using say "ADD" instead, you will get the error message

> No definition for relation
> trying ADD(......)

This is because the relation/command name "ADD" is not one of the defined command names of micro-PROLOG or the SIMPLE front-end system that we are using. If you get either error message the sentence has not been accepted, so try again with a new **add** command. (If you correctly spell **add** and you get an error message of the form:

> Error: 2

this probably means that you have forgotten to **LOAD SIMPLE**.)

You do not have to type all of the bracketed sentence on a single line; indeed, some sentences may be longer than the display line of your computer. As you come to the end of the display line, check that what you have typed on that line is correct and edit it if need be.

When you are satisfied that there is no mistake, hit the **RETURN** or **ENTER** key. You will now get the prompt

> 1.

instead of the usual command prompt "&." This indicates that micro-PROLOG knows that the current command is not complete. Actually, the "1" indicates that micro-PROLOG is still waiting for the single right bracket that marks the end of the sentence to be added. The "." is the read prompt that micro-PROLOG always displays when it is ready to read from the keyboard.

If you have used brackets within the sentence, and later we shall make considerable use of bracketed lists within sentences, the prompt may be "2." or "3." or even some higher number. The number is always the number of right brackets needed to properly finish the sentence. You will find this right bracket prompt very useful when we start using lists.

Different kinds of relationship

A relationship such as "father-of" holds between pairs of individuals, in this case between a 'father' and a 'child'. It is a *binary* relation. Not all relationships are between pairs, some relate three or more individuals, and some are properties that apply to single individuals. The genders "male" and "female" are properties.

(More technically, they are *unary* relations.) The relation of *someone* giving *something* to *someone* is a three place relation (a *ternary* relation). Sentences giving facts about these non-binary relations have a slightly different syntax.

Sentences about properties are written in the *postfix* form

name-of-individual name-of-property

in which the name of the property follows the name of the individual. Sentences about all other relations are written in the *prefix* form

relation-name(individual-name .. individual-name)

in which the relation name precedes a bracketed list of the individuals related by the relation.

The form:

name-of-individual relation-name name-of individual

used for sentences about binary relations is called *infix* form.

Examples of sentences for non-binary relations are:

Henry male
Gives(Henry Mary book)
SUM(2 3 5)

The prefix form of sentence is the most general form. Sentences for binary relations and for properties can be also be entered using the prefix form. Thus,

father-of(Henry-Snr Henry)
is-male(Henry)

are accepted equivalents of

Henry-Snr father-of Henry
Henry male

but the infix and postfix forms are arguably more readable. Even if you enter sentences about binary relations or properties in the prefix form micro-PROLOG will display them in the binary and postfix forms when you list or edit the program.

A technical term - argument of a relation

A fact tells us that certain individuals are related by some relation. In mathematics and logic the individuals are called the *arguments* of the relation. We also talk about the first argument, the second argument, etc., of the relation. This names the argument by its position in the list of arguments of the prefix form of sentence for the relation. In the sentence

Gives(Henry Mary book)

"Henry" is the first argument, "Mary" the second and "book" the third.

System note - the use of spaces - The spaces separating the names of the individuals and the names of the relations are necessary. In micro-PROLOG spaces and the new lines generated by hitting the **RETURN** or **ENTER** key are word separators. However, micro-PROLOG only knows about the new lines that result from the hitting of the **RETURN** or **ENTER** keys. An automatic new line caused by your typing beyond the end of the previous line is ignored by micro-PROLOG. It does not count as a separator.

The number of separators you use does not matter, but failure to use a separator may mean that micro-PROLOG makes into one name what you intended to have as two names.

You do not always need to use a separator: micro-PROLOG can sometimes detect the end of one word and the beginning of the next by a change of character type. For example, a "(" or ")" always signals the end of the word that precedes it so you never need to follow or precede a bracket with a space.

For more detailed information on what is or is not understood by micro-PROLOG as a word boundary, we refer the reader to the reference manual for the implementation you are using. *If in doubt, use a space.*

The converse of the need to use spaces as separators is the need to hyphenate phrases such as "father of" in order to make it *one* name, not two.

Adding some more facts

Carrying on, let us enter some more family relationship facts.

&.add(Elizabeth1 mother-of Henry)

```
&.add(Katherine mother-of Mary)
&.add(Henry father-of Elizabeth2)
&.add(Ann mother-of Elizabeth2)
&.add(Henry father-of Edward)
&.add(Jane mother-of Edward)
&.add(Henry-Snr male)
&.add(Henry male)
&.add(Elizabeth1 female)
&.add(Katherine female)
&.add(Mary female)
&.add(Elizabeth2 female)
&.add(Ann female)
&.add(Female(Jane))
&.add(Male(Edward))
```

Notice that we slipped in some "mother-of" facts and some facts about who is male and female. We can add sentences of any relationship at any time using the **add** command. The sentences are collected together by name of relationship. The vocabulary of a program consists of the names of the relationships and the names of the individuals; the vocabulary defines the "things" that a subsequent query can talk about. Our vocabulary so far is

Henry-Snr
Henry
Mary
Elizabeth1
Katherine   } Names of individuals
Elizabeth2
Ann
Edward
Jane

father-of
mother-of   } Names of relations
Male
Female

Notice that we have used numerals in the names "Elizabeth1" and "Elizabeth2" to distinguish the two Elizabeths. Numerals and "-" and all the letter characters of the keyboard all count as alphabetic characters in names. The only restriction is that the name cannot begin with a numeral. So,

   4jane

is not allowed although

   jane4

is. In fact, micro-PROLOG will interpret the

   4jane

as 4 jane

that is, as the number "4" followed by the separate name "jane". This is an example of the situation where micro-PROLOG interprets a change in character type as equivalent to the insertion of a separating space.

   Names made up of letters, numerals and "-" are just one type of name. They are called *alphanumeric constants*. Other kinds of constants - symbolic constants and quoted constants can also be used as names. We refer the reader to the micro-PROLOG Reference Manual for details. We shall mostly use alphanumeric constants as names.

The accept *command*

   The last two facts about the male and female properties that we added were expressed in the prefix form. There is a special command that speeds up the entering of a set of facts that are expressed in the prefix form: this command is **accept**. If you enter

   accept female

you will get the prompt

   female.

Now enter the list of arguments for the **female** fact that you want to enter, in this case a list of one argument. You will again get the name of the relation as a prompt. You can continue in this way, not having to type the name of the relation, only the list of arguments, until you have no more facts to enter about the relation. You signal this by entering **end** when you receive the relation name prompt.

Using accept, the following interaction could have been used to enter all the **male** and **female** facts that we have added so far.

```
 &.accept male
male.(Henry-Snr)
male.(Henry)
male.(Edward)
male.end
&.accept female
female.(Elizabeth1)
female.(Katherine)
female.(Mary)
female.(Elizabeth2)
female.(Ann)
female.(Jane)
female.end
```

The **emphasized** text is what we entered, the prompt being supplied by micro-PROLOG.

Listing and saving a program

We can display our data base program by using another command **list**. This command can be used to display on the screen all the sentences entered, or just those for a specified relation. To list the full program we type:

```
&.list all
Henry-Snr father-of Henry
Henry father-of Mary
Henry father-of Elizabeth2
Henry father-of Edward
Elizabeth1 mother-of Henry
Katherine mother-of Mary
Ann mother-of Elizabeth2
Jane mother-of Edward
Henry-Snr male
Henry male
Edward male
Elizabeth1 female
Katherine female
Mary female
Elizabeth2 female
Ann female
Jane female
&.
```

The sentences are grouped according to the name of the relation that they are about, not the order in which they were entered. However, the listing of the sentences for each relation does correspond to the order in which they were entered.

We can choose a particular relation and list that. For instance:

```
&.list mother-of
Elizabeth1 mother-of Henry
Katherine mother-of Mary
Ann mother-of Elizabeth2
Jane mother-of Edward
&.
```

We can save the current state of the data base on disk (or onto cassette tape if that is used by your computer) giving it a unique name of our choice, as follows:

```
&.save FAMILY
```

This copies all the sentences of the current program into a named file on backing store. The sentences still remain in the data base. However, on a subsequent occasion, we can retrieve these sentences and have them automatically added to any data base simply by typing:

&.load FAMILY

Editing by adding and deleting sentences

Editing of a micro-PROLOG program can be achieved by deleting a whole sentence and adding a new one to replace it. Let us suppose that the name of Elizabeth2's mother has been misspelled, and that it should be "Anne". The simplest way to remove the sentence "Ann mother-of Elizabeth2" is to use:

&.delete(Ann mother-of Elizabeth2)

This use of **delete** is the opposite of **add**. If the bracketed sentence given as the argument to the command is in the program, the **delete** command removes it. If it is not in the program, you will get a message telling you that there is no such sentence. You will get this message unless there is an *exact* match between the sentence to be deleted and some sentence of the current data base.

There is another way to delete a sentence, we can refer to it by its position in the listing of the sentences for its relation. In the listing of the relation "mother-of" given above the sentence "Ann mother-of Elizabeth2" was the third sentence to be listed. So, instead of giving the sentence to delete we can use an alternative form of the **delete** command in which the sentence is identified by its relation name and its position.

&.delete mother-of 3

Having deleted the sentence, using either form of the **delete** command, we can add the new version:

&.add(Anne mother-of Elizabeth2)

If we now list the "mother-of" relation we will get:

```
&.list mother-of
Elizabeth1 mother-of Henry
Katherine mother-of Mary
Jane mother-of Edward
Anne mother-of Elizabeth2
&.
```

The new sentence

Anne mother-of Elizabeth2

is now listed at the end because it was entered last.

Let us now correct the spelling of "Ann" in the "female" relation. This time we will *replace* the sentence "Ann female" with "Anne female". We do this by deleting the old sentence and adding the new one so that it occupies the same position in the listing of "female" sentences. The following are the commands needed together with the micro-PROLOG responses.

```
&.list female
Elizabeth1 female
Katherine female
Mary female
Elizabeth2 female
Ann female
Jane female
&.delete female 5
&.add 5 (Anne female)
&.list female
Elizabeth1 female
Katherine female
Mary female
Elizabeth2 female
Anne female
Jane female
&.
```

We have used a variant of the **add** command in which the position which the added sentence is to occupy is given.

add 5 (Anne female)

makes the added sentence the fifth sentence in a new listing of the relation. It does this by inserting it between the current fourth and fifth sentences, which is where the deleted sentence was.

Editing using the line editor

A quicker way to change a sentence about a relation, especially when the change required to the text is small, involves using the line editor for the computer you are using. You invoke the line editor using the **edit** command. Like the second form of delete, this identifies the sentence to be edited by the name of its relation and its current position in the listing of the sentences for the relation.

edit female 5

will result in

5 (Anne female)

being displayed ready for editing using the line editor.

System note - the line editor on your computer - For details of how to use the editor and how to exit when you have finished consult the micro-PROLOG documentation which is specific to the computer you are using.

Notice that the position of the sentence is given along with the bracketed sentence. By editing the position, say changing it from 5 to 4, you can reposition the sentence. Do not delete the brackets surrounding the sentence. Just as when you add a sentence, micro-PROLOG needs the brackets to delimit the text of the sentence when you exit the line editor.

Summary of program development commands

All of the following commands operate on the current program which is held in the user workspace area by micro-PROLOG. In giving the general form of each command we shall use angle brackets to denote some syntactic form. For example, we shall use sentence to indicate that any sentence can be used.

add   (i) add (<sentence>)

will add its bracketed sentence argument to the end of the current listing of sentences for its relation.

(ii) add n (<sentence>)

will add the bracketed sentence as a new n'th sentence in the listing of sentences for its relation. If there are currently less than n sentences it becomes the new last sentence. Otherwise, it is inserted between the current n-1'th sentence and the current n'th sentence.

delete   (i) delete (<sentence>)

will remove <sentence> from the current program.

(ii) delete <relation name> n

will remove the n'th sentence in the current list of sentences for the named relation.

list   (i) list <relation name>

lists all the sentences for the named relation in the current program.

(ii) list all

lists all the sentences in the workspace program.

save   save <file name>

will save all the sentences of the current state of your program in a file on backing store.

System note - micro-PROLOG files - The given file name must be different from the name of any relation of the program, and different from the name of any command. If it is not you will get the "File error" message and the save operation will be aborted. Try again using a different name. We suggest you use all capitals in the names of files to avoid clashes with relation names.

The name attached to the saved program file on backing store may be slightly different from the <file name> you give in the command although you can always refer to the file from within micro-PROLOG using the given <file name>. For example, for micro-PROLOG under CP/M, the directory name of the file will always end with ".LOG". Moreover, if you inspect or list the saved program file outside micro-PROLOG you will find that the sentences of your program have not been saved in the form in which you entered them. They are saved in a special compiled form that uses the *standard* syntax of micro-PROLOG.

kill   (i) kill <relation name>

deletes *all* sentences for the named relation.

           (ii) kill all

deletes all sentences from the workspace program. **You should only use this command after you have saved the program** - it clears the workspace for a fresh program.

edit   edit <relation name> n

Allows the current n'th sentence for the named relation to be edited using the line editor of the micro-PROLOG system you are using. The sentence (in brackets) and its position will be displayed ready for editing. By changing the position number you can reposition the sentence within the listing of sentences for its relation. You can change the position without changing the sentence if you just want to reposition. You can also change the relation name of the edited sentence. The position number is then the position that will be used when the edited sentence is added to the listing of sentences for the changed relation name.

QT   QT.

this command exits from the micro-PROLOG to the host system. As with "kill all", you should save your workspace program before using it. The "." after the "QT" is important. It is needed because all micro-PROLOG commands must have at least one argument. In this case the argument is the (ignored) ".". Any argument can be used.

           QT goodbye

will work just as well, but is not so brief.

Exercises 1-1

System note - save your program now - If you are following the text with a computer, at this stage you should save the program that has been developed, using the command:

save FAMILY

Before you attempt Exercise 2 you should clear the workspace of the family relations sentences using the command

kill all

After each exercise we suggest you save the current workspace and then clear it before entering the sentences for the next exercise. Answers to all the exercises are given in an Appendix.

1. Using the program developed above:

a. Show how you would edit the program to change the spelling of "Katherine" to "Catherine" in each sentence in which it appears using delete and add commands. Do this in such a way that the new sentences are in the same positions in the program as those they replace.

b. Add the two sentences necessary to express the information that Henry-Snr had a son called Arthur. Add these new sentences so that they will be listed at the beginning of the sentences for their relation.
   Clear the workspace before you attempt the next exercise.

2. Set up a data base of sentences describing countries in different continents using the following vocabulary:

Names of Individuals

Washington-DC	USA	North-America
Ottawa	Canada	Europe
London	United-Kingdom	Africa
Paris	Italy	
Rome	Nigeria	
Lagos	France	

Names of Relations

capital-of
country-in

As examples, your data base should contain the sentences:

Washington-DC capital-of USA
USA country-in North-America

Save this data for future use using the **save** command and then
clear the workspace.

3. Set up a data base of simple sentences describing the books of
different kinds written by different people. Use the following
vocabulary:

Names of Individuals

Tom-Sawyer	Mark-Twain	Novel
For-Whom-The-Bell-Tolls	Ernest-Hemingway	Play
Oliver-Twist	Arther-Miller	
Great-Expectations	Charles-Dickens	
Macbeth	William-Shakespeare	
Romeo-And-Juliet		
Death-Of-A-Salesman		

Names of Relations

type
written-by
writer

For example, you should have the sentences

Tom-Sawyer written-by Mark-Twain
Tom-Sawyer type Novel
Mark-Twain writer

in your data base. Save this data for future use with the **save**
command then clear the workspace.

4. Set up a data base describing the structure of a bicycle using
the vocabulary:

Names of Individuals

bicycle	wheel	pedals
frame	spoke	saddle
brake-system	hub	handle-bars
brake-cable	brake-block	lighting-system
gear-selector	chain	dynamo
lights	electric-flex	gear-cogs

Names of Relations

part-of

For example, your data base should contain the sentences:

wheel part-of bicycle
spoke part-of wheel
hub part-of wheel

Use the **accept** command to enter the sentences. Again, save the workspace sentences for future use and clear the workspace.

5. Set up a data base of your own family using the relation names of the example. Save it in the file MYFAMILY for future use and clear the workspace.

1.2   Queries

We now look at how a micro-PROLOG data base program is queried. This is done via one of the query commands. We shall illustrate the query commands using the FAMILY data base developed in 1.1. If this data base is not in the workspace (test this by trying to list the sentences for the "father-of" relation) clear the workspace and then load the FAMILY data with a "load FAMILY" command.

Confirmation

The simplest form of query is the **is** query which asks for confirmation of some fact. We explain this and other queries by posing some example questions in English. Below the questions we give the micro-PROLOG equivalent and the answers given by micro-PROLOG. A brief explanation is provided of points arising from the query.

Is Henry the father of Elizabeth2?
&.is(Henry father-of Elizabeth2)
YES

The query is asking about a particular member of the "father-of" relation described by the micro-PROLOG sentence "Henry father-of Elizabeth2". The is query is asking whether this sentence is in the data base. As with the add command the sentence to be 'looked up' must be bracketed. There is a match between the query sentence and the sentence

Henry father-of Elizabeth2

in the data base, so the answer is "YES", an abbreviation for "Yes, fact is confirmed".

Is Katherine the mother of Edward?
&.is(Katherine mother-of Edward)
NO

In this case there was no match between the query sentence and a sentence in the current data base so the answer is "NO", short for "No, fact is not confirmed".

Is the mother of Mary known?
&.is(x mother-of Mary)
YES

In this query we are trying to find out whether the data base contains a sentence that records who the mother of Mary is. The "x" stands for the mother, whose name is unknown to us. micro-PROLOG searches the sentences of the "mother-of" relation, looking for a sentence of the form

x mother-of Mary.

It finds the sentence

Katherine mother-of Mary

and so returns the answer "YES". It does not tell us that the unknown x is Katherine. To retrieve this information we need to use a different form of query - the **which** query described below.

Variables in queries

The letters x, y, z, X, Y, Z are variables of micro-PROLOG. The variable in a query is a very simple concept: it stands for some unknown individual. It is a **place holder**, ready to be filled in by a name. Variables are the formal equivalent of pronouns in English. Where in English we would say something, someone, it or he, in micro-PROLOG we use a variable.

Just as pronouns cannot be used in English as names, without risk of ambiguity, so in micro-PROLOG variables cannot be used as names of individuals or relations. You cannot enter a fact about an individual whose name is x!

The variable names of micro-PROLOG were chosen so that this problem is highly unlikely to arise. Even so, if ever you do want to use x as a name, you can do so by quoting it with quotation marks. "x" is not a variable. It can be used either as the name of an individual or the name of a relation. For more information on quoting and name conventions consult the micro-PROLOG Reference Manual.

The letters x,y,z,X,Y,Z are actually variable prefix letters. A variable prefix may be be followed by a positive integer subscript made up of a sequence of decimal digits. Variables are different if they have different prefixes or different subscripts. Thus x and y are different, x2 and y2 are different, and x1 and x2 are different. The variables x1 and x01 are not different because 1 and 01 are the same integer number.

Data Retrieval

To retrieve the names of unknown individuals we use the **which** form of query.

Who is the father of Edward?
&.which(x : x father-of Edward)
Henry
No (more) answers

A **which** query has two components separated by a colon. The second component is the *query condition*. In this case it is a simple sentence pattern

>   x father-of Edward

The first component is the *answer pattern*. Here it is the single variable x of the query condition. More generally, the answer pattern is a sequence of variables that appear in the query condition.

>   In answering a **which** query micro-PROLOG finds *all* the instances of the query condition that are facts that can be confirmed. In doing this it 'fills in' the variable slots of the query condition with the names of individuals, which are then displayed in accordance with the answer pattern. In this case, there is only one instance of

>   x father-of Edward

that can be confirmed. This is the instance with x = Henry. It is confirmed because

>   Henry father-of Edward

is a sentence of the data base. So we get the answer

>   Henry

followed by the message that there are no more answers.

Conjunctive queries

>   Queries with several conditions can be expressed directly in both **is** and **which** form.

>   Is Henry-Snr the father of Henry and of Edward?
>   &.is(Henry-Snr father-of Henry
>   1.and Henry-Snr father-of Edward)
>   NO

>   Recall that the prompt "1." means that micro-PROLOG is expecting at least one right bracket before it considers that the query is complete.

For an **is** query with a conjunctive condition to receive the answer YES all of its conditions must be confirmed. If they can't all be confirmed then the answer NO is returned. In this case the second sentence is not contained in the data base, so the answer to the *conjunctive* query is "NO".

Notice how in micro-PROLOG we must make explicit the question "is Henry-Snr the father of Edward" that is implicit in the English phrase "and of Edward".

> Who is both a child of Henry-Snr and
>   the father of Elizabeth2?
> &.which(x : Henry-Snr father-of x and
> 1. x father-of Elizabeth2)
> Henry
> No (more) answers

> Who are the daughters of Henry?
> &.which(x : Henry father-of x & x female)
> Mary
> Elizabeth2
> No (more) answers

Notice that in this query we have used "&" as an abbreviation for "and". This is an abbreviation that micro-PROLOG understands.

> Who is a mother (of somebody)?
> &.which(x : x mother-of y)
> Elizabeth1
> Katherine
> Jane
> Anne
> No (more) answers

We do not get the names of the children because the unknown child y of the query condition is not given in the answer pattern.

> Who are all the mother, child pairs?
> which(x y : x mother-of y)
> Elizabeth Henry
> Katherine Mary
> Jane Edward
> Anne Elizabeth2
> No (more) answers

Who are all the father, son pairs?
which(x y : x father-of y & y male)
Henry-Snr Henry
Henry Edward
No (more) answers

In this query the answer pattern is the pair of variables x y both
of which appear in the query pattern. They are the unknown
father and unknown son referred to in the query pattern. Note
that we must use the vocabulary of the data base. The data base
does not include any facts that directly describe the father-son
relationship, so we describe what we want using the "father-of"
and "male" relations. We had to do the same thing in the earlier
query to find the daughters of Henry. We had to characterize a
daughter as a female child.

Summary of query commands

is   This has the form:

    is(<condition> [and ... <condition>])

where each <condition> is a simple sentence in which one or more
individuals may be named by variables. This query checks to see
if each of the given conditions can be confirmed using the facts
in the data base. It responds "YES" if each can be confirmed,
and "NO" if not. If the same variable occurs in more than one
condition it denotes the same unknown individual.

which   This has the form:

    which(<answer pattern> : <condition> [and ... <condition>])

This query returns the answers to the query condition or the
conjunction of conditions that follow the ":". Each answer is
some instance of the <answer pattern> in which variables are
replaced by the names of individuals that satisfy all the query
conditions. The answer pattern is a variable or sequence of
variables that appear in the query conditions.

The different variables of the answer pattern *must* be
separated by spaces. After all the different answers have been
given the message "No (more) answers" is displayed. The ":"
separating the two components of the query is important. If you

miss it out you will get the error message that there is a missing colon and the query will not be answered. This is because without the ":" micro-PROLOG cannot tell where the <answer pattern> ends and where the first query condition begins.

The command name **all** is an accepted alternative to **which**.

one   The form of the query is:

one(<answer pattern> : <condition> [and ... <condition>])

The **one** query is similar to the **which** query except that after each answer is found and displayed micro-PROLOG interrupts the query evaluation and waits for an input to indicate whether it should look for more answers or stop. It prompts for this input with the message "more?(y/n)". If you respond by entering **y** (for yes) then the next solution is sought. If you enter **n** (for no) the evaluation stops. For example, we might ask for the children of Henry one at a time:

```
&.one(x : Henry father-of x)
Mary
more?(y/n)y
Elizabeth2
more?(y/n)n
&.
```

Because we quit the evaluation before micro-PROLOG was sure that there were no more answers we do not get the usual terminating message "No (more) answers". We just get the "&." prompt to indicate that it is ready for another command.

System note - syntax errors - if there is a mistake in the syntax of any of the query commands you will get an error message identifying the error and the query will not be answered. micro-PROLOG usually displays the part of the query in which the syntax error occurs. For example, if one of the conditions is not a valid simple sentence you will get the message

Syntax error: <condition> not a valid simple sentence form

If the condition contains variables the variable names in the displayed condition will probably not be the same as the ones that you used in the query. This is because micro-PROLOG forgets variable names, it just remembers the positions that each variable occupies in the query.

So, when it prints out the error message it assigns new variable names to the variable positions in the condition. We shall say more about this renaming of variables in the next chapter.

Finding the names of your relations

Each time you **add** a sentence about a new relation to your program the **add** command records the name of the new relation in a **dict** sentence added to your program. You can therefore find out what relation names you have used with the query

all(x : x dict)

or equally:

list dict

When you do a **list all** what you get is a listing for all the relations recorded by a **dict** sentence.

When you get rid of all the sentences about a relation using a **kill** command the **dict** sentence for the relation will be automatically deleted. However, it will not be removed if you get rid of each of the sentences one by one using **delete**. So the fact that the relation name is displayed in answer to the **dict** query does not *guarantee* that it has any defining sentences. To check if there are defining sentences for some relation R use the query

is(R defined)

A "YES" answer tells you that there is at least one sentence for the relation, a "NO" reports that their are no sentences for R. The **defined** relation can only be used for checking. Unlike the **dict** relation it cannot be used to find the names of the relations that you have used which are still defined. To do this use **dict** and **defined** together in the query

all(x : x dict & x defined)

Predefined relations and modules

micro-PROLOG contains several predefined relations some of which we shall meet in the next section. micro-PROLOG does not allow you to alter the definitions of these predefined relations. If you accidentally try to add a sentence for one of these relations you will get the error "Cannot add sentences for R" where R is the name of the relation.

You will get the same message if you try to add a sentence about one of the command or relation names defined by the SIMPLE front-end program. For example, if you try to add a sentence about the is relation. Even though SIMPLE is a micro-PROLOG program its definitions are protected in this way because it comprises three special forms of program called modules.

Modules are named collections of relation definitions that explicitly export the names of certain relations. Only the exported relations can be used by other programs and their definitions are protected from accidental alteration. Modules are more fully described in Chapter 7 which also tells you how you· can convert one of your programs into a protected module.

You can find out the names of the relations exported by SIMPLE by using the query:

    all(x : x reserved)

The answer will be a list of names that you should not use for the names of your relations. You can use this query to remind you of the command names such as which and all because these are included in the list of reserved names.

Exercises 1-2

1. Using the FAMILY data base developed in this chapter, give or find the answers to the following queries and give an English equivalent for each query:

a.   is(Jane mother-of Elizabeth2)
b.   is(Henry-Snr father-of x)
c.   which(x : Henry-Snr father-of x)
d.   is(Katherine mother-of x and x female)
e.   all(x : Henry father-of x and x male)
f.   which(x y : x father-of z & z father-of y)

2. Using the vocabulary of the FAMILY data base, express these English questions as micro-PROLOG queries:

a.   Is Katherine the mother of Edward?
b.   Who is a father (of somebody)?
c.   Is Jane the mother of someone whose father is Henry-Snr?

d. Who has Henry as their father and Katherine as their mother?

3. Using the geographical data base started in Exercise1-1, express these English questions as micro-PROLOG queries:

a. Is Rome the capital of France?
b. Is Washington-DC the capital of a country in Europe?
c. Which are the capitals of countries in Europe?
d. Is the capital of Italy recorded?
e. For which North-American countries is the capital known?
f. For which continents are the capitals of countries known?

4. Using the books data base started in Exercise 1-1, give the answers to the following micro-PROLOG queries and for each query give an equivalent English question:

a. is(Oliver-Twist written-by William-Shakespeare)
b. is(x written-by Mark-Twain and x type Novel)
c. which(x y : x type Play and x written-by y)
d. which(x : x type Novel and x written-by Charles-Dickens)
e. which(x : y written-by x)

5. Using the bicycle parts data base of Exercise 1-1 express the following as micro-PROLOG queries:

a. Which are the parts of a bicycle?
b. Is a dynamo part of a bicycle?
c. Is a spoke part of something?
d. Which part of a bicycle is a dynamo part of?
e. Which are the parts of the braking-system?

1.3   Arithmetic relations

micro-PROLOG is not particularly well suited for applications which need a lot of routine numerical work. However, we can do arithmetic using four built-in arithmetic relations SUM, TIMES and LESS and INT and we can use arithmetic expressions in query conditions. We shall introduce arithmetic expressions in Chapter 4. Here we shall illustrate the use of the arithmetic relations since they are used and queried in exactly the same way as data base relations. Arithmetic expressions are ultimately evaluated using the SUM and TIMES relations.

Although each arithmetic relation is implemented by a machine code program, so as to make use of the hardware operations of the machine, we can think of each relation as being defined by an implicit data base of facts. This is why we can query them in the same way as we query relations defined by a real data base of facts.

Addition and Subtraction using the SUM relation

The **SUM** relation is a three argument relation such that

SUM(x y z) holds if and only if z = x + y.

The *implicit* data base describing the relation contains sentences such as SUM(2 3 5) and SUM(-3 10.6 7.6). We do addition & subtraction by querying this implicit data base.

Uses of the **SUM** *relation*

Checking:

&.is (SUM(20 30 50))
YES

Adding:

&.which(x : SUM(5.6 -2.34 x))
3.26
No (more) answers

Subtracting:

&.which(x : SUM(x 34 157))
123
No (more) answers

or:

&.which(x : SUM(34 x 157)
123
No (more) answers

Restrictions on the use of SUM

A query condition for the SUM relation can have at most one *unknown* argument. This constraint would not apply if there was a real data base for the relation. It applies because micro-PROLOG simulates the data base and for efficiency supports only a restricted range of query patterns. This means that a query such as

which(x y : SUM(x y 10))

will not be answered. It will result in a "Too many variables" error message. Try it! The "Too many variables" message is the one you will get when you try to use any of the built-in relations of micro-PROLOG and there are too many unknown arguments.

Syntax of numbers

The above queries made use of both integers and floating point numbers. All the arithmetic relations take arguments that are either integers or floating point numbers. If you mix the two types of number micro-PROLOG automatically converts the integers to floating point numbers.

A *positive integer* is a sequence of decimal digits *without* any preceding "+" sign. Indeed, you *must not* use a "+" to indicate that a number is positive. If you do you will get an error when the query is evaluated.

A *negative integer* is a sequence of decimal digits with a preceding "-" sign. Thus:

234 7056 89004

are all positive integers and

-34 -56004 -11000

are all negative integers.

A *positive floating point number* is a sequence of decimal digits (again *without* a preceding "+" sign) which contains a "." decimal point. It can be optionally followed by an integer exponent expressed as the letter "E" followed by an integer. For example:

>   23.45 2.345E1 0.02345E3 2345.0E-2

are all different representations of the same floating point number. The "." in a floating point number must always be preceded by at least one digit, which can be 0. The exponent is the power of 10 by which the number preceding the exponent should be multiplied.

A *negative floating point number* has the same form as a positive floating point number except that it is preceded by the "-" sign. Thus:

>   -34.678 -0.0783E-34 -100.05

are all negative floating point numbers.

System note - floating point numbers - The form 2.345E1 is the standard form for the number 23.45. Floating point numbers can be entered in any form but they are displayed (in most implementations of micro-PROLOG) in their standard form. That is, they are expressed as a number between -10 and 10 with the appropriate exponent. When this exponent is 0, that is when the number does lie between -10 and 10, the exponent is suppressed. That is why the number 3.26E0 which was the answer to one of the above queries was displayed without the exponent as 3.26.

All implementations of micro-PROLOG handle integers in the range -32767 to 32767 and floating point numbers with at least 8 digits of accuracy and exponents in the range -127 to 127. Some implementations may handle larger numbers. If the evaluation of an arithmetic condition would give an answer that is too small to represent as a floating point number you will get the "Arithmetic underflow" error message. If it would give a number that is too large to represent as a floating point number you will get the "Arithmetic overflow" message. If a condition with integer arguments has an answer that is too large to represent as an integer the answer will be given as a floating point number.

Conversion and testing of number types

The INT relation has two forms of use. It can be used as a property relation to test if a number is an integer, or more exactly to test if the number is an integer or a floating point number that does not have a fraction part. It can also be used as a binary relation to find the integer part of a floating point number.

Uses of **INT**

Testing:

&.is(45 INT)
YES

&.is(4.67 INT)
NO

&.is(3.567E3 INT)
YES

Use for conversion

which(x : 3.45 INT x)
3
NO (more) answers

which(x : -3.56498E3 INT x)
-3564

Restrictions on use the of **INT**

When it is used as a property relation the single argument must be given. It can only be used to test, not to find an integer number.

When it is used as a binary relation, the first argument must be given and the second one must be unknown, that is, represented as a variable. The evaluation of the condition will give the variable the value of the integer part of the first argument. So, in the two argument form **INT** cannot be used as a test that some number is the integer part of another. It can only be used to find an integer part. To test that some number is the integer part of another we must use **INT** and then another micro-PROLOG primitive relation **EQ** to test that the found integer part is identical to the given value.

&.is(6.78 INT x & x EQ 6)
YES

The placing of the EQ test after the INT condition is important: we shall discover why in Section 1.4.

Multiplication and division using TIMES

The TIMES relation is such that

TIMES(x y z) holds if z = x * y

Uses of the TIMES relation

Checking a product:

&.is (TIMES(3 4 12))
YES

Checking for exact division:

&.is(TIMES(3 y 12) & y INT)
YES

&.is(TIMES(3 y 11) & y INT)
NO

Multiplying:

&.which(x : TIMES(5 4.3 x))
2.15E1
No (more) answers

Division:

&.which(x : TIMES(x 24 126))
5.25
No (more) answers

&.which(x : TIMES(24 y 126) & x INT y)
5
No (more) answers

&.is(TIMES(x 3 10) & TIMES(x 3 10))
NO

System note - accuracy of floating point numbers - The NO answer to the last query may surprise you, but it should not. The result of dividing 3 into 10 cannot be accurately represented as a floating point number. The answer that micro-PROLOG gives is 3.3333333 which is only a close approximation of 10 divided by 3. So, when micro-PROLOG multiplies this result by 3 to check the second condition it gets 9.9999999 and not 10. You must be careful when using floating point numbers in any programming language to remember about such rounding errors.

Restriction on **TIMES** *queries*

The restrictions on the use of **TIMES** are the same as those for **SUM**. At most one argument can be unknown, but this can be any of the three arguments. This covers the use for multiplication and division.

Testing for order using the **LESS** relation

The primitive **LESS** relation can only be used for checking.

LESS(x y) holds if x is less than y in the usual ordering of the numbers

Uses of LESS

&.is(3 LESS 4)
YES

&.is(4 LESS 3)
NO

&.is(TIMES(3 x 10) & TIMES(3 x y) &
1. SUM(y z 10) & z LESS 0.1E-5)
YES

LESS can also be used for comparing two names. The ordering used is that of the dictionary. LESS(x y) holds for words x and y if x comes before y in a dictionary. Example:

&.is(FRED LESS FREDDY)
YES

&.is(ALBERT LESS HAROLD)
YES

&.is(SAM LESS BILL)
NO

The alphabetical ordering of the characters that can appear in the names is the ASCII ordering of all the keyboard characters. In this ordering "-" precedes all the numerals which come before all the capital letters which come before all the lower case letters.
So, we have

SAM LESS Sam

Sam1 LESS Samantha

Sam-1 LESS Sam1

Exercises 1-3

1. Answer the following micro-PROLOG queries:
a.   is(SUM(9 6 15))
b.   which(x : SUM(4 18 x))
c.   which(x : SUM(x 23 40))
d.   is(9 LESS 10)
e.   is(SUM(9 8 x) and x LESS 19)
f.   which(x : TIMES(9 7 x))
g.   is(TIMES(11 8 80))
h.   which(x y : TIMES(4 z1 14) & z1 INT x & TIMES(x 4 z2) &
         SUM(z2 y 14))

2. Write micro-PROLOG queries to ask the following English questions:
a.   What is 9 plus 7?
b.   What is the integer part of the result of 65 divided by 7?
c.   What is the result if you add 29 and 53, and divide the total by 2?
d.   Can 93 be exactly divided by 5?
e.   Is the result of multiplying 17 and 3 less than 50?

1.4   Evaluation of queries

This is an appropriate point to say something about the way in which micro-PROLOG evaluates queries.
When querying a data base of simple sentences we can, for

the most part, ignore the way that queries are evaluated. However, we shall see that the ordering of the conditions in a conjunctive query can affect the time that micro-PROLOG takes to answer the query. Unless an error occurs, it *will not* affect the answers that we get. Choosing an ordering that facilitates the evaluation is part of the pragmatics of using micro-PROLOG.

For certain conjunctive queries, for example the query:

which(x : TIMES(37 51 y) & SUM(y 73 x))

we *must* know about the order of evaluation of the component conditions. Does micro-PROLOG solve the **SUM** or the **TIMES** condition first? If it is the **SUM** condition we will get a "Too many variables" error message because there are two unknown arguments y and x. If micro-PROLOG answers the **TIMES** condition first there will be no problem providing the answer obtained for the unknown y is 'passed on' to the **SUM** condition before it is solved.

Fortunately (in this case) this is exactly what micro-PROLOG does. micro-PROLOG evaluates conjunctive queries by solving the conditions in the left to right order in which they are given passing on any values for variables that it has found. So, by the left to right ordering in which we give the conditions we *control* the evaluation order.

The ordering of the conditions is the control component of the query. The conjunction of the conditions is the logical component. In posing a query our primary concern should be a correct logical description of what we want to ask or retrieve. Our secondary concern should then be with the ordering of the conditions for efficient and error free evaluation.

Evaluation of **is** queries with one condition

The simplest form of query is the **is** query of the form

is(C) where C is a simple sentence without variables

micro-PROLOG evaluates this query by searching through the sentences in the data base that are about the relation of the condition C. It does not search the whole data base. micro-PROLOG stores the sentences about each relation in a list, the ordering of the sentences on the list being the order in which they are displayed by the **list** command. micro-PROLOG runs down this list, comparing C with each sentence in turn. If it finds an exact match between C and a sentence in the list it terminates the search and gives the answer "YES". If it reaches the end of the list of sentences without finding a match, it displays the "NO" answer.

Example 1

    is(Henry male)

The sentences in the FAMILY data base about "male" are stored in the order

    Henry-Snr male
    Henry male
    Edward male

because this is the order in which they are listed by the "list male" command. First micro-PROLOG compares the query condition

    Henry male

with the sentence

    Henry-Snr male

that heads the list. The sentences do not match because "Henry" and "Henry-Snr" are different names. Since this match fails, micro-PROLOG then moves on to the next sentence. We now have an exact match, so micro-PROLOG terminates the search and gives the answer "YES".

    If we pose the query

    is(Edward3 male)

micro-PROLOG compares "Edward3 male" with each sentence in turn. In no case is there an exact match. So we get the answer "NO".

is query with a sentence pattern

An **is** query of the form

is(C)   where C is a simple sentence pattern, i.e. a simple
            sentence with at least one variable standing for an
            unknown individual

is answered in much the same way. The only difference is that
when looking for an exact match micro-PROLOG is allowed to
give each variable in C a *value* which is the name of some
individual.

Example 2

is(x father-of Elizabeth2)

The sentences for the father-of relation are stored in the order

Henry-Snr father-of Henry
Henry father-of Mary
Henry father-of Elizabeth2
Henry father-of Edward

micro-PROLOG compares the sentence pattern

x father-of Elizabeth2

with each sentence in turn. There is an exact match with the
third sentence when the variable x has the value "Henry". At this
point micro-PROLOG terminates the search and gives the answer
"YES".

Example 3

is(x father-of x)

This query is asking whether the data base contains any fact that
says that someone is their own father. micro-PROLOG will give
us the answer "NO", but it is instructive to see why.
    It tries to match the sentence pattern

    x father-of x

with each of the above sentences. It gets a partial match with the first sentence

    Henry-Snr father-of Henry

by giving x the value "Henry-Snr". This makes the sentence pattern become the sentence:

    Henry-Snr father-of Henry-Snr

But it is not an exact match because by giving x this value micro-PROLOG must replace both occurrences of x in the sentence pattern by the name "Henry-Snr". This creates a mismatch between the names of the children. The same thing happens in the attempt to match all the other sentences of the data base. So the query is answered, "NO".

    Now consider the query

    is(x father-of y)

In answering this query, micro-PROLOG does not encounter the same problem because it can give the different variables x and y different values. In fact, there is an immediate match with x=Henry-Snr and y=Henry.

    In answering a query micro-PROLOG can give different variables different values, but it may also give them with the same value. Thus, if we had a data base that contained just the single "likes" sentence

    Tom likes Tom

then both

    is(x likes x)

and

    is(x likes y)

would be answered affirmatively. In the second query we are asking whether the data base knows anything about some x liking some y. It does, when x and y are the same person Tom. This convention that different variables can stand for the same unknown person micro-PROLOG inherits from symbolic logic. To insist that different variables name different individuals we must add an extra condition that says just that. We shall see how we can do this in Chapter 3.

Evaluation of **which** queries with one condition

The single condition **which** query is of the form

which(P : C)   where P is an answer pattern and C is a
                  simple sentence pattern

micro-PROLOG takes the sentence pattern C and compares it with each of the sentences for its relation in the data base. A match of C with a sentence in the data base results in each variable of C being given a value. For each match of C with a data base sentence the answer pattern P is displayed with its variables replaced by the values for that match.

Example 4

which(x : Henry father-of x)

The sentences of the data base are compared with the query pattern in the listing order given above. There is no match with the first sentence

Henry-Snr father-of Henry

because the fathers "Henry", "Henry-Snr" do not match. There is a match with the second sentence,

Henry father-of Mary

providing x = Mary. Because it has found a sentence that matches the query pattern micro-PROLOG has found one answer to the query. It therefore displays the answer pattern, x, with x replaced by its value "Mary". We get the first answer:

Mary

The evaluation continues with the attempt to match the

query pattern "Henry father-of x" with the remaining sentences:

> Henry father-of Elizabeth2
> Henry father-of Edward

There is a match with the first of these providing x = Elizabeth2. So we get the second answer:

> Elizabeth2

There is also a match with the last sentence, providing x = Edward. This gives us the last answer

> Edward
> No (more) answers

Evaluation of conjunctive **which** queries

We illustrate the method of evaluation by two examples. We shall describe the method more formally in the next chapter.

Example 5

> which(x : Henry father-of x & x male)

This query is a restriction on the query of example 4 to find only the male children of Henry. What micro-PROLOG has to do is to find all the names that can replace x such that both

> Henry father-of x

and

> x male

are sentences of the data base.

It finds all these x's by initially ignoring the second condition of the query. It starts by looking for all the x's that satisfy

> Henry father-of x

We know that there are three sentences of this form, the first one being

Henry father-of Mary

micro-PROLOG matches the query condition with this sentence and finds a possible answer, x=Mary, for the conjunctive query. At this point micro-PROLOG interrupts the search for solutions to the first condition in order to see whether this value for x is compatible with the second condition of the query, the condition "x male". It sees whether it can find a successful match for this condition if x has the value "Mary". This is equivalent to finding a successful match for the query condition

Mary male

It tries to confirm this condition by searching the list of sentences about the "male" relation. Since it does not find the sentence "Mary male", it cannot confirm the extra condition on x for the value x=Mary. It therefore returns to its interrupted search for all the solutions to

Henry father-of x

It finds the next solution to this with the match against the sentence

Henry father-of Elizabeth2

This gives the value x=Elizabeth2. Again, micro-PROLOG interrupts the search for other solutions to the "father-of" condition to check if "x male" can be confirmed when x=Elizabeth2. That is, it checks to see if the condition

Elizabeth2 male

can be confirmed. This attempt also fails. So micro-PROLOG again returns to its interrupted search for all the x values that satisfy the first condition

Henry father-of x

It finds the next possible value for x with the match against

Henry father-of Edward

which makes x = Edward. Interrupting the search once more, micro-PROLOG tries to confirm the second condition "x male" with x = Edward which is the condition

Edward male

This time it succeeds, for the sentence "Edward male" is in the data base. micro-PROLOG has at last found an answer to the compound query, which it immediately displays.

Since the query requires all solutions, micro-PROLOG once more returns to its interrupted search for x's that satisfy "Henry father-of x". There are no more because micro-PROLOG has already looked at all the sentences that match this pattern. It therefore displays the message "No (more) answers".

The method of evaluation of the query

which(x : Henry father-of x & x male)

can be captured in the *control* reading

for all the x that satisfy the condition Henry father-of x
 if x is male, display x

Example 6

which(x z : x father-of y & y father-of z)

This is a request for all the pairs of people in the paternal grandfather relation. The answers to this query are the names assigned to x and z for each *solution* to the conjunctive condition of the query. A solution is an *assignment* of values to variables in this query pattern such that each of its sentences become facts in the data base. In this case, it is an assignment to x, y, z such that

x father-of y *and* y father-of z

are both sentences of the data base.

Again, micro-PROLOG searches for all the solutions to both conditions by initially ignoring the second condition. It starts by looking for all solutions to the first condition

x father-of y.

It finds the first solution with the match against the sentence

Henry-Snr father-of Henry

which makes x=Henry-Snr, y=Henry. At this point micro-
PROLOG interrupts its search for all the solutions to the first
condition. It now looks for *all* the solutions to the rest of the
query which are compatible with this solution (x=Henry-Snr,
y=Henry) to the first condition. In other words, it looks for *all*
solutions to the condition

y father-of z (with x=Henry-Snr, y=Henry)

This is the condition

Henry father-of z.

There are three solutions to this:

z=Mary, z=Elizabeth2, z=Edward.

These three solutions for z give three solutions:

x=Henry-Snr, y=Henry, z=Mary
x=Henry-Snr, y=Henry, z=Elizabeth2
x=Henry-Snr, y=Henry, z=Edward

to the conjunctive condition

x father-of y & y father-of z.

As micro-PROLOG finds each z solution it displays the answer
pattern "x z" with the variables replaced by their solution values.
Hence micro-PROLOG gives us:

Henry-Snr Mary
Henry-Snr Elizabeth2
Henry-Snr Edward

as its first three answers to the query.
    When micro-PROLOG has found all the answers to the
second condition "y father-of z" for y=Henry it can only find
more answers to the query by returning to its interrupted search

for all solutions to first condition "x father-of y". The next solution it finds is

   x=Henry, y=Mary

produced by the match with the sentence

   Henry father-of Mary.

micro-PROLOG again interrupts the search for all the solutions to "x father-of y", to find all the solutions to the remaining condition

   y father-of z (with x=Henry, y=Mary)

This is the condition

   Mary father-of z

There are no solutions to this condition for there are no matching sentences in the data base. So the x=Henry,y=Mary solution to the first condition is not compatible with the second condition and does not lead to any solutions to the conjunctive query. Once more micro-PROLOG returns to its search for the solutions to "x father-of y". The last two solutions it finds are:

   x=Henry, y=Elizabeth2
   x=Henry, y=Edward

On finding each solution micro-PROLOG again interrupts its search to look for all solutions of the second condition "y father-of z" with the found value of y. The first solution of these two solutions causes it to look for all solutions to

   Elizabeth2 father-of z,

and the second causes it to look for all solutions to

   Edward father-of z.

In each case, there are no solutions; there are no values for z that make them sentences of the data base. So micro-PROLOG finds no more answers to the original query.
   The method of evaluation of

which(x z : x father-of y & y father-of z)

can be expressed in the control reading

> for all the x and y that satisfy x father-of y
> find each z that satisfies y father-of z
> and display x and z

Evaluation of conjunctive **is** queries

The evaluation of an **is** query with a conjunctive condition proceeds in exactly the same way as that of a conjunctive **which** query. micro-PROLOG starts off as though it were trying to find *all* the solutions for the conjunction of conditions given in the query. It stops as soon as it finds one solution to the query, giving the answer "YES". If it cannot find any solution, we get the answer "NO".

System note - tracing queries using the SIMTRACE program - if you are using a computer to follow the examples and the exercises you can use a special program called SIMTRACE to follow through the evaluation of both **which** and **is** queries. This program will be on the distribution disk or tape along with the SIMPLE front-end program. To use the trace program do a

load SIMTRACE

command. Now, instead of using **all** or **which** use **all-trace** and instead of **is** use **is-trace**.

As an example, if you pose the query

all-trace(x : Henry-Snr father-of x & x male)

you will be taken step by step through the evaluation of the query. The first thing you will see is the message

(1) Henry-Snr father-of X trace?

and the evaluation will suspend waiting for your response. The "(1)" tells you it is the first condition of the query. Notice that the "x" of the query has become "X". This is the variable renaming that micro-PROLOG does which we have already mentioned. When a condition is displayed by the trace program the first variable in the condition will always be named "X", the second "Y", the third "Z" and so on in the sequence X, Y, Z, x, y, z, X1, Y1, ...

For tracing you should respond by entering **y** (that is, type **y** and then hit the **RETURN** or **ENTER** key). If you do not want tracing of this condition enter **n**. With the **y** response micro-PROLOG will take you through its scan of sentence for "father-of" telling you whether there is a successful match or not. With the **n** response it will just tell you when it has solved the condition. When the condition is solved you will get the message

(1) solved : Henry father-of Mary

with the variable replaced by the value found by the successful match with a sentence. The trace will then move on to the next condition, replacing the x variable of that condition with the value it has found. You will then get the prompt:

(2) Mary male trace?

If you respond by entering **y** you will be taken through the attempts to match the condition with each sentence about "male". When it has unsuccessfully tried the last sentence you will get the message

failing (2)

and the trace will return to find the next solution to the first condition and so on. You always get the "failing" message for a condition when micro-PROLOG has reached the end of the list of sentences for its relation even if a match with an earlier sentence had been successful. So, just before the end of the evaluation of the query you will get the message

failing (1)

to indicate that all the sentences for "father-of" have been scanned. You will then get the finish message

No (more) answers.

Try **all-trace** and **is-trace** with several queries until you understand the evaluation method.

For more information on the use of the trace program consult the chapter on SIMPLE in your Reference Manual. There are other responses that you can make when prompted with "trace?". In particular, **q** will quit the evaluation of the traced query.

To get rid of the trace program when you have finished using it you can do a

&. kill simtrace-mod

command. "simtrace-mod" (all lower case) is the name of the single module contained in the SIMTRACE program. This is another use of kill. It can be used to get rid of a whole set of relation definitions wrapped up as a module just by giving the name of the module. All the modules supplied with the micro-PROLOG system have names of the form "<name>-mod".

Exercises 1-4

1. We will add further sentences to our geographical data base, giving information about the latitude and longitude of each city, using the form

   city location (latitude longitude)

with figures given in degrees. Figures North and East are given as positive integers, figures South and West as negative integers.

   Washington-DC location (38 -77)
   Ottawa location (45 -76)
   London location (51 0)
   Paris location (48 2)
   Rome location (41 12)
   Lagos location (6 -3)

Give the micro-PROLOG queries that correspond to the following English questions:

a.   Which cities are North of London?
b.   Which cities are West of Rome?
c.   Is there a European country whose capital is North of Rome and South of London?
d.   Which countries in Europe have capitals that are East of London?
e.   In which country and continent is there a city that is South and West of Rome?

2. I have been sent on a shopping expedition, with a data base describing the financial situation.

   Wallet contains 98
   Cheese costs 84
   Bread costs 40
   Apple costs 12

Obtain answers to the following questions, using micro-PROLOG queries:

a.   How many apples can I afford to buy?
b.   Can I afford to buy the bread and the cheese?
c.   How much is left in my wallet after I have bought the cheese and
     one apple?
d.   How much more money will I need in order to buy five apples
     and three loaves of bread?

3. Add information about the year of publication to the books data
base using sentences such as:

> Oliver-Twist published 1849
> Great-Expectations published 1853
> Macbeth published 1623

> Guess the dates if need be.

Pose the following as micro-PROLOG queries:
a.   Was Oliver-Twist published in 1850?
b.   What was published in 1623?
c.   When was Tom-Sawyer published?
d.   Were Oliver-Twist and Great-Expectations published in the same
     year?
e.   Was Macbeth published before Romeo-And-Juliet
f.   What was published before For-Whom-The-Bell-Tolls
g.   Was anything published before 1600?

1.5   Efficient queries

Now that we know how micro-PROLOG evaluates queries,
particularly conjunctive queries, we can see that the way in which
we pose a query can effect the efficiency with which micro-
PROLOG finds the answers. Thus,

> which(x : Henry father-of x and x male) and
> which(x : x male and Henry father-of x)

are equivalent queries and will produce exactly the same set of
answers. However, in answering the first query, micro-PROLOG
will use the condition, "Henry father-of x" to find values for x
that it checks with the "x male" condition. In answering the
second, it uses the condition "x male" to find the different values
for x which it then checks with the "Henry father-of x" condition.
So the queries are not *control* equivalent. Their respective control
readings are

For all the x that satisfy Henry father-of x
    if x satisfies x male, display x

For all the x that satisfy x male
    if x satisfies Henry father of x, display x

In a much larger data base than our FAMILY data base, where there will be far fewer children of Henry than males, the first query will be answered more efficiently. For each child of Henry it will do a search through all the sentences for the "male" relation. In evaluating the second query, for each male recorded in the data base it will search through all the sentences for the "father-of" relation. As a general rule, when a query has two or more conditions on a variable we should put first the condition which will have the fewest number of solutions.

2. Rules

Often we want to ask the same conjunctive query many times, in which case it becomes tedious to be have to repeat the same conjunction of conditions. It would be convenient if we could in some way abbreviate the query condition. Also it would be useful to be able to draw conclusions from the facts in the data base. For example, that Henry-Snr is the father of Henry implies that he is a parent of Henry. We would like to be able to conclude "Henry-Snr parent-of Henry" without having to have this as an explicit fact in the data base. To be able to draw conclusions and to abbreviate queries we need to use rules.

2.1   Turning queries into rules

If we look at Exercise 1-2(1).f we see that we are really asking for all instances of the paternal grandfather relation defined by the conjunctive condition of the query:

which(x y : x father-of z and z father-of y)   (A)

The pairs x y which are produced as answers to the query are all the pairs in the "paternal-grandfather-of" relation that the data base knows about.

If we often wanted to find instances of this relation it would be more convenient if the data base recorded all the instances

    Henry-Snr Mary
    Henry-Snr Elizabeth2
    Henry-Snr Edward

that are given as answers to the query. A straightforward way to do this, is to *explicitly* record them by adding facts about the "paternal-grandfather-of" relation:

    Henry-Snr paternal-grandfather-of Mary
    Henry-Snr paternal-grandfather-of Elizabeth2   (1)
    Henry-Snr paternal-grandfather-of Edward

We could now get the effect of query (A) with the simpler query

which(x y : x paternal-grandfather-of y)   (B)

There is an alternative to this explicit recording of the instances of the new relation defined by a query. We can add just one sentence that links the new relation to the conjunctive query condition that defines it. This new sentence is a *rule* that gives an *implicit* definition of the new relation. The rule is expressed using a new form of sentence, the *conditional sentence*. The **which** query:

which(x z : x father-of y and y father-of z)

becomes the rule:

x paternal-grandfather-of y if x father-of z   (2)
                                        and z father-of y

A conditional sentence is added to the program in just the same way that simple sentence facts are added:

add(x paternal-grandfather-of y if x father-of z
and z father-of y)

Rule (2) is equivalent to the set of facts (1). When used to answer query (B), it has the effect of transforming it into our original query (A).

The **logical** (or **descriptive**) reading of the rule is:

x is a paternal grandfather of y if
        x is the father of z and
        z is the father of y, for some z.

The **control** (or **imperative**) reading reflects the way it is used to solve query conditions for the "paternal-grandfather-of" relation. We should read it as:

To solve: x paternal-grandfather-of y,
        solve the conjunction : x father-of z and z father-of y

For different specific uses we can elaborate this control reading. For example, for the finding grandchildren use it can be read:

To find a y such that x paternal-grandfather-of y for given x
    find a z such that x father-of z
    then find a y such that z father-of y

For the finding grandfather use, it is read:

To find a x such that x paternal-grandfather-of y for given y
    find an x and z satisfying x father-of z
    such that z father-of y can be confirmed

Using several rules

Sometimes it takes more than one "which" query to completely 'cover' a relation. For example, if we want a list of parents and children, because we do not have this information explicitly stated, we would have to use the two queries:

which(x y : x father-of y)   (C)

which(x y : x mother-of y)   (D)

We can transform these two queries to two rules for the "parent-of" relation in the same way we did for the "paternal-grandfather-of" relation. Taking (C) and (D) in turn we get the two rules:

x parent-of y if x father-of y   (3)

x parent-of y if x mother-of y   (4)

Adding these to the program gives us two rules which together define the "parent-of" relation. Both rules contribute towards the definition. In general, many rules can contribute towards a definition of a relation, and we can even describe a relation by a mixture of facts and rules.

In technical English our two micro-PROLOG rules can be read:

x is a parent of y if x is the father of y   (rule 3)

x is a parent of y if x is the mother of y   (rule 4)

Providing the data base contains all the facts about the mother and father relationships for some group of people, the definition of the "parent-of" relation provided by these two rules is just as good as a set of simple sentences giving all the facts about the relation. Indeed, they are better. By having "parent-of" defined by rules we automatically augment the instances of this relation that we can retrieve whenever we add new "father-of" or new "mother-of" facts. If the relation was described by facts we should also have to explicitly add new "parent-of" facts. The way they are used is indicated by the following control reading of the two sentences:

> To solve a condition of the form : x parent-of y,
>   solve the condition : x father-of y.

or

>   solve the condition : x mother-of y.

Here, the *or* is a non-deterministic branch giving an alternative way of solving the condition to be used after the first method has been tried.

The two rules give micro-PROLOG two different ways of solving conditions about the new relation "parent-of". They are a complete program, because logically they together cover all the instances of the relation implicitly given by the "father-of", "mother-of" facts of the data base.

To answer the query:

> which(x : x parent-of Elizabeth2)

micro-PROLOG will use both rules. Using the first rule transforms the condition of the query into:

> x father-of Elizabeth2

and the second rule transforms it into:

> x mother-of Elizabeth2

We therefore get the two answers:

> Henry
> Mary

They come in this order, because rule (3) comes before rule (4) and so will be used first.

Variables in rules

If we list the rules for the relation we get:

```
&.list parent-of
X parent-of Y if
      X father-of Y
X parent-of Y if
      X mother-of Y
&.
```

Again the rules are listed in the order that they were added. But notice that micro-PROLOG has changed our lower case "x" and "y" to upper case "X" and "Y". It can do this because the actual variable names used in a rule are not important. It can replace a variable, without affecting the meaning of the rule, providing the replacement appears in exactly the same position as the variable it replaces. micro-PROLOG changes variable names but never violates this constraint. It actually 'forgets' the original variable names and remembers only the positions that they occupied in the rule.

Conditional Sentences

The rules we have used so far are examples of conditional sentences. A *conditional sentence* is a sentence of the form

    <simple sentence> if <condition> [and ... and <condition>]

where each condition is a simple sentence.

A conditional sentence is technically termed an *implication*. The *conclusion* (technically the *consequent*) is the simple sentence on the left of the "if". The *condition* of the sentence (technically the *antecedent*) is the single condition or the conjunctive condition on the right of the "if".

Any sentence that contains variables is a *rule*. So far we have only used simple sentences without variables and conditional sentences with variables. The former we have called *facts*. We can also have conditional sentences without variables, e.g.

    Bill likes Jim if Jim likes Bill,

and we can have simple sentences with variables, e.g.

    Bill likes x   (Bill likes everyone).

In the next chapter we shall have frequent need of these simple sentence rules. For the time being we shall continue to use only facts (simple sentences without variables) and conditional rules (conditional sentences with variables).

The set of all the facts in a micro-PROLOG program is its data base. The conditional rules enable us to abbreviate queries by defining new relations in terms of the relations of the data base. When queried about these new relations micro-PROLOG uses these rules to interrogate the data base.

Logical reading of a conditional rule

Suppose we have a conditional rule of the form

    S if C

Let $y1,...,yk$ be the variables of the sentence that *only* appear in the antecedent C. We can read the rule as the implication:

    S if C, for some $y1,...,yk$.

It is understood that each variable $x1,..,xn$ in the consequent S represents an arbitrary individual. The rule says that for any $x1,..,xn$ the conclusion S is true whenever the condition C is for some $y1,...,yk$.

We can now see why the rule:

    x paternal-grandfather-of y if
        x father-of z &
        z father-of y

is read as:

   x is the paternal grandfather of y if x is the father of z
       z is the father of y, **for some z**.

The "for some z" is tagged on because z only appears in the condition of the rule.

Control reading of: S if C

The general purpose control reading is:

to answer a condition of the form: S,
        answer the condition: C.

For particular uses of the rule, that is for cases where we can assume that certain arguments of the relation of S are given whilst the others are to be found, we can often refine this general purpose control reading.

Exercises 2-1

1. Using the FAMILY data base, add rules to define the following relations:

a.   x maternal-grandmother-of y
b.   x father-of-son y
c.   x mother-of-daughter y

2. Using the geographical example developed in Exercise 1-1(2), complete these rules:

a.   x city-in Europe if .....
b.   x North-of London if .....
c.   x West-of y if .....

Use these rule defined relations to pose the following queries:

d.   What cities are there in Europe?
e.   Is anywhere north of London?
f.   Which places are north of London and west of Rome?

3. Using the books data base developed in Exercise 1-1(3), express the following information as rules added to the program:

a.   A book is classified as fiction if it is a novel or a play. Give two rules of the form: x fiction if ...
b.   Anything written by William-Shakespeare or Charles-Dickens is a classic.

Give rules of the form: x classic if...

c. Any book published after 1900 is contemporary literature. Give a
rule of the form: x cont-literature if ...

Use these relations to pose the following:

d. Which books are classics?
e. Who wrote books published before 1900?
f. Which books of fiction are also contemporary literature.

Rules can use rule-defined relations

The relations that we have defined using rules can
themselves be used in rules to define further relations. We can
build up a hierarchy of such relations with the data base relations
at the bottom. We can, for instance, define the relationship
"grandparent-of" in terms of "parent-of". In semi-English we would
say:

Somebody x is a grandparent of somebody y
        if x is the parent of z and z is a parent of y, for
some z.

We can add a conditional sentence to our program expressing this
rule:

x grandparent-of y if
        x parent-of z and
        z parent-of y

The general purpose control reading of the rule is:

To answer a condition of the form x grandparent-of y,
        answer the conjunctive condition:
        x parent-of z and z parent-of y

We leave the reader to give the refinements of this control
reading for the special cases of finding a grandchild and finding a
grandparent. The control reading for the checking use is:

To check that x grandparent-of y for given x and y
        find a z such that x parent-of z
        such that z parent-of y can be confirmed

The "grandparent-of" rule makes use of the "parent-of"

relation which is itself defined by rules. This does not matter. micro-PROLOG can use this rule defining the grandparent relation independently of whether the parent relation is defined explicitly by facts in the data base, or implicitly by rules. It discovers which is the case, and behaves accordingly, when it reduces a condition about "grandparent-of" to the conjunctive condition about "parent-of".

The program so far

Our program, from simple beginnings, has now grown somewhat. To conclude its development at present, let us list it in its current state, to see what our changes have produced.

```
&.list all
Henry-Snr father-of Henry
Henry father-of Mary
Henry father-of Elizabeth2
Henry father-of Edward
Elizabeth1 mother-of Henry
Katherine mother-of Mary
Jane mother-of Edward
Anne mother-of Elizabeth2                                 facts
Henry-Snr male
Henry male
Edward male
Elizabeth1 female
Katherine female
Mary female
Elizabeth2 female
Anne female
Jane female
x paternal-grandfather-of y if
          x father-of z and
          z father-of y
x parent-of y if
          x father-of y                                   rules
x parent-of y if
          x mother-of y
  x grandparent-of y if
          x parent-of z and
          z parent-of y
&.
```

System note - Suspending the screen display - This program is sufficiently large to not fit onto a single screen. micro-PROLOG allows you to suspend the display on the screen temporarily so that you can read the information at leisure. For details of how to do this for your particular version consult the Reference Manual. (For example, on CP/M and MSDOS systems you type control-S to stop the display and control-S again to restart it.)

Exercises 2-2

1. Give micro-PROLOG rules that define
a.   x grandfather-of y
b.   x grandmother-of y
c.   x child-of y
d.   x grandchild-of y

2. Answer the following micro-PROLOG queries about the FAMILY data base:
a.   which(x : x parent-of y)
b.   one(x : Henry-Snr grandfather-of x)
c.   is(Henry parent-of x and y grandfather-of x)

3. Give the micro-PROLOG queries for the following English questions:
a.   Who was Edward's paternal grandmother?
b.   Who are the mothers of Henry-Snr's grandchildren?
c.   Did Katherine have a male child?
d.   Who was the mother of a male child of Henry?

More on answer patterns

So far answers to queries have just been values for variables given in the answer pattern of the query. We can also have text displayed with each answer. We simply insert the text in the answer pattern of the query. As an example, consider the query:

What are the names of mothers and their children?
which(x y : x mother-of y)
Elizabeth1 Henry
Katherine Mary
Jane Edward
Anne Elizabeth2
No (more) answers

We just get the pairs of names, which is not very informative. We can also get the answers in the form:

Elizabeth1 is the mother of Henry
Katherine is the mother of Mary
etc.

in which the inserted text "is the mother of" helps us to interpret
the answer. Each of these answers are instances of the answer
pattern

x is the mother of y

To get the message, we use this pattern instead of the answer
pattern "x y" of the original query:

&. which(x is the mother of y : x mother-of y)
Elizabeth1 is the mother of Henry
Katherine is the mother of Mary
Jane is the mother of Edward
Anne is the mother of Elizabeth2
No (more) answers

We have simply added text to the answer pattern to affect the
form of our displayed answers. The text is only coincidentally
similar to the query pattern "x mother-of y". We can insert *any*
text into the list of variables of an answer pattern. It has *no*
effect on the query evaluation. The only constraint is that the
variables must be separated from the text by spaces. If they are
not, they will not be recognized as variables and their values will
not be displayed.

2.2   How queries involving rules are evaluated

We shall just consider the case of the evaluation of which
queries. The other query forms are answered in almost the same
way. The only difference is that for a one query we can quit the
evaluation each time an answer is found by entering n when
prompted, and for an is query the evaluation is always stopped
when one solution to the query condition is found.
    In describing the way that micro-PROLOG answers which
queries with rule-defined relations we shall describe the general
method used by micro-PROLOG to find all the solutions to a
conjunctive query. This method applies whether the relations of
the conjunction are defined by facts, by general rules, or a

mixture of the two.

A conjunctive **which** query is of the form:

&.which(P : C & C′ ..)

where C and C′ etc. are simple sentences. The query conditions C, C′... will contain variables, some or all of which will appear in the answer pattern P.

What micro-PROLOG must do is find all the different ways in which the variables of the conjunction of conditions can be given values so that each of the conditions becomes a sentence in the data base, or a sentence that can be inferred from the data base using the rules. Each set of values is a solution to the conjunctive condition of the query. For each solution, micro-PROLOG displays the answer pattern P.

micro-PROLOG begins its search for all the solutions to the conjunction of conditions by looking for all the different ways it can solve the first condition C. As soon as it solves C it interrupts its search for further solutions to C. If C contained variables the solution will have given values to these variables.

micro-PROLOG now looks for *all* the solutions to the rest of the conjunctive query that are compatible with these found values. In effect, it 'passes on' the values for the variables that *solve* C to the rest of the query.

When it has found all the solutions to the rest of the query that are compatible with this first solution to C, it returns to find the next way to solve C. On finding the next solution, it again immediately passes any variable values of this solution on to the rest of the query.

Only when it has found all the solutions to the rest of the query compatible with this second solution to C does it return to look for the third solution to C. It continues in this way until it can find no more solutions to C.

Backtracking

The way that micro-PROLOG searches for all the solutions to a conjunctive condition is called a *backtracking* search. When micro-PROLOG finds a solution to the first condition C, and passes it on to the remaining conditions C′ &.., it is 'tracking forward'. When it returns to find the next solution for C, it is 'tracking backward', or *backtracking*.

The evaluation of a conjunctive **which** query is a forwards and backwards shuffle through the conditions of the query. Let us suppose that there are three conditions

     C & C' & C".

micro-PROLOG finds the first solution to C and passes it on to

     C' & C".

It now looks for all the solutions to C' & C" that are compatible with this solution to C. It again starts by looking for a solution to the first condition C'.

     It tries to solve C' with the variable values given by the first solution to C. If it can do this, it moves forward to C". It tries to solve C" with the variable values given by the solution to C & C' that it has just found.

     When it has found all solutions to C" (compatible with the values for the variables of C and C'), it backtracks to look for the next solution to C'. It shuffles backwards and forwards between C' and C" until it has found all the solutions of

     C' & C"

compatible with the first solution to C. At that point, it backtracks to look for the next solution to C.

     The process of 'passing' on solutions to the rest of the query represents a flow of 'information' from left to right in the query. The first condition in which a variable appears is the *generator* of values for that variable. These values are passed on to the other conditions of the query in which the variable appears.

Rules

     This backtracking search for all the solutions to a compound query applies irrespective of whether the relations in the query are defined by facts, rules or a mixture of the two. The difference occurs only when micro-PROLOG picks off a condition C in the query and starts to look for a solution to that condition.

     Let us suppose that the condition C refers to a rule defined relation R. micro-PROLOG searches for solutions to the condition as for a data base relation. It scans the list of sentences about R looking for a match with the query condition. It scans them in the order in which they were added to the program (the order in which they are listed by the list command).

The extra complication is that it now has to match the query condition with the consequent of a rule, which may contain variables. Then, even when it has found a match, it has not yet found a solution. It must interrupt its scan of the sentences for R to find a solution to the query given by the condition of the rule. Each solution to **this** auxiliary query is a solution to the condition C.

Each time it finds a solution to the auxiliary query micro-PROLOG interrupts its search to pass the solution on to any remaining conditions of the original query. Now, backtracking to find the next solution to C means backtracking to look for the next solution to the auxiliary query. When it has found each solution to the auxiliary query, it returns to its scan of the program sentences for the relation R. Each rule with a consequent that matches C gives rise to an auxiliary query. The solutions to each of these auxiliary queries combine to give all the solutions to C.

Summary of evaluation method

The evaluation method can be summarised by:

To find all the solutions to a conjunctive query:
for each way of solving the first condition find all the compatible solutions of the remainder of the query.

To find all the solutions to a single condition
for each matching sentence, if it is a conditional rule then find all the solutions to the conditions of the rule, otherwise the matching sentence gives the solution.

Matching sentences are found by searching down the list of sentences for the relation of the condition.

Example evaluation

Let us illustrate the invocation of rules during the evaluation of a query by a simple example. Consider the query:

which(y : Henry-Snr grandfather-of y)   (E)

We shall assume that the rule

>   x grandfather-of y if
>   x father-of z and   (5)
>   z parent-of y

has been added to the program. (This was one of the answers to Exercise 2-1.) micro-PROLOG must find all the values for the variable y that are solutions to the query condition:

>   Henry-Snr grandfather-of y   (F)

There is only one sentence in the program about this relation, the rule (5) given above. Now, remember that micro-PROLOG forgets the variables used in a rule. It remembers only their positions. When it starts to match a condition with the consequent of the rule it gives the variables of the rule names. It always gives them names that are different from the variable names used in the query. Let us suppose it gives the x variable of the rule the name x1, the y variable the name y1, and the z variable the name z1. micro-PROLOG must match the query condition (F) with the consequent

>   x1 grandfather-of y1

of the rule

>   x1 grandfather-of y1 if
>   x1 father-of z1 and
>   z1 parent-of y1

Matching is now a little more complicated. To obtain a match, variables of the query condition and variables of the rule may be given values. In this case only variables of the rule are affected. The values x1 = Henry-Snr and y1 = y give an exact match. Notice that y1 has a value which is not the name of an individual but the name of a variable in the query. With x1 and y1 given these values the antecedent of the rule becomes the conjunctive condition

>   Henry-Snr father-of z1 and z1 parent-of y

The task of finding all the solutions of

Henry-Snr grandfather-of y

has become the task of finding all the solutions of the new conjunctive condition

Henry-Snr father-of z1 and z1 parent-of y   (G)

This is solved in the usual way. micro-PROLOG starts by looking for a solution to the condition "Henry-Snr father-of z1". It finds the first solution, z1=Henry, by matching with the fact

Henry-Snr father-of Henry

micro-PROLOG immediately suspends its scan of the "father-of" sentences to find all the solutions to the next condition

z1 parent-of y

that are compatible with z1=Henry. It must find all the solutions to the condition

Henry parent-of y   (H)

We now have another rule-defined relation. This time there are two rules, which with renamed variables are:

x2 parent-of y2 if x2 father-of y2
x3 parent-of y3 if x3 mother-of y3.

The query condition "Henry parent-of y" matches the first rule when x2=Henry, y2=y, and it matches the second rule when x3=Henry,y3=y. micro-PROLOG tries these rules one at a time, in the above order. After the successful match with the first rule, micro-PROLOG replaces condition (H) by the condition

Henry father-of y   (J)

The three solutions y=Mary, y=Elizabeth2, y=Edward of this condition are solutions of (H). All these solutions of (H) paired, with the solution z1=Henry for the first condition of (G), are solutions of (G). Finally, the y values of the solutions of (G) are solutions of the single condition (F) of the original query. So the first three answers to (E)

> Mary
> Elizabeth2
> Edward

will be displayed as each solution to (J) is found. When all the solutions have been found micro-PROLOG backtracks to find more ways of solving (H). It uses the second rule for "parent-of". This gives rise to the auxiliary query condition

> Henry mother-of y

to which there are no solutions.

Remember (H) was produced when micro-PROLOG found the first solution to the first condition of

> Henry-Snr father-of z1 and z1 parent-of y

To find more solutions to the this conjunctive condition, and hence more solutions to the original query, it returns to the task of finding all the solutions to the first condition

> Henry-Snr father-of z1

It continues its scan of the data base of sentences for "father-of". There are no more sentences which match the condition. micro-PROLOG must now backtrack to the original query condition

> Henry-Snr grandfather-of y

to see if there are other sentences in the data base about "grandfather-of". There are no more sentences so the search for solutions stops.

System note - Tracing the evaluation - In Section 1.4 we briefly described a utility module in the file SIMTRACE that can be used to trace the evaluation of queries. If you are using a computer we strongly recommend that you load SIMTRACE and use its **all-trace** command to trace the above query. Try it on several queries with rule-defined relations until you understand the evaluation method. During the trace, the rule sentence that is being used to try to match a query condition is identified by its position in the listing of sentences for its relation together with the conclusion of the rule. If there is a successful match, the new conditions introduced by the preconditions of the rule are displayed as:

new query: <preconditions of the rule>

Now, when you are prompted with a condition of the new query and asked whether it should be traced you will find that the condition is identified by a list of numbers not just a single number. For example, an identifier "(1 3)" will tell you that it is the first condition of the query introduced by using a rule for the third condition of the original query. The first number always gives the position in the current query. The rest of the list is the history back to the original query.

2.3   Recursive descriptions of relations

So far our rule-defined relations have been such that they could be dispensed with. Queries using these relations could always be expanded to longer queries that used only the relations of the data base. This is because each rule defined a new relation solely in terms of previously defined relations. There are some relations that cannot be so simply defined. These are relations that can only be described *recursively*, by definitions that refer back to the relation being defined. For such relations the use of rules is essential.

As an example, suppose that our FAMILY data base had many generations in it, and that we wanted to query the data base to find all the ancestors of Edward. If we knew that the data base referred to exactly four generations of ancestors of Edward we could find all of them with the query:

which(x1 x2 x3 x4 : x1 parent-of-x2 and
          x2 parent-of x3 and
          x3 parent-of x4 and
          x4 parent-of Edward)

But if we do not know how many ancestors are given in the data base we cannot find all the ancestors with a single query. This is because we cannot know how many "parent-of" conditions will be needed to chain back to the earliest recorded ancestor. To find all the ancestors with a single query, we need to define the relation "ancestor-of".

If we wanted to explain to someone who their ancestors were we might say:

Your ancestors are your parents and all the ancestors of your parents.

This is a recursive (i.e. coming 'back on itself) definition because the explanation makes use of the concept being explained. If they 'think through' the definition it tells them that their ancestors are:

> their parents
> their grandparents (who are the parent ancestors of
> their parents)
> their great-grandparents (who are the parent ancestors
> of their grand-parents)
> their great-great-grandparents (who are the parent
> ancestors of their great-grandparents),

> .
> .

and so on until the records run out.

We can express this recursive definition as the pair of micro-PROLOG rules:

> x ancestor-of y if x parent-of y
> x ancestor-of y if z parent-of y and
> x ancestor-of z

The logical reading is quite simply:

> x is an ancestor of y if x is a parent of y.
> x is an ancestor of y if z is a parent of y
> and x is an ancestor of z, for some z.

The general purpose control reading of the two rules is:

> To solve a condition the form : x ancestor-of y
> solve the condition : x parent-of y.

> To solve a condition of the form : x ancestor-of y
> solve the conjunctive condition:
> z parent-of y & x ancestor-of z

Notice that the definition comprises a recursive rule and a non-recursive rule. All recursive definitions must have at least one non-recursive rule or fact otherwise they are completely circular.

Given the task of finding all the ancestors of Edward with a query:

   which(x : x ancestor-of Edward)

micro-PROLOG will begin by using the first rule to replace the condition of the query with the condition

   x parent-of Edward

When all the solutions to this condition have been found, and the parents of Edward are found and listed, it will backtrack to use the second rule to find more ancestors of Edward. This converts the condition into

   z parent-of Edward and x ancestor-of z

Since the rule defining a parent as a father comes first, the condition "z parent-of Edward" will be solved with z=Henry who is the the father of Edward. Given this value for z, micro-PROLOG looks for all solutions to the second condition which is now

   x ancestor-of Henry

When this has been answered, and all the ancestors of Henry have been found, micro-PROLOG backtracks to the second way of finding a parent of Edward. It finds his mother Jane. It then finds and lists all her ancestors.

System note - tracing "ancestor-of" - Again we suggest that you use **all-trace** to follow the evaluation of this query and other queries involving "ancestor-of" on a computer. You will have to add the two rules defining the relation to your program.
     Notice the effect of the order of the two rules for "ancestor-of" on the way that ancestors are found. If the recursive rule is placed before the non-recursive rule the distant ancestors are found before the parent ancestors. But also notice that the ordering in which the recursive rule is second is crucial if we use the definition to answer the query:

   which(x y : x ancestor-of y)

Hand evaluate this query or follow it through using **all-trace**. Then follow it through with the recursive rule first. You will find that micro-PROLOG never finds an answer because it continually re-uses the recursive rule on the "ancestor-of" condition introduced by the use of the rule. (If you use **all-trace** you can quit the trace by entering **q** when prompted.) The moral is: put recursive rules defining a relation after the non-recursive rules especially if the definition is to be used to find all instances of the relation.

Separate definition of inverse relations

Logically our two rules defining the ancestor relation also define the inverse relation "descendant-of". To find the descendants of Henry we could use the query

which(y : Henry ancestor-of y)

micro-PROLOG will again begin by using the first rule to find and list the children of Henry. It will then backtrack to expand the query using the second rule to replace the query condition by

z parent-of y and Henry ancestor-of z

The finding of all solutions of this derived query condition is a very inefficient search for the descendants of the children of Henry. For in order to try to satisfy the condition "z parent-of y" it will find each parent/child pair recorded in the data base and check to see if the found parent is a descendant of Henry. The only way to avoid this inefficiency is to give a separate definition of the "descendant-of" relation, a definition that will be logically equivalent to the definition of "ancestor-of" but which will have a different control behaviour.

In particular, when used for finding descendants it will generate the same kind of directed search as does the "ancestor-of" definition when used to find ancestors.

The problem with the use of the "ancestor-of" definition for finding descendants relates to the flow of values via the variables of the rule. The rule:

x ancestor-of y if z parent-of y and x ancestor-of z

gives efficient retrieval if y is given. For then the first condition "z parent-of y", with y known, has a much smaller set of possible z values to pass on to the "x ancestor-of z" condition. To get a similar flow for the case when x is given and y is to be found, we should use the given x, find a child z of x, then find all the descendants of z.

To optimize the finding of descendants, we must separately

define the "descendant-of" relation by the rules:

> y descendant-of x if
>   x parent-of y
> y descendant-of x if
>   x parent-of z and
>   y descendant-of z

These constitute a correct alternative definition of the relation that holds between two people x and y when x is an ancestor of y and, equivalently, when y is a descendant of x. For purely pragmatic reasons, we should use these rules for finding descendants and the ancestor rules for finding ancestors. For checking whether two people are in the ancestor/descendant relation either set of rules can be used. The queries:

> is(Henry ancestor-of Edward)
> is(Edward descendant-of Henry)

are logically equivalent and micro-PROLOG does comparable work in answering each query. To answer the first it walks over the family tree beginning at Edward, for the second it begins at Henry. If the families described in the data base have on average more than two children, the "ancestor-of form" of the query is more efficiently answered. Why?

The contrast between the "ancestor-of" rules and the "descendant-of" rules is reflected in the control reading of their respective definitions for the finding descendants use. For this use the "ancestor-of" program is read:

> To find a y such that x ancestor-of y for given x
>   find a y such that x parent-of y

or

>   find a y and z such that z parent-of y and
>   check that x ancestor-of z can be confirmed
>   for the found z

The "descendant-of" rules are read:

> To find a y such that y descendant-of x for given x
>   find a y such that x parent-of y

or

>   find a z such that x parent-of z for the given x
>   and then find a y such that y descendant-of z

for the found z

We leave the reader to give appropriate control readings for each definition for the finding ancestors and for the checking uses.

To observe the differences between the use of the "ancestor-of" definition and the use of "descendant-of" definition trace a few queries using the relations with **all-trace**.

Exercises 2-3

1. Answer the following micro-PROLOG queries, using the FAMILY data base:
a.   which(x is male grandchild of y :
            x grandchild-of y & x male)
b.   one(x is a wife of Henry :
            y child-of Henry & x mother-of y)
c.   which(x : x ancestor-of Edward)
d.   which(x : x descendant-of Elizabeth1)
e.   is(Henry descendant-of Mary)
f.   which(x : x descendant-of Henry-Snr and x female)

2. We have used the built-in relation **LESS** in queries. This can also be used to define rules for other relations. For instance, to define the relation "lesseq" (which means less than or equal to) we need just two rules:

    x lesseq x

This rule simply states that everything is less than or equal to itself. The other rule is:

    x lesseq y if x LESS y

This rule says that if two numbers (or words) are in the **LESS** relation then they are also in the lesseq relation.

a.   Define the relation "greater-than".
b.   Define the relation "greateq" (greater than or equal to).
c.   Define the relation "divisible-by" in terms of **TIMES**.

Notice that because of the restrictions on the use of the arithmetic primitives your rules for these relations can only be used for confirming.

3. Using the books data base, add rules defining the relations:
a.   x Nineteenth-Century-Author : x has written a book published in the 19th century.
b.   x Contemporary-Playwright: x has written a play published in the 20th century.

Add a rule to express the following information:
c.   A book is available from the time it is published. Do this by defining the relation "x available-at y" which holds when x is a book and y is a year later than the year of publication.

Express the following questions as micro-PROLOG queries:
d.   What books were available in 1899?
e.   What works of nineteenth century authors were available in 1980?

4. The bicycle parts data base of Exercise 1-1(4) made use of a single relation "part-of" to describe the structure of a bicycle. This was actually the *direct* part of relation which was why the query

    is(lights part-of bicycle)

gets the answer "NO" even though lights are indirectly part of a bicycle since they are part of the electrical system which is part a bicycle. What we need to do is define the relation "indirect-part-of". This bears the same relation to "part-of" as the relation "descendant-of" bears to "parent-of".

a.   Define the relation: x indirect-part-of y
b.   Define the relation: x indirectly-contains y

Add these definitions to the parts data base and use them to answer the questions:

c.   What are all the indirect parts of a bicycle?
d.   What parts indirectly contain spokes?

Recursive description of arithmetic relations

    In the above exercise some new arithmetic relations were defined in terms of the arithmetic primitives. If we use recursive definitions we can define every arithmetic function as a micro-PROLOG relation.
    Let us first consider the factorial function. The factorial of a positive integer N is the product of all the numbers between 1 and N:

1*2*....*N

Since this product can be written as

(1*2*...*(N-1))*N   when N>1

we can see that the factorial of a number greater than 1 is the factorial of (N-1) multiplied by N. This gives us the recursive characterization we need. As we have already remarked, every recursive definition must have at least one non-recursive sentence. In the case of factorial, the non-recursive rule will be a fact which defines factorial when N=1.

Let us use "x factorial y" to mean that y is the factorial of the positive integer x. The following two sentences give us a complete recursive definition of the relation:

    1 factorial 1
    x factorial y if
            1 LESS x &
            SUM(x1 1 x) &
            x1 factorial y1 &
            TIMES(x y1 y)

If we add them we can use them to find factorial values with queries such as:

    which(x : 6 factorial x)

The control reading of the rules for the use to compute factorial values is:

    To find a y such that x factorial y for given x
        if x=1,y=1 or
        if 1 LESS x
                subtract 1 from x to give x1
                find y1 such that x1 factorial y1
                multiply y1 by x to get y

Because of the test restriction on the use of LESS the definition can only be used when the first argument is given. It can therefore only be used for finding factorials or for testing that a pair of numbers are in the "factorial" relation.

&.is(3 factorial 6)
YES

If we try to use the definition to find the factorial of a negative number or a non-integer number micro-PROLOG's use of the definition will ultimately fail to solve the query condition. For a negative number, neither rule applies. For a positive non-integer number the use of the recursive rule will eventually reduce the condition to the task of finding the factorial of a number less than 1 and again neither rule will apply. This failure is entirely appropriate, since the "factorial" relation is only supposed to relate positive integers. We could extend the relation by replacing "1 factorial 1" by the rule:

x factorial 1 if x lesseq 1

Now it is defined for all numbers greater than or equal to one. Try the new definition to find the factorial of 4.5. You will need to enter the definition of "lesseq" given in Exercise 2-3(2).

Recursive definition of a range of integers

The definition of "factorial" cannot be used compute the inverse of the factorial function because of the test only restriction of **LESS**. But let us suppose that the relation could be used to generate as well as test to see how our factorial definition might have been used to find a number whose factorial is a given value. In solving a condition in which y is given and x is to be found, the rule

x factorial y if
    1 LESS x &
    SUM(x1 1 x) &
    x1 factorial y1 &
    TIMES(x y1 y)

will try to use the condition "0 LESS x" to generate candidate values of the number x greater than 0. The factorial of each candidate value will then be computed and checked against the given y. If **LESS** were defined in such a way that it would generate different integer values for x in the order 2,3,4.... then the use of the rule would be an iterative search through the sequence of values to find a number whose factorial is y. In fact, we know that the value of x can never be more than y. So for a definition of the factorial relation for the inverse use we can replace the condition

   1 LESS x

by the stronger condition

   x between (2 y)

where "x between (y z)" holds when y <= x and x < z. Let us see if we can define this relation in such a way that it can be used to generate all the x's in a given range (y z).

   Let us first try to get a non-recursive rule. What number is definitely in the range y <= x < z. The number y is, providing y is less than z. This gives us a non-recursive rule:

   y between (y z) if y LESS z

This covers the case of x being at the left end of the interval. We now look for a recursive rule for "x between (y z)" to cover the case when x is inside the interval. What conditions guarantee that a value x other than y is between y and z. The conditions that y+1 is less than z and that x is between y+1 and z. This gives us a recursive rule:

   x between (y z) if
        SUM(y 1 y1) &
        y1 LESS z &
        x between (y1 z)

   Now let us turn to its use by micro-PROLOG to find all the numbers in a given range.
   In answering the query

   all(x : x between (1 3))   (A)

micro-PROLOG will first use the non-recursive rule which will give x the value 1 and reduce the condition "x between (1 3)" to

   1 LESS 3

which will be solved. This gives the first answer to the query. Backtracking will then result in the use of the recursive rule which transforms (A) into

SUM(1 1 y1) & y1 LESS 3 & x between (y1 3)

When the first two conditions are solved this becomes the single condition

x between (2 3)

which will give all the remaining answers to the original query.

Again the non-recursive rule will be applied to find the first value $x = 2$ that satisfies this condition and then the use of the recursive rule reduces it to

SUM(2 1 y1) & y1 LESS 3 & x between (3 3)

This time the second condition cannot be confirmed for the value $y1 = 3$. So this last application of the rule fails to find more solutions. The answer to the query is therefore

2
3
No (more) answers

For the use to find a number in a given range the control reading of the "between" program is

To find an x such that x between (y z) for given y,z
    if y LESS z, let $x = y$
or
    add 1 to y to get y1 then
    if y1 LESS z, find an x such that x between (y1 z)

Defining inverse factorial

Let us now return to the definition of the factorial relation. We can define the inverse relation "fact-of" by a single rule:

y fact-of x if x between (1 y) & x factorial y

The extra condition "x between (1 z)" is logically redundant but is there to act as a generator of candidate values for x when y is given. Each candidate value is tested by the condition "x factorial y" which uses the old definition to check if its factorial is y. The definition should not be used to find a y given x for with y a variable the evaluation of "x between (1 y)" will result in a "Too many variables" error when the·condition "1 LESS y" is checked. However, like the "factorial" definition it can be used for checking that a pair of numbers are in the factorial relation.

For the inverse factorial use it has the control reading

> To find an x such that y fact-of x for given x
> find an x in the range 1 to y
> such that x factorial y is confirmed

Defining the property of being a divisible integer

A positive integer x has a proper divisor if there is some integer between 2 and x that divides x. This gives us the definition:

> x has-divisor if y between (2 x) & TIMES(y z x)

The definition can be used as a micro-PROLOG program to test if a number has a divisor. Coupled with a "between" condition it can be used to find all the divisible numbers in a given range.

> all(x : x between (2 10) & x has-divisor)

will give you all the divisible integers between 2 and 10.

Exercises 2-4

1. Consider the following two rules about greatest common divisors:

Rule (A): The greatest common divisor of a pair of equal positive integers is their common value.

Rule (B): The greatest common divisor of a pair of unequal positive integers is the greatest common divisor of the smaller integer and their difference.

Encode these properties of the relation as a recursive micro-PROLOG definition of the relation

> (x y) GCD z

which holds when x and y are positive integers and z is their greatest common divisor. Rule (B) will need to be expressed as two rules, one for the case when x is less than y and the other for the case that y is less than x. Use your definition to find the greatest common divisor of different pairs of positive integers.

2. The definition of "between" given above excludes the upper end of the interval. Add an extra rule so that it is included. Where must you position the rule so that the upper limit is the last value given when you are trying to find all the numbers in an interval.

3. Define the property "even" that holds if a number is divisible by 2 using the TIMES relation. Use this relation and "between" to define

    x even-num-in (y z) :
        x is an even integer in the range y <= x < z

Use the definition to find all the even numbers in the range 1 to 100.

4. Pose a query to find all the pairs of positive integers whose product is 12. You need to use "between".

5. Define the relation

    x divisor-of y :
            x is an integer between 2 and y that exactly divides y

Use your definition to find all the positive integer divisors of some integer.

3. Lists

3.1 List as Individuals

So far we have only seen how to handle facts that referred to single individuals. Sometimes it is more convenient to have a fact that refers to a list of individuals. This is quite common in English. We say:

John enjoys football, cricket and rugby

which is a fact that relates John to the list (football cricket rugby) of games that he enjoys. We can represent this compound fact in micro-PROLOG by three simple sentences:

John enjoys football
John enjoys cricket   (1)
John enjoys rugby

We can also represent it by a single sentence:

John enjoys (football cricket rugby)   (2)

in which we collect together the games that John enjoys as a list (football cricket rugby). The query:

&.which(x : John enjoys x)

used with this single sentence program (2) will produce the response:

(football cricket rugby)
No (more) answers

because the pattern "John enjoys x" matches the data base sentence only when x is this list. The advantage of using lists in place of single individuals is that we often get a more natural and compact representation of information. The disadvantage is that we must sometimes do some work to get at the individuals in a list. With the information about John represented by the three sentences (1) we can directly query the data base about individual games. The query:

&.is(John enjoys football)

will return the answer "YES". But for representation (2) the query will get the answer "NO". This is because there is no sentence in the data base that exactly matches the query. To find out if John enjoys football we must be able to get at the components of the list of games (football cricket rugby).

Exercises 3-1

1. You have this micro-PROLOG program which is an alternative representation of the bicycle parts data:

(wheel frame pedals saddle handle-bars
     lighting-system brake-system) part-of bicycle
(hub spokes gear-cogs) part-of wheel
(brake-cable brake-block) part-of brake-system
(dynamo lights electric-flex) part-of lighting-system

Answer these micro-PROLOG queries:
a. which(x : x part-of y)
b. is(x part-of dynamo)
c. which(x : y part-of x)
d. is(dynamo part-of lighting-system)

2. Re-express the books data base information using lists of words for titles and author names. For example, the sentence:

Oliver-Twist written-by Charles-Dickens
becomes
(Oliver Twist) written-by (Charles Dickens)

This enables us to separate authors' surnames from their first name. "written-by" is now a relation between a list of words of the title and a list of the names of an author.

3.2   Getting at the members of a list of fixed length

To get at the components of a list we have to elaborate the idea of patterns and pattern-matching introduced earlier. To illustrate these ideas, let us look at a different way of representing information about family relationships which makes use of lists.

Initially we recorded the parent-child information by having separate sentences giving each of the children of each parent. Using lists we can collect together all the information about a particular family in one sentence of the form:

(father mother) parents-of (all their children)

The facts of the family relations data base are now sentences such as:

(Henry Sally) parents-of (Margaret Bob)
(Henry Mary) parents-of (Elizabeth Bill Paul)
(Bill Jane) parents-of (Jim)
(Paul Jill) parents-of (John Janet)

The sentence

(Bill Jane) parents-of (Jim)

records the only child of Bill and Jane in a list with just one name. In this case, we might have expressed this information in the sentence

(Bill Jane) parents-of Jim

But then our facts about families would not have been all of the same form. In some we would have lists of children, in some just single names. It is important that all sentences about a relation all have a uniform pattern. micro-PROLOG retrieves data by matching sentences with patterns, and patterns are critical when we use lists. So, for uniformity, we have recorded the only child in a list of one name.

The expression "(Jim)" is a list because of the brackets. If we drop the name altogether, writing "()", we have a list of no names: we have an **empty** list. We can use the empty list to record information about couples with no children. We can have a sentence such as:

(Samuel Sarah) parents-of ()

This records the fact that Samuel and Sarah are to be treated as a couple but it also tells us they have no children. (If we had been using the "father-of", "mother-of" relations to record the family data we would have to record this information using an auxiliary relation "partner-of".)

System note - use **accept** - If you are following the text using a computer enter the above "parents-of" facts using **accept**. When you give the list of the two arguments of the relation remember that each argument is now itself a list. So, the above fact is represented in the prefix form required by **accept** as

   parents-of ((Samuel Sarah) ())

   Suppose that we now want to retrieve the children of Henry. The data giving Henry's children is contained in all the sentences of the form:

   (Henry y) parents-of x

So the query is:

   which(x : (Henry y) parents-of x)
   (Margaret Bob)
   (Elizabeth Bill Paul)
   No (more) answers

   Consider the sentence pattern

   (x y) parents-of (x1 x2 x3)

This will match any fact in the data base about a family with three children x1, x2, x3. We can therefore use this to retrieve information about all the three-child families.

   all (children x1 x2 x3 father x mother y :
        (x y) parents-of (x1 x2 x3))
   (children Elizabeth Bill Paul father Henry mother Mary)
   No (more) answers

Here we have used an answer pattern to rearrange the retrieved data and to give some documentation.
   The pattern

   (x y) parents-of z

matches every fact in the data base about families. In this pattern x is the father, y is the mother and z the list of children. We can, therefore, define "father-of-children" and "mother-of-children" relations with the rules:

> x father-of-children z if (x y) parents-of z
> y mother-of-children z if (x y) parents-of z

Then a typical query to find the children of Jill would be:

> which(z : Jill mother-of-children z)
> (John Janet)
> No (more) answers

We get a list of children because we have defined "mother-of-children" as a relation between an individual and the list of children with the same father.

Exercises 3-2

1. Using the notation for the empty list, give a definition of the relation "x childless-wife" in terms of "parents-of".

2. Using the example program above, answer the following micro-PROLOG queries:
a.   which(x : (Bill x) parents-of y)
b.   which(x y : (z x) parents-of (x y))
c.   is((Henry x) parents-of (y z X))
d.   which(x : (x y) parents-of z)
e.   all(x father y mother z child X child : (x y) parents-of (z X))
f.   which(x : Paul father-of-children x)

3. Using the new books data base, answer the following micro-PROLOG queries:
a.   which(x : (Oliver Twist) written-by (Charles x))
b.   is((Great x) type Novel)
c.   which(x y : x written-by (Mark y))
d.   which(x was a great playwright : (Macbeth) written-by x)
e.   which(x : (x y) written-by z)

Lists of lists

Just as the individuals of a relation can be lists, so the individuals, more technically the *elements*, of a list can be lists. Indeed we can arbitrarily mix names of individuals with lists, with lists of lists, and so on. There is no constraint on the mix that we can have or the degree to which we can have nested list structures. As an example

((a b) c () ((d) e))

is a list of four elements. The first element is a (sub)list of two names "a" and "b". The second element is a name, "c". The third is the empty list "()", and the fourth is a list comprising a (sub)list of one name "(d)" and the name "e".

Of course, if we do use such nested structures to record information we should normally stick to one 'pattern', the pattern that we can then use to get at the components of the structure.

We can use lists of lists to put more information into each fact of our family data base. Instead of having each person represented just by their name we could represent them by a list of data about them. For example, we could use a list of two elements comprising the name and age. We would then have facts such as

((Bill 53) (Jane 47)) parents-of ((Jim 17))

The above definitions for "father-of-children" and "mother-of-children" are still valid. The only difference is that they now define relations between a list (representing a single parent) and a list of lists (representing a list of children). To find the children of Jane we must use the query

which(x : (Jane y) mother-of-children x)
((Jim 17))
No (more) answers

Notice that we have named Jane with the list (Jane y). This is because we know that she is denoted by such a two-element list in which the second element is her age. By giving the age as a variable in the query we do not need to guess the age. The answer we get is a list of lists telling us that she has one seventeen-year old child named Jim.

Terms

We are now in a position to give a complete description of the syntax of the allowed arguments relations. The argument of a relation can be term, where a *term* is:

a constant (i.e. a name)
a number
a variable
a (possibly empty) list of terms

3.3   Getting at the members of a list of unkown length

Using a list representation of family relationships we are still not able to check, with a single query, whether or not someone is some particular child's mother. The trouble is that a single pattern cannot cover all the different size lists of children that we can get back in response to a mother-of-children query. The rules:

y mother-of-child x1 if (x y) parents-of (x1 x2)
y mother-of child x2 if (x y) parents-of (x1 x2)

define the mother-of-child relation for families with two children because such families are recorded by sentences of the form "(x y) parents-of (x1 x2)". Each rule selects out one of the pair of children (x1 x2). But we also need a rule to cover single-child families:

y mother-of-child z if (x y) parents-of (z)

and rules for three, four and even bigger size families.
We can make do with a single rule:

y mother-of-child z if
(x y) parents-of Z and z belongs-to Z

if we could define the relation "z belongs-to Z" that holds for every element z that appears in an arbitrary size list of individuals Z.

Heads and Tails

An arbitrary size list is of the form

(x1 x2 ... xn)
 | ‾‾‾‾‾‾‾‾‾
head tail

Let us call the first element in the list, x1, the **head** of the list. If we take away the head element we are left with a list (x2 ... xn) which we shall call the **tail** of the list. The tail of a list that only contains one element, is the **empty** list ().

One rule about membership of an arbitrary size list is:

The head of a list is a member of the list   (3)

Another is:

Something is a member of a list if
   it is a member of its tail   (4)

Just like our recursive definition of the "ancestor-of" relation these two rules enable us to check whether any individual appears on a list.

To formalise these as micro-PROLOG rules we need to have a pattern that enables us to talk about the head and the tail of a list. This is the pattern (x|y).

We read the pattern as:

(x|y) is a list which is the element x
   followed by the list y.

The "|" stands for "followed by". Without the "|" sign the pattern (x y) denotes a list of two elements x and y. The "|" between the x and y signals that y is not the second element of a two element list, but that it is the list of all the elements that follow x on a list of arbitrary size.

If micro-PROLOG matches (x|y) against the list (A B C D) it gives x the value A and y the value (B C D). If it matches (x|y) against the list (A), comprising just the element A, then x is given the value A and y the value (). This is because (A) is the element A *followed* by no other elements. Or looked at another way, it is the element A *followed* by the empty list (). Other examples of the use of "|" in list patterns are:

(x y | z)

This denotes a list of two individuals x y followed by some remainder list z. Since z can be the empty list, the pattern denotes any list of two or more individuals. Matched against the list (A B C D) we get the values x=A, y=B, z=(C D). It fails to match the list (A) because this only has one element.

(x y z | Z)

is a list of three individuals x y z followed by some remainder list Z. It denotes any list of at least three elements.

We can describe a list of at least **n** individuals by having **n** different variables before the "|". We should always follow the "|" with a variable or another pattern that describes a list. For example, (x1 x2|(x3 x4)) is the list x1 x2 followed by the list of two elements x3 x4. In other words, it denotes the list of four individuals (x1 x2 x3 x4).

In this case, there is no point in using the "|". Indeed there is only a point in using "|" when we do not know anything about the remainder of the list, i.e. when we describe it by a variable that can match any remaining list of elements.

If we are using lists of lists we use nested list patterns. The pattern

((x y) | Z)

represents any list which starts with a sub-list of two elements. It matches the list

((a b) c) with x=a,y=b,Z=(c)

The pattern

((x|Y) | Z)

describes any list that begins with a sublist which has at least one element, the element x. It matches

((a)) with x=a,Y=(),Z=()
((a b) c) with x=a,Y=(b),Z=(c)

Exercises 3-3

1. What values if any, are assigned to the variables when (x y z|Z) is matched against:
a. (A B C D E)
b. (A B C D)
c. (A B C)
d. (A B)
e. (A)
f. ()

2. Give the pattern that represents
a. a list of three elements whose second element is a sublist of two elements.
b. a list whose first element is a sublist of at least two elements.

3. What values are given to x and y when the list patterns
    ((A B)|x) and (y C|y) are matched.
Hint: ((A B)|x) matches any list that has as its first element the sublist (A B).

4. Give a different representation of the bicycle parts data of the form:

    (component number) part-of component

For example,

    (wheel 2) part-of bicycle
    (spokes 60) part-of wheel

Define the relations

    (x y) indirect-part-of z:
        y number of x's are contained in z
    z indirectly-contains (x y):
        z contains y number of x's

in an analogous way to the relations defined in Exercise 2-3(4). Do not forget to multiply the number of components in the recursive rules. The answer to

    which(y : (spokes y) indirect-part-of bicycle)

should be 120 not 60.

Belongs-to

Using the "|" pattern, we can express our rules (3) and (4) about "belongs-to" directly as micro-PROLOG rules:

X belongs-to (X|Z)   (5)
X belongs-to (Y|Z) if X belongs-to Z   (6)

Let us illustrate how this definition is used by micro-PROLOG to find all the elements on a list (A B C D E). If we ask:

all(x : x belongs-to (A B C D E))

we first get the answer

A

This is produced by the attempt to use the first sentence, rule (5), to find a solution to the query condition

x belongs-to (A B C D E)   (7)

The condition is matched against

X belongs-to (X|Y)   (the first rule (5))

Matching X with x makes X=x. So, when the second argument (X|Y) is matched against (A B C D E) micro-PROLOG is really matching (x|Y) against the list. This makes x=A and Y=(B C D E). Since there are no preconditions to the rule the successful match immediately results in an answer to the query, the answer A. micro-PROLOG now backtracks to try the second sentence for "belongs-to" in order to find more solutions to the query condition. It now matches (7) against

X belongs-to (Y|Z)   (the conclusion of the rule (6))

This results in the values X=x, Y=A, Z=(B C D E). With these values for the variables the precondition of the rule becomes

x belongs-to (B C D E)   (8)

All the solutions to this condition are all the remaining solutions to the original query condition (7).

    micro-PROLOG continues in this way, first using rule (5) then rule (6), until it has found all the elements of (B C D E). The last element E is found when it applies rule (5) to the derived condition

    x belongs-to (E)   (9)

But micro-PROLOG does not yet know that it is the last answer. There is still a sentence about the relation, namely rule (6), that it has not yet used to try to find a solution to this condition. The application of rule (6) matches (9) against

    X belongs-to (Y|Z)

This results in the values $X=x$, $Y=E$, $Z=()$ and the reduction of (9) to the new condition

    x belongs-to ()

    Neither sentence for "belongs-to" matches this condition, so it has no solutions. This failure to match with either sentence is what tells micro-PROLOG that there are no more solutions to be found and so the evaluation of the query stops. The full answer to the query is therefore:

    A
    B
    C
    D
    E
    No (more) answers

System note - tracing "belongs-to" -If you are using a computer, load SIMTRACE and trace the evaluation of the query by using **all-trace**.

    We can now get at the individual children of Jill. Assuming the simpler representation in which people are denoted just by their names, we can either use the query

    which(x : Jill mother-of-children Z & x belongs-to Z)

or we can add the rule

y mother-of z if (x y) parents-of Z & z belongs-to Z

and use the query

which(x : Jill mother-of x)

In either case we will get the answers

John
Janet
No (more) answers

Notice that "mother-of" is a rule-defined relation that is the same as the fact-defined relation of Chapter 1.

Exercises 3-4

1. You have this micro-PROLOG program:

(English Welsh Gaelic) spoken-in United-Kingdom
(English French) spoken-in Canada

Answer these micro-PROLOG queries:
a.   which(x : x spoken-in Canada)
b.   which(x : (x|y) spoken-in z)
c.   which(x : y spoken-in United-Kingdom and x belongs-to y)
d.   is (x spoken-in United-Kingdom and y spoken-in Canada and z belongs-to x and z belongs-to y)
e.   Give a definition of the relation "x British-language" which is defined to be a language spoken both in the United-Kingdom and Canada.
f.   Assuming that the languages have been listed in order of importance in each case, give a definition of the relation x Minor-language : x a language of some country but not the most important spoken language of the country.

2. Answer these micro-PROLOG queries:
a.   which(x : x belongs-to (R O B E R T) and x belongs-to (B O B))
b.   is(x belongs-to (A L F) and x belongs-to (F R E D))

The spaces between the letters in these queries are important; spaces separate the members of a list. The list (R O B E R T) has six elements, each of which is a single letter. However, the list (ROBERT) has just one element, the word "ROBERT". It has one element because there are no separating spaces.

   In the answer to query b. you will get the letter "B" twice. This is because there are two ways of showing that the "B" of "(R O B E R T)" also appears on (B O B). In answering the conjunctive query, micro-PROLOG finds each letter in (R O B E R T) as a candidate value for x. For each value it looks for all ways of showing that the found x is also on the list (B O B). Each time it succeeds in doing this, it displays that value for x. If (R O B E R T) had been given as (R O B B E R T), with the two B's instead of one, "B" would be displayed four times. micro-PROLOG would find it twice, and each time twice confirm that it is also on the list (B O B).

3. Using the program developed in Section 3.2, give definitions of:
a.   x parent-of-children y
b.   x child-of y

   In each case make use of the "belongs-to" relation.

Alternative uses of "belongs-to"

   In Exercise 2 above the "belongs-to" program is used both for finding and for checking. The program is more versatile than that. We can use it to find all the lists with a given element. Since there are an infinite number of such lists, we must use the **one** query that allows us to finish when we have seen enough answers.

   one(x : 2 belongs-to x)
   (2|X)
   more?(y/n)**y**
   (X 2|Y)
   more?(y/n)**y**
   (X Y 2|x)
   more?(y/n)**n**

The answers are not particular lists but list patterns. The first answer (2|X) is the pattern representing any list that begins with 2. The second answer (X 2|Y) represents any list on which 2 is the second element. The third answer is any list on which it is the third element and so on. We can even use the program to find all instances of the relation with the query

   one(x X : x belongs-to X)

What do you think the answers will be?

Control reading of the "belongs-to" rules

The two rules:

X belongs-to (X|Y)
X belongs-to (Y|Z) if X belongs-to Z

can be given different control readings depending on the use. For the use to find an element on a list the appropriate reading is as the non-deterministic program:

(1) To find an element x on a given non-empty list (y|Y)
>   return x = y

or

>   find an element x on the tail list Y

For the use to check if a given element is on a given list the appropriate reading is:

(2) To check if something x is on a non-empty list (y|Y)
>   check if x = y

or

>   check if x is on the tail list Y

(3) For the non-terminating use to find a list on which an element occurs it is read:

To find a non-empty list Z on which x occurs
>   return the list pattern Z = (x|Y) or
>   find a list Y on which x occurs and return the list
>   pattern Z = (y|Y) where y is a variable not on Y

This use has an infinite number of solutions because the 'else' branch will always apply to each recursively derived condition to find a list on which x occurs.

3.4   The length of a list

A very useful list program is the "has-length" program which is a definition of the relation between a list and its length. There are just two sentences in the "has-length" program, a fact and a rule:

() has-length 0
(x|X) has-length z if X has-length y and SUM(y 1 z)

The logical reading of these rules is:

The empty list () has length 0

A non-empty list (x|X) has length one more than the length of its tail sub-list X

As with the "belongs-to" relation the control reading is best linked with a particular use. Let us first examine some different uses.

To find the length of the list (A B C D) we use the query

which(x : (A B C D) has-length x)
4
No (more) answers

To check that the list has length 4 we use

is((A B C D) has-length 4)

The finding length and checking length uses are to be expected. The rules can also use be used (somewhat inefficiently) to find a list pattern of a given length, or to find all instances of the "has-length" relation.

one(x : x has-length 4)
(X Y Z x)
more? (y/n)n

and

one(x y : x has-length y)
() 0
more? (y/n)y
(X) 1
more? (y/n)y
(X Y) 2
more? (y/n)y
(X Y Z) 3
more? (y/n)n

System note - tracing "has-length" - If you have a computer handy, define "has-length" and try the queries. Better still, trace their evaluations using **all-trace**. Stop the evaluation of the first query after it has given you the one list pattern of length 4. If you do not micro-PROLOG will continue indefinitely and fruitlessly trying to find another pattern of length 4. (If you use **all-trace** you can follow through the initial steps of this fruitless search.) Keep responding with **y** to the second query until you get tired of seeing the answers. There an infinite number of answers to the query. It is important that you add the "has-length" fact before the rule. If you do not you will not get any answers to either of these queries.

Control readings

The different control readings reflect the way micro-PROLOG will use the definition to find a solution for each type of use.

(1) For the use to find the length of a given list it is read:

> To find the length z of a given list Y
>   if Y=(), return z=0

or

> if Y is of the form (x|X),
>   find the length y of X, return z=(y+1)

(2) For the use to find some instance of the relation it is read:

> To find a Y and z satisfying Y has-length z
>   return Y=() and z=0

or

> find an X,y satisfying X has-length y
> return the list pattern Y=(x|X) and the number z=(y+1)
> where x is a variable not on X

(3) For the use to find a list pattern of a given length it is read:

> To find a list Y of a given length z
>   if the length z=0, return Y=()

or

> find a pair X and y that satisfies X has-length y such
> that the condition y=(z+1) can be confirmed
> return the list pattern Y=(x|X) where x is a variable
> not on X.

Notice that for this third 'inverted' use the same program is also used as a generator of pairs X,y of lists and their lengths which are checked by the condition $y=(z+1)$ on the length. It is not the most efficient way to find a list pattern of a given length. But there is another more serious disadvantage. We know that there are an infinite number of X,y pairs satisfying the condition "X has-length y". This means that micro-PROLOG's backtracking search will enter a bottomless pit if there is an attempt to find a second solution to a condition to find a list pattern of a given length. To see how this can happen let us examine the evaluation of the query:

> one(x : x has-length 4)   (A)

We assume that the sentences for "has-length" are as originally given, with the fact before the rule.

micro-PROLOG first tries to use the fact

> () has-length 0

to match the query condition

> x has-length 4

It fails to get a match, since 4 and 0 are different. It can only solve the condition by using the rule, which with renamed variables, is

> (x1|X1) has-length z1 if
>   X1 has-length y1 & SUM(y1 1 z1)

There is a successful match with the query condition providing $x=(x1|X1)$ and $z1=4$. micro-PROLOG reduces the condition of (A) to

> X1 has-length y1 & SUM(y1 1 4)   (B)

The answer to (A) is

> (x1|X1)

where X1 has the value given by the solution to (B).

The condition "X1 has-length y1" of (B) becomes a generator for candidate values for X1 and y1 with the y1 value checked with the SUM(y1 1 4) condition. Now we know that there are an infinite number of solutions to the "X1 has-length y1" condition and that the solutions will be generated in order of increasing length. When the solution X1=(x2 x3 x4), y1=3 is generated we get the answer (x1 x2 x3 x4) to query (A).

This is, of course, the only answer. But micro-PROLOG does not know this. It will happily continue generating more and more candidate solutions for the condition "X1 has-length y1" checking if the value of y1 is one less than 4. If we let it, after giving us the only answer, micro-PROLOG will enter a bottomless pit in its search for a second answer. It will not be able to detect that are no more answers.

This is similar to the problem that can arise if we do not choose a judicious ordering for the rules of a recursively defined relation. In this case, the problem is that the ordering of the preconditions of the rule

> (x|X) has-length z if
>   X has-length y & SUM(y 1 z)

is not appropriate for the use in which the length is given and a list of that length is to be found. For this use, we should put the SUM(y 1 z) condition first. But if we do this we shall have a problem with the finding length use. For then micro-PROLOG will encounter the problem of trying to find a solution to SUM(y 1 z) with both the arguments y and z unknown. As with the "ancestor-of" relation of Chapter 2 we need a separate definition of the inverse relation, "length-of".

The two sentences,

> 0 length-of ()
> y length-of (x|X) if
>   y INT & 0 LESS y &
>   SUM(z 1 y) & z length-of X

are a definition of the relation with an ordering of the preconditions of the rule that limits the use to queries in which the length of the list, which must an positive integer, is given. But for that use, it is an efficient, safe program. We can even use it to evaluate the query

> which(x : 4 length-of x)
> (X Y Z x)
> No (more) answers

This time, micro-PROLOG stops when it has found the only answer, and tells us there are no more answers.

System note - tracing "length-of" - Follow through the evaluation by hand or trace it using the **all-trace**. You will see that the evaluation stops because the condition SUM(z 1 y), with y given, only has one solution and because the attempt to use the recursive rule to solve the final condition "0 length-of x4" will fail when it reaches the **LESS** condition of the rule. As with the definition of "between" given in Chapter 2, the **LESS** condition is logically redundant but is necessary in order to forstall an infinite recursion when the rule is applied to a condition with a non-positive length.

Conclusion

To find the length of a list use the "has-length" relation defined by the sentences:

() has-length 0
(x|X) has-length z if
     X has-length y and SUM(y 1 z)

To find a list of variables of a given length, use the "length-of" relation defined by the sentences:

0 length-of ()
y length-of (x|X) if
     y INT & 0 LESS y &
     SUM(z 1 y) & z length-of X

For this use a suitable control reading of the "length-of" program is:

To find a list Y of variables of a given length y
    if the length y=0 return the list Y=()

or

    check that y is an integer & y > 0, subtract one from y
    to give z and then find a list X of variables of length
    z, then return the list pattern Y=(x|X) where x is a
    variable not on the list X

To check that a given list has a given length, use either relation. For the checking use the "has-length" program can be read:

To check that a given list Y· has a given length y
  check that Y=() and y=0

or

if Y has the form (x|X), find the length of the list X
and then check that this is one less than the given
length y

whereas the "length-of" program is read:

To check that a given list Y has a given length y
  check that y=0 and Y=()

or

if Y has the form (x|X) check that the length y is a
positive integer, subtract 1 from y to give z, check that
z is the length of X

Do not use either relation to find some instance of the
relation that will be checked by a second condition. This is
because there are infinite number of answers to the condition

X has-length y

and micro-PROLOG's backtracking evaluation will enter a
bottomless pit generating all the different solutions. This problem
will not arise with "length-of". Instead, micro-PROLOG will give a
"Too many variables" error message when trying to answer

y length-of X

This is because it will try to evaluate an **INT** condition with the
argument unknown.

Taking into account these sorts of restrictions on the use of
micro-PROLOG programs, particularly programs that embody a
recursive definition or use the arithmetic primitives, is part of the
pragmatics of programming in the language.

Incidentally, the "has-length" program has no problem
finding the length of a list of variables. The query

which(x y : 4 length-of x & x has-length y)

will produce the response

(X Y Z x) 4
No (more) answers.

Try it!

Exercises 3-5

1. Use the "has-length" program to define a rule which gives the number of children a mother has, and find out how many children Jill has.

2.
a. Pose the query: Who has five children? (use the "has-length" program in your query.)
b. Pose the same query, but this time use "length-of".

3. What answers will you get to the query
   all(x : 3 length-of x & 2 belongs-to x)

Unification and the EQ relation

We can get answers to queries that contain variables because micro-PROLOG uses a powerful pattern matching method called *unification*. In a unification two patterns can be matched. The result of such a unification is an assignment of values to the variables of the two patterns so that each pattern becomes identical. The assignment of values produces a common instance of each pattern. Moreover, this common instance is always the most general common instance. That is, if a variable can be left unassigned it is left unassigned. So the common instance may be itself a pattern.

An example of this unification of patterns is the matching of

(X Y |Z) and ((x y)|z)

The most general instance of the two patterns is

((x y) Y |Z)

The assignment X=(x y), z=(Y|Z) reduces each pattern to this most general common instance. It is a most general common instance because any other common instance, for example ((a b) c |Z)

can be obtained by assigning values to its variables. The
assignment x=a, y=b, Y=c converts

((x y) Y |Z)

into this other common instance.

The matching that micro-PROLOG performs whenever it
compares a condition with a simple sentence always produces an
assignment of values that produces a most general common
instance. If there is no such assignment, the match fails. The
match also fails if there are no variables to be given values and
the condition and sentence are not identical.

An example of a pair of patterns that cannot be unified is

(A y y) and (x x C)

There is no common instance because the first pattern insists that
the second and third elements are the same and the second insists
that the first and second elements are identical. This means that a
common instance must have all three elements identical. This is
not possible since the first list already contains an A and the
second a C.

There is a primitive relation of micro-PROLOG called **EQ**
the evaluation of which is an attempt to unify its two arguments.
Its built-in definition is the single rule

x EQ x

It holds only if its two arguments are identical or can be made
identical by a unification match. The query

which((x y b) : (x y b) EQ (z () z))

will give the answer

(b () b)

since this is the only common instance of the two list pattern
arguments of the **EQ** condition.

Using the **EQ** relation we could rewrite every rule so that
the consequent only had variables as arguments. Thus, the rule

x belongs-to (x|y)

is equivalent to

x belongs-to z if z EQ (x|y)

However, rules with patterns in the consequent are generally more readable than rules with **EQ** preconditions.

Building a chain of descendants

The "length-of" program can be used to construct a list of variables given a length. Programs that can be used to construct lists are exceedingly useful. We shall deal with them more fully in Chapter 5. We shall complete this section by giving a program that is similar to "length-of". It can be used to find a list of intermediary parents that connect two individuals in a parent-of chain. It is a program that defines the relation

(x y) have-descendant-chain X:
    y is a descendant of x and
    X is the list of intermediary parents.

Its definition is:

(x y) have-descendant-chain () if
    x parent-of y
(x y) have-descendant-chain (z|X) if
    x parent-of z and
    (z y) have-descendant-chain X

The logical reading of the two rules is:

() is the descendant chain between x and y
    if x is a parent of y

(z|X) is the descendant chain between x and y
    if z is some offspring of x and
        X is the descendant chain between z and y

For the use to find descendant chains connecting a pair of given people the control reading of the pair of rules is:

To find the descendant chain between given x and y
   return the list () if x is a parent of y or
   find an offspring z of x,
   find the descendant chain X between z and y,
   return the list (z|X)

It can also be used to check that a pair have a given descendant chain, to find pairs connected by a given chain, even to find all x y pairs with their connecting descendant chains.

The program is a classic example of how the data base handling and the list processing sides of micro-PROLOG co-operate. When used to find the ancestor chain between two individuals, the recursive 'walk' over the "parent-of" data base that is performed is combined with the construction of a list. This list reflects the sequence of steps needed to 'complete' the descendant link between the pair of individuals.

Exercises 3-6

1. Using the program for "have-descendant-chain", pose and answer these questions:
a.   What is the list of descendants between Arthur and Robert?
b.   How many generations are there between Jane and Robert?
c.   Give all the pairs of people separated by one intermediary parent, i.e. the grandparent, grandchild pairs.

   Make use of the following facts:

   Jane parent-of Arthur
   Arthur parent-of Peter
   Mary parent-of Peter
   Peter parent-of Robert

2. Define "is-a-great-grandparent-of" in terms of "has-descendant-chain".

3.5   Answer sets as lists

We shall now look more closely at the relationship between information represented by facts about individuals and the same information represented by facts about lists of individuals. We started the chapter by observing that a lot of facts can often be more compactly represented using lists. For example, in the family relationship data base we can have a single fact giving both parents and all the children instead of several facts describing each "father-of", "mother-of" relationship.

These two representations of the family information both contain essentially the same information. The "parents-of" facts relating both the parents to their children implicitly contains the "father-of", "mother-of" relations. Indeed we have already seen how we can define the "father-of" and "mother-of" relations in terms of the "parents-of" relation using "belongs-to". The definition of "father-of" is:

> x father-of y if
> (x z) parents-of Y and y belongs-to Y

Using "belongs-to" we can always define relations over individuals in terms of relations over lists of individuals. Can we do the reverse definition? Can we define the "parents-of" relation in terms of the "father-of" and "mother-of" relations? The answer is YES.

The complex condition isall

We make use of a complex condition of micro-PROLOG called isall. A complex condition is like the simple sentence conditions we have seen so far, except that it involves a combination of one or more simple sentences. We shall briefly introduce the isall condition here. It is more fully described together with the other types of complex condition in micro-PROLOG in the next chapter.

What isall does is wrap up all the answers to a query as a list. Consider the query:

> all(y : Henry father-of y)

The answer to this query is all the children of Henry. micro-PROLOG displays them as:

> Mary
> Elizabeth2
> Edward
> No (more) answers

Using isall we can put all these answers into a list in the reverse order in which they are displayed. Thus, the query:

which(x : x isall (y : Henry father-of y))

has one answer:

(Edward Elizabeth2 Mary)
No (more) answers

We can use **isall** to define the relation "father-of-children" in terms of the "father-of" relation. The latter relates a father to a single child, the former relates him to the list of all his children. The rule defining the relation is:

x father-of-children Y if
      Y isall (z : x father-of z)

We can also use **isall** to define the "parents-of" relation using both the "father-of" and "mother-of" relations. Its definition is:

(x y) parents-of Z if
      Z isall (z : x father-of z and y mother-of z)

and its logical reading is:

x and y are the mother and father of all the children of list Z
      if Z is the list of all the children of x
      that are also children of y

Just like a **which** or **all** query the condition of an **isall** can be any conjunctive condition.

The **isall** condition has many useful applications, all stemming from its ability to make available in a list all the answers to some query. For example, coupled with "length-of" we can use it define a relation that gives the *number* of children when we only have the "parent-of" relation for individuals.

x has-no-of-children y if
      z isall (X : x parent-of X) & z has-length y

Exercises 3-7

1. Give a query which asks how many male children someone (Peter, say) has.

2. Suppose that we extend the FAMILY data base by giving family names with facts such as:

    Henry-Snr family Smith
    Elizabeth1 family Smith
    Charles family Jones
    George family Clarke

Pose the following questions as queries that use **isall**:
a.   What is the list of people in the Smith family?
b.   How many Jones's are there?

3. Give the rules which define the relation: x is the last element of a list y.
Hint: The last member of a list with only one element is that element. The last element of a list of at least two elements is the last element of the tail of the list.

4. Define the relation "(x y) adjacent-on z" which holds when the pair of elements x and y are next to each other somewhere on the list z.
Hint: treat the two cases:
a.   x and y are the first two elements of the list,
b.   x and y are adjacent elements on the tail of the list.

    Test out your answers to 3 and 4 on various forms of query.

System note - interrupting execution - you can always interrupt the evaluation of a query that you think may have got into a bottomless pit by hitting the appropriate break keys. Consult the documentation for your implementation of micro-PROLOG to find which are the break keys for your implementation. (As an example, the control-C combination will abort any query or command if you are using a CP/M or MSDOS micro-PROLOG.)

5. In the introductory chapter we gave the rules

    x greater-of (x x)
    x greater-of (x y) if y LESS x
    y greater-of (x y) if x LESS y

defining the "greater-of" relation. Use the relation in a recursive

definition of "x max-of Y" : x the greatest number on the non-empty list Y. Treat the two cases:
a.   Y only has one element
b.   Y has more than one element.

6. The "belongs-to" relation defined by the pair of sentences

   x belongs-to (x|Z)
   x belongs-to (y|Z) if x belongs-to Z

is a relation between a list and its 'top-level' elements. It does not allow us to get at the elements of any sublists that might be on the list. Thus, the query

   is(b belongs-to (a (b) c)

will be answered "NO" because "b" is not a top-level element of the list. It is an element of the sublist "(b)" which is a top-level element. The query

   is((b) belongs-to (a (b) c)

will get the answer "YES". Now consider the relation "somewhere-on" defined by

   x somewhere-on X if x belongs-to X
   x somewhere-on X if y belongs-to X & x somewhere-on y

What answers will you get from the query

   which(x : x somewhere-on ((a b) () (c (d e) f) g)

Give an alternative definition of "somewhere-on" that does not make use of "belongs-to".
Hint: the definition is similar to that for "belongs-to" except that you need an extra rule for the case when the first element of the list is a sublist of at least one element.

Part II
Logic Programming using micro-PROLOG

4.   Complex conditions in queries and rules

At the end of the last chapter we introduced the **isall** condition. **isall** is an example of a complex condition that can be used in queries and the condition side of rules. There are several other complex conditions that we can use. In this chapter we introduce these other complex conditions and we give a more complete description of **isall**. We also describe the use of **is-told** which we can use to make micro-PROLOG query us for information whilst it is answering one of our queries.

4.1   Negated conditions

Sometimes the condition that we want the retrieved data to satisfy is more naturally expressed by giving a positive condition that it must satisfy and then giving an extra negative condition that it must *not* satisfy.

As an example, suppose that we wanted to retrieve all the descendants of Henry-Snr who do not themselves have any children, or rather, who do not have any children recorded in the data base. What we want are the x's such that

   x descendant-of Henry-Snr

can be confirmed, but for which the extra condition

   x parent-of y

cannot be confirmed. In micro-PROLOG we express this negative condition using **not**. We pose the query:

   which(x : x descendant-of Henry-Snr &
            not x parent-of y)

Since it is a general property of micro-PROLOG that any query expression can be used as the right-hand side of a rule, negated conditions can also be used in rules. Thus, the rule:

    x childless-descendant-of z if
            x descendant-of z and
            not x parent-of y

generalizes the query and defines the property of being a childless descendant.

Syntax of negated conditions

Syntactically, we have a new type of condition. Until we met the **isall** condition in the last chapter conditions were just simple sentences. A *negated condition* has the form:

    not C

where C is a single condition or a bracketed conjunctive condition. In other words, if we want to negate several conditions we must surround them with brackets. The brackets are needed to tell micro-PROLOG the extent of the negation.

We can have nested negations, for one or more of the conditions in a negated conjunction can be another negated condition.

The descriptive reading of a negated condition in a query or rule is:

    It is not the case that C for some y1,..,yk

Here, y1,..,yk are all the variables of C that *do not* appear elsewhere in the query or rule. They are the *local* variables of the negated condition. Variables that appear in C which also appear elsewhere are its *global* variables.

The rule defining "childless-descendant-of" is read:

    x is a childless descendant of z if
            x is a descendant of z &
                    it is not the case that
                            x is a parent of y, for some y

We say, "some y" because y is a local variable of the negated condition. The x is global because it appears elsewhere in the rule.

The query

which(x : x male & not (x father-of y & y male))

finds all the men who do not have sons. The negated condition is read as

x is not the father of *some* male y

because y is local to the condition.

Another example of the use of negation is in the query:

all(x : x city-of England & x population-is y &
          not y LESS 10000)

Used with a data base of cities and their populations it will give all the English cities of the data base that have a population greater than or equal to 10000.

Restrictions on use of **not**

A negated condition can only be used for *checking* values already given to its global variables. It *cannot* be used for generating candidate values for these global variables. This means that in a query a negated condition must be *preceded* by a positive condition for each of its global variables. In the evaluation of the query these positive conditions will be used to find values for the variables that the negated condition checks.

Control reading

The checking restriction on the use of negation is reflected in its control reading:

to confirm a condition : not C
     check that the query is(C) cannot be confirmed.

After the evaluation no variable of C will have a value. In other words, the evaluation of the negated condition

not C

becomes the evaluation of the query

    is(C)

with a "NO" answer interpreted as "YES" and a "YES" answer interpreted as "NO".

Let us see what happens if we ignore the positioning rule for negative conditions. Suppose we posed the query about the childless descendants of Henry-Snr as:

    which(x : not x parent-of y & x descendant-of Henry-Snr)

When micro-PROLOG evaluates the query it will now encounter the condition "not x parent-of y" with x not yet given a value. The evaluation of the condition reduces to the evaluation of

    is(x parent-of y)

which will, of course, be confirmed. (We have at least one person who is the parent of someone.) Confirmation of the is query is failure to confirm the negated condition. So micro-PROLOG will immediately print out

    No (more) answers.

This incorrect answer is a consequence of not placing the negative check on x after the positive generator for x which is the condition "x descendant-of Henry-Jnr".

For safety micro-PROLOG should give us an error message when it reaches a negative condition in which there is a global variable which has not been assigned a value. This would stop it giving an incorrect answer to the above query because x is a global variable of the negated condition without a value when the condition is checked.

micro-PROLOG does not give such an error message because to check that each global variable has a value each time a negated condition is evaluated would be a time consuming test. The decision was made to put the responsibility for ensuring that negated conditions will only be used for checking onto the programmer.

You must make sure that negative conditions will only be used for *checking* by a suitable ordering of the conditions of the query or rule. In practice this is not a problem.

Negated equalities

One of the most common uses of negation is a negated EQ condition. This confirms that the arguments of the EQ are not identical, or rather, cannot be unified.

Suppose that we wanted to define the relation

x brother-of y.

We must find some query condition that defines the brother relation. Two individuals x and y are brothers if:

they are male	x male & y male
they are different people	not x EQ y
they have a common parent	z parent-of x & z parent-of y

This gives us the rule:

        x brother-of y if
            x male & y male &
            not x EQ y &
            z parent-of x & z parent-of y

The negated condition "not x EQ y" has global variables x and y but it comes after the positive conditions "x male" and "y male" that will be generators of candidate values of these variables if the rule is used to find a pair of brothers.

Checking versus generating rules

When we use **not** in a rule we need not always make sure that it is preceded by positive conditions for its global variables. But, if we do not do this, we should make sure that the rule is only used for checking values of the global variables which are given in the condition to be solved.

As an example, consider the rule:

        x childless if not x parent-of y

This is read:

> x is childless if it is not the case that
> x is a parent of y, for some y.

Because the global variable of the negated condition must have a value when the condition is evaluated this rule can only be correctly used for *checking* that someone is childless. It *cannot* be used for *finding* childless people. For generality of use we would need to add an extra condition:

> x childless if x person & not x parent-of y

Here "person" is defined by the two rules:

> x person if x male
> x person if x female

This rule can be used both for checking and generating. When used for checking that someone is childless the "person" condition is redundant. Thus, if we *only* use the childless condition as a checking condition, the shorter restricted use rule might be preferred. But to use rules that can only be used as checking rules is to live dangerously. micro-PROLOG does not check that the restriction is adhered to. If you make a mistake, and try to use the rule to generate, you will get incorrect answers.

The rule that has the "person" condition also has another merit. It makes sure that only *people* are confirmed as childless. The shorter rule will confirm the condition "6 childless" because 6 is something for which there is no "parent-of" fact. So the condition

> not 6 parent-of y

will be solved.

not with belongs-to

We can use a negated condition to check that something is not on a list. As an example, the query:

> which(x : x belongs-to (a cow jumped over the moon)
>   & not x belongs-to (a the))

will give us all the words in the list (a cow jumped over the moon) which are not one of the articles (a the).

The query:

which(Z : Z isall
        (x : x belongs-to (P A L I N D R O M E)
          & not x belongs-to (A E I O U)))

gives the answer

(M R D N L P)

which is a list of all the non-vowels in the letters of PALINDROME.

Exercises 4-1

1. Give a definition of an odd number that makes use of the "even" number definition of Exercise 2-5.

Notice that your programs for "even" and "odd" can only be used for testing the relations they define.

2. Answer the following micro-PROLOG queries:

a.   all(x : x belongs-to (the quick brown fox) and not x belongs-to (how now brown cow))
b.   which(x : x isall (y : y belongs-to (F R E D) and not y belongs-to (D O R I S)))

3. Using the relations of the FAMILY program:

a.   Define the relation "a-man-with-no-sons".
b.   Define the relation "a-mother-with-no-daughters".

4. We can extend the BOOKS program into a library loan system. Records of book issues can have the form:

Issue (Name Title Author Issue-Date Due-Date)

for instance, the sentence:

Issue((Jim Gunn)
      (Oliver Twist)(Charles Dickens)
      (4 6 80)(18 6 80))

records the fact that Jim Gunn borrowed Oliver Twist, by Charles Dickens, on 4th June 1980, and is supposed to return it by the 18th. Our records of book returns can have the form:

Return (Name Title Author Return-Date)

for instance:

Return((Jim Gun)(Oliver Twist)(CharlesDickens)(12 6 80))

tells us that Jim Gunn returned his book on the 12th of June (before it became overdue)

a.   Add the following definition to your program:

A book is overdue if it has been issued, it has not been
returned, and the date is after the Due-Date.

Assume that the data base has an assertion "(....) date" which gives the current date as a list of three numbers in the order (day month year).

b.   Give the definition of "after" that you will use.
c.   Add the following rule to your program as a definition of the property "Banned":

Anybody who has an overdue book is banned from the library.

5. In Section 2.3 we defined the relation "has-divisor" in terms of "between" and "divides". Define "prime" in terms of "has-divisor" using not. Your definition can only be used for checking that a number is prime, i.e. that it has no divisors. Give the query to find all the prime numbers between 2 and 15.

6. An atomic part is a part with no sub-parts. Define "atomic-part" in terms of the "part-of" relation used for the bicycle parts data base. Give the query to find all the indirect atomic parts of a bicycle.

4.2   The isall condition

The isall condition is another form of complex condition. At the end of Chapter 3 we had some examples of its use.

Syntax of **isall** conditions

An isall condition has the form:

L isall (A : C)

where (A : C) are an answer-pattern and a query-condition as in a which query and L is a variable or a list pattern. The condition is read:

L is a list of all the A's such that C for some y1,..,yk

Here, y1,..,yk are the local variables of C, the variables that only appear in C. The global variables of C are the variables that also occur outside the isall condition somewhere else within the query or rule in which the isall is used.

Restrictions on use

As with negated conditions, when the isall condition is evaluated all the global variables of C must have values. So in a query we must precede an isall condition with generator conditions for its global variables, and in a rule we must have preceding generators or make sure that the global variables will be given values when the rule is used. micro-PROLOG does not check that the global variables of C have values when it evaluates the isall condition. As with not it is likely to give incorrect answers if they do not have values.

Generate use

Usually, the L argument of the isall condition will be a variable. The evaluation of the condition then generates a single value for the variable which is the list of all the answers to the query "all(A : C)" **in the reverse order** that they are found.

Checking use

In general, it is not wise to give L as a particular list and use the isall in a checking mode. This is because the condition will only be confirmed when the given L is identical to the list of answers that would be constructed in the generate use of the condition. Only if there is an exact match will the condition be solved. Thus, the query:

    is((Tom Dick Peter) isall (y : Mary mother-of y))

may fail to be confirmed even though Tom, Dick and Peter are the only answers to the query:

    which(y : Mary mother-of y)

This happens if the evaluation of this query would generate the answers in a different order from the reverse of the list (Tom Dick Peter). In Section 4.3 we shall see how we can get around this problem using a relation that checks that two lists have the same elements irrespective of the order.

     If the given list L is empty, or only contains one element, this problem of exact ordering of the elements does not arise. So isall can be safely used to check that there are no answers or that some individual is the only answer.

    is(() isall (x : Tom father-of x))

checks that Tom has no children. It is equivalent to the query

    is(not Tom father-of x)

The query

    is((Bill) isall (x : Tom father-of x))

checks that Bill is the only child of Tom.

     Finally, the list L can be given as a list of variables. The query:

    which(x1 x2 x3 z :
          (x1 x2 x3|z) isall (y : Mary mother-of y))

checks that there are at least three children of Mary, and if there are, gives us the names of three of them as the values of x1, x2 and x3. The names of any other children will be in the list value of z. The query

    which(x : 3 length-of x & x isall (y : Mary mother-of y))

checks that there are exactly three children and gives us their names. It uses the relation "length-of" that we discussed and defined in Chapter 3 to generate the list of three variables that is passed on to the **isall** condition. In this case we could equally have used "has-length" and the query

which(x : x isall (y : Mary mother-of y) & x has-length 3)

Only the evaluation behavior is different.

Control reading

The way an **isall** condition is evaluated is reflected in the alternative control reading:

To solve the condition : L isall (A : C)
        generate the list of answers to all(A : C) in the
        reverse of the order that they are found,
        then unify L with this list of answers

After the evaluation no variable of C will have a value.

Notice that any duplicate answers to "all(A : C)" appear as duplicates on the list L.

micro-PROLOG generates a reverse list of answers because in some implementations there is a very efficient implementation of the the **isall** construct that adds each answer to the front of a partial list of answers as it is found. It adds it to the front rather than the back of the partial answer list because adding elements to the front of a list is a much faster operation than adding them to the back.

In the next chapter we shall define a relation that can be used to add elements to the back of a list. We shall also define relations that can be used to reverse a list, to order a list or to remove duplicate elements. They can be used to manipulate the answer lists produced by **isall**.

Use of **isall** and "belongs-to"

The rule:

X intersection-of (Y Z) if X isall
        (x : x belongs-to Y & x belongs-to Z)

defines the relation that is satisfied when x is a list of all the individuals that appear on the lists Y and Z. Because of the restrictions on the use of isall it should only be used for construction of an intersection list. Notice that if Y or Z contains a duplicate of a common member this duplication will be repeated on the list X. But X will be without duplicates if Y and Z are without duplicates.

The rule:

> X difference-between (Y Z) if
>   X isall (y : y belongs-to Y & not y belongs-to Z)

defines the relation that holds when X is the list of elements on Y that are not on Z. It should only be used for finding X given Y and Z. The constructed list X will be without duplicates if Y is without duplicates.

Exercises 4-2

1. Using the relation "member-of-either" defined by the two rules:

> x member-of-either (y z) if x belongs-to y
> x member-of-either (y z) if x belongs-to z

give a rule for the relation "x union-of (y z)" that can be used for constructing a list x of all the individuals that are members of y or z.

2. Define the "subset-of" relation: x subset-of y holds when all the elements of x also belong to y. (Hint: x is a subset of y if x is the intersection of x and y.) We will revisit this example later.

3. Define the relation: X set-union-of (Y Z) which is the same as "union-of" except that its use will always give a list X without duplicates if Y and Z are without duplicates. Define it in terms of the "union-of", "intersection-of" and "difference-between".

4. Exercise 3-7(6) asked for a recursive definition of the relation "x somewhere-on Z" which holds when x is on Z or is somewhere on a sublist of Z. The definition allows x to be a list. The following sentences define a restricted form of this relation "x individual-on Z" which holds when x is a non-list element somewhere on the list Z. In other words, it excludes the sub-list elements.

> x individual-on (x|Z) if not x LST

x individual-on ((y|Y)|Z) if x individual-on (y|Y)
x individual-on (y|Z) if x individual-on Z

The relation **LST** is a primitive test relation of micro-PROLOG that is confirmed only when its argument is a list. (Specifically, LST is true of the empty list: "()", and the list pattern: "(X|Y)" where X and Y are any terms.)

An example use of "individual-on" is:

all(x : x individual-on ((a b) () (c (d)))
a
b
c
d
No (more) answers

Use "individual-on" and **isall** to define the relation

x flattens-to y

which holds when y is a list of all the individuals that appear somewhere on x. As an example,

((a (b c)) d e ((f)) (() (g (h (i j)))))

flattens to (j i h g f e d c b a). What happens to the order in which you get the elements of the flattened list if you reorder the sentences defining "individual-on" so that the last rule becomes the first rule?

Generate and check

Sometimes we want to check that the answers to a query all satisfy some condition. In the next section we will show how this can be tested directly with a single **forall** condition. As an exercise in the use of **isall** we show how it can be done using **isall** together with a recursively defined check on the answer list.

Suppose that we have a family data base and that we want to find all the men who only have sons. Earlier, we had the query

all(x : x male & not (x father-of y & y male))

to find all the men who do not have a son. To find those who only have sons is to find those who do not have a daughter. We can therefore replace the "y male" condition in the above query by "y female", or, to give an example of the use of a nested negation, by the condition "not y male". The query

all(x: x male & not(x father-of y & not y male))   (A)

is read as

> all the x's such that
>> x is male and it is not the case that
>> x is the father of some y who is not male

We can also express the query using **isall**. A male x satisfies the condition if all the answers to the query

all(y : x father-of y)

are male. By wrapping up these answers as a list using **isall**, we can check the condition using the "all-male" relation defined by:

() all-male
(u|x) all-male if u male & x all-male

This is the property that holds for a list if it is a list of males. The query to find all the men who only have sons can be posed:

all(x : x male & Z isall (y : x father-of y) & Z all-male) (B)

Notice that this query, and query (A) above, are both satisfied by men who have no children at all. This is a correct and strict interpretation of the condition "only have sons". If we wanted to insist that each man had at least one child we could replace the "x male" condition of both query (A) and query (B) by the condition "x father". This is defined by the single rule:

x father if x father-of y.

(A) and (B) are equivalent ways of expressing the same query. There is a third way using another complex condition.

all(x : x male & (forall x father-of y then y male))   (C)

This uses the **forall** condition we are about to describe. It has the effect of testing that all the children of x are male without the need to construct the list of these children. In this respect it is similar to query (A). Notice that in (A), (B) and (C) the global variable x of the complex condition of each query has a preceding generator, "x male".

4.3   The forall condition

Syntax of forall conditions

A forall condition has the form:

(forall C then C')

where C and C' are single conditions or conjunctive conditions. The outer brackets are essential. They tell micro-PROLOG where the C' ends and the next condition after the forall starts.

Logical reading

Its logical reading is:

for all the x1,..,xk such that C then C'

where x1,..xk, are all the local variables of the forall condition that appear in both C and C'.

The forall condition of query (C) of the preceding section is read

for all the y such that x is the father of y then y is male

Restrictions on use

The global variable restriction applies. All global variables of the condition, variables of C and C' that appear elsewhere in the query or rule, must have values before the condition is evaluated. Again, micro-PROLOG does not check that this constraint is satisfied. If it is not satisfied, micro-PROLOG's evaluation of the condition may not be correct. As with not and isall you must precede the condition with generators for its global variables, or make sure the rule in which it appears will only used for checking given values of the global variables.

The control reading

> to check the condition (forall C then C')
> > answer the query all(x1 x2 ..xk : C)
> > > as each answer is generated check that C' holds for
> > > that set of values of the shared local variables
> > > x1,..,xk
> > >
> > > if C' does not hold for some answer fail the **forall**
> > > condition and abandon the search for solutions to C
> > >
> > > if C' holds for every found answer, or if there are
> > > no solutions to C, report the **forall** condition as
> > > solved.

At the end of the evaluation no variable of the **forall** condition
will have a value.

Equivalent double negation

> The **forall** condition

> (forall C then C')

is equivalent to

> not (C and not (C'))

> It is equivalent because the double negation holds only if
there is no solution to

> C and not(C')

There is no solution to this conjunction of conditions if there is
no solution to C, or any found solution to C is such that when
it is passed on to not(C') this condition cannot be confirmed, i.e.
C' can be confirmed. These are exactly the same conditions under
which the **forall** condition is confirmed.

We had an example of this equivalence with the alternative
query conditions:

> x male & not(x father-of y & not y male)

x male & (forall x father-of y then y male)

in which C is "x father-of y" and C' is "y male". (In the double negation form brackets are not needed around the "y male" because it is a single condition.)

The **forall** form is easier to read and understand. However, micro-PROLOG converts all **forall** conditions into double negations before it evaluates them. The double negation form can therefore be viewed as the definition of **forall**.

Example uses of **forall**

(1) The rule:

X subset-of Y if
   (forall x belongs-to X then x belongs-to Y)

can be used to check that all the members of a list X are members of Y. The rule:

X same-elements-as Y if X subset-of Y & Y subset-of X

can be used to check that all the members of X are members of Y and vice-versa.

Notice that this defines a set equality with sets represented by lists of their elements. It can also be used to check if some list is just a permutation of the elements of another list. The relation can be used in conjunction with **isall** to check whether some particular set, represented as a list, is the set of answers to some query.

As an example, suppose that we wanted to check that Mary's children were Tom, Dick and Peter. The query

is(x isall (y : Mary mother-of y) &
               x same-elements-as (Tom Dick Peter))

checks this. It does not depend in any way on the order in which the answers to (y : Mary mother-of y) are placed on the answer list x. The use of "same-elements-as" is therefore the way round the restriction on the test use of **isall** that we discussed earlier.

(2) An ordered list is a list such that for all pairs of adjacent elements the condition "x lesseq y" holds. This gives us the rule:

X ordered if (forall (x y) adjacent-on X then x lesseq y)

This specification-like rule can be used for checking the ordered condition. The relation "(x y) adjacent-on X" which holds when (x y) are a pair of adjacent elements on a list X can be defined by:

(x y) adjacent-on (x y | X)
(x y) adjacent-on (z | X) if (x y) adjacent-on X

This definition of the relation was the answer to Exercise 3-7(5). The relation "lesseq" was defined in Exercise 2-3(3).

Exercises 4-3

1. Using the relations of the books data base, i.e. "writer", "written-by", "type", "published", define the following relations. Use **forall**.
a.   x novelist : x is a writer whose books are all novels.
b.   x modern-author : x is a writer whose recorded books are all published in the twentieth century.

2. Use **forall** to define:
a.   x positive-nums : x is a list of numbers greater than 0.
b.   x all-male : x is a list of names of males.

3. Define the relation disjoint(X Y): X and Y are lists with no common element. Define it using:
a.   **not**
b.   **isall**
c.   **forall**

   Any of these definitions can be used for testing the relation (but only for testing).

4. In Exercise 4-1(5) you were asked to define "prime" in terms of "has-divisor" using **not**. Give an alternative definition in terms of "divides" using **forall** and **not**. This should read as a high school definition of the property of being a prime number. Use your definition to test the property.

4.4   The or condition

In Chapter 2 when we defined "parent-of" in terms of "father-of" and "mother-of" we used two rules:

x parent-of y if x father-of y
x parent-of y if x mother-of y

Using **or** we can compress them into one rule:

x parent-of y if (either x father-of y or x mother-of y)

micro-PROLOG's use of this single rule is equivalent to its use of the two rules. When asked to solve a condition about "parent-of" it will search "father-of" sentences first because this is the **either** branch condition. Only when it has exhausted all the sentences defining "father-of" will it use the sentences defining the **or** branch condition "mother-of".

The **or** condition is particularly useful in queries. To avoid its use in

all(x: (either x in London or x in New-York) &
      x supplies IBM)

we would need to use two queries or first define "x in-L-or-NY" using the two rules:

x in-L-or-NY if x in London
x in-L-or-NY if x in New-York

We could then use the single query

all(x : x in-L-or-NY & x supplies IBM)

The use of the **or** condition makes the query easier to understand and quicker to pose.

Syntax of **or** conditions

The condition has the form

(either C or C')

where C and C' are single conditions or conjunctive conditions.

As with **forall** the outer brackets are needed to tell micro-PROLOG where C' ends. The conditions in C and C' can be any conditions. They can be simple sentences, negated conditions, **isall** conditions, **forall** conditions or nested **or** conditions.

An example use of a nested **or** is the query

all(x : (either x lives-in London or
         (either x lives-in New-York
          or x lives-in Paris)))

Note the necessary use of the inner brackets around the inner **either..or...**

Logical reading

The condition (either C or C')
     is read as : either C or C'

Control reading

To solve a condition of the form (either C or C')
     solve the condition C

or

     solve the condition C'

Here, the **or** is a non-deterministic branch giving an alternative solution path to be tried after the first C branch has been fully explored.

Single rules for list relations

If we want to absorb two rules defining a list relation into a single rule we usually have to make use of explicit **EQ** conditions to specialize or replace the list patterns used in the conclusions of the separate rules. The two rules:

> x belongs-to (x|y)
> x belongs-to (y|z) if x belongs-to z

can be expressed as the single rule

> x belongs-to (y|z) if (either x EQ y or x belongs-to z)

The condition "x EQ y" specializes the pattern (y|z) to the pattern (x|z) of the first of the pair of rules. In this case the single rule gives a readable and clear definition of the relation. However, more often than not the use of separate rules with different list patterns in the conclusion of each rule gives a clearer definition than a single either..or.. rule. The pair of rules:

> () has-length 0
> (z|Z) has-length y if Z has-length y1 & SUM(1 y1 y)

are a far clearer definition of "has-length" than the single equivalent rule:

> x has-length y if
>   (either x EQ () & y EQ 0
>   or x EQ (z|Z) & Z has-length y1 & SUM(1 y1 y))

Exercises 4-4

1. In Exercise 4-2(1) you were asked to define the relation "union-of" using isall and the auxiliary relation "member-of-either". Give a direct definition of "union-of" in terms of "belongs-to" using an either..or.. condition. This is an example of a clearer definition using either..or...

2. Give a single rule definition of the relation "last-of" that you defined in Exercise 3-7(3).

3. Give a single rule definition of the relation "adjacent-on" which you defined in Exercise 3-7(4).

4.5   Expression Conditions

At the end of Chapter 1 we introduced the primitive arithmetic relations of micro-PROLOG. To evaluate an arithmetic expression such as (3 * 5 + 9) using these relations we have to use the conjunction of conditions

TIMES(3 5 x) & SUM(x 9 y)

where y is the value of the expression and x is an intermediate variable used to help compute y. Most programming languages allow you to directly enter expressions like (3 * 5 + 9) and many of them compile such expressions into a sequence of operations as represented by the conjunction of the **TIMES** and **SUM** conditions. So it is with micro-PROLOG.

System note - using expressions on smaller computers - on some micro-computers you may have to load an extra program which extends the SIMPLE front end so that it can recognise and compile expressions. When we **add** a sentence or pose a query that contains expressions SIMPLE converts the expression into a conjunction of conditions. When we **list** a program in which expressions were used the same relation is used to de-compile the conjunction of conditions back into expression form.

Expressions can be used in two new kinds of condition: *equality conditions* and *expression conditions*.

Equality conditions

An equality condition has the form

E1 = E2

where E1 and E2 are expressions. The relation is an elaboration of the primitive **EQ** relation that was introduced in Chapter 3. The difference is that when an = condition is solved the two arguments are evaluated before they are compared using **EQ**. When one of the expressions is just a variable, the effect is to give it the value of the other expression.

Examples

x=(y * 67 + z)

can be used to give **x** the value of the bracketed expression if **y** and **z** have values at the time that the condition is evaluated. If they do not, there is a "Too many variables" message as when you directly use one of the arithmetic primitives and the condition has two many unknown arguments.

$$(x \ y)=((2*z) \ (z/45))$$

will cause (x y) to be matched against the list comprising the values of $(2*z)$ and $(z/45)$. It is therefore equivalent to the conjunction of equalities

$$x=(2*z) \ \& \ y=(z/45)$$

The equality

$$24=(2*x*x \ + \ 7*x)$$

can be used to check that some given value of x satisfies the equation:

$$2x^2 \ + \ 7x \ = \ 24$$

It cannot be used to *find* the roots of the equation. To find an integer root of the equation in the range 1 to 24 we can use the **between** relation as in the query:

which(x : x between (1 24) & $24=(2*x*x \ + \ 7*x)$)

In Exercise 1-4(2) you were asked to give the query to find how much money is needed to buy five apples and three loaves. Using only the arithmetic primitive relations the query is:

which(x : Apple costs y & Bread costs z &
            TIMES(y 5 X) & TIMES(z 3 Y) & SUM(X Y x))

Using an equality condition it is

which(x : Apple costs y & Bread costs z &
            x = $(y*5 \ + \ z*3)$)

Syntax of expressions

Formally, an *expression* is

a constant

a number
a variable
an arithmetic expression
a function call

or

a list of expressions

As we shall see arithmetic expressions and function calls are both just special kinds of lists. Notice the similarity between the definition of expression and the definition of term that we gave in Section 3.2. A term is an ordinary argument of a relation, an argument that does not contain any arithmetic expressions or function calls.

Syntax of arithmetic expressions

An **arithmetic expression** is a list of the form

(\<expression\> \<operator\> \<expression\>)

where the operator is one of

*	for multiplication
% or /	for division
+	for addition
- or ~	for subtraction

The outermost brackets of an arithmetic expression are essential - an arithmetic expression is a three-element list whose second element is an operator. However, if the expression arguments of this operator are also arithmetic expressions the *inner* brackets around them may be dropped in accordance with the following rules:

A *, / or % is evaluated before an adjacent +, ~ or -

For a pair of adjacent *, / or % operators the left one is evaluated first.

For a pair of adjacent +, ~ or - operators the left one is evaluated first.

The % is the main division operator with / an accepted synonym. If you use / in an expression in an added sentence you will find that it has been converted into a use of % when you list the sentence.

Likewise, - is the main subtraction operator with ˜ an accepted synonym. All uses of ˜ will be converted to uses of -. However, in general you should use ˜ when you enter expressions rather than -. This is because of the other syntactic roles of - to indicate that a number is negative and to hyphenate names. Thus, in the expression (x ˜ 4) the use of ˜ will be recognized as a use of the subtraction operator. If you use (x-4) this will be interpreted as a list containing the single hyphenated name "x-4". Likewise, the expression ((x*7) ˜ 6) will be recognized as equivalent to ((x * 7) - 6), but ((x*7)-6) will be interpreted as the list of expressions ((x * 7) -6), i.e. as a list of two elements comprising the value of (x * 7) and the number -6.

If you do use - make sure that you always surround it with spaces. Spaces are not needed around the other operators.

Examples of arithmetic expressions

(x*y+3/z) is equivalent to ((x * y) + (3 % z))
(x+y/(5+z)) is equivalent to (x + (y % (5 + z)))
(x*y/5 ˜ z) is equivalent to ((x * y) % 5) - z))

Function call expressions

Function calls are another form of expression. They allow program defined relations to be used as functions in expressions.

Examples

Suppose the relations **div** and **mod** are defined by the rules:

div(x y z) if TIMES(y z1 x) & INT(z1 z)
mod(x y z) if div(x y z1) & z=(x ˜ y*z1)

INT is the primitive of micro-PROLOG that we introduced in Chapter 2 which can be used to test if a number is an integer or to find the integer part of a number, as here. So, **div(x y z)** can be used to find the integer divisor **z** of **x** and **y** and **mod(x y z)** can be used to find the remainder **z** of the integer division of **x** by **y**. For both **div** and **mod** the last argument is functionally determined by the first two arguments. To use "div" and "mod" in expressions we declare that the last argument of each relation is a function of the preceding arguments with the commands:

    function div
    function mod

These two commands add the two sentences:

    div func
    mod func

to our program which record that they are special **func** relations. It is the presence of these **func** sentences that enables the expression compiler to recognize the use of "div" and "mod" in expressions as function calls. We can now use "div" and "mod" in expressions:

    x=((mod 85 23)*34)
    y=(div z (X * 6))

Thus, a function call in an expression is a list that begins with the name of a **func** ·recorded relation. The rest of the list are the arguments needed to find the value of the call. The function call (mod 85 32) has the value that would be given to x by an evaluation of the relational condition mod(85 32 x).

Syntax of function calls

A **function call** is a list of the form

    (R E1 .. En-1)   (A)

where **E1**...**En-1** are expressions and **R** is a n-ary relation name that has been declared a function with the command

    function R

The expressions are the first n-1 arguments of what would otherwise be given as a relational condition of the form

    R(V1 .. Vn-1 x)   (B)

where V1 .. Vn-1 are the values of the expressions E1 .. En-1.
    The value of function call (A) is the value that would be

given to x when (B) is solved.

Warning

If you forget to declare that some relation R is a function before using it in an expression the expression parser will not compile the function call into a relation condition. It will leave it as a list within the expression. However, whenever it ignores a list that might be intended as a function call the expression compiler warns you about this by giving you the message

R assumed not to be a function

If the function call was in a query you will now get the wrong answers. If it was used in an added sentence you can easily recover from this mistake. Declare R as a function with a

function R

command and edit the sentence. Just call the editor and then immediately exit the editor. The editor de-compiles the compiled form of the original sentence, mapping compiled expressions back into expression form. It re-compiles the expressions on exit. This time the use of R as a function call will be recognized because of the declaration.

You can always discover what functions have been declared using

which(x : x func)

or

list func

If you kill a relation that has been declared a function the func sentence for the relation will be automatically deleted.

Nested expressions

Function calls can be arguments to arithmetic operators and arithmetic expressions can be arguments to function calls. This is because each is just another form of expression and both take any expression as an argument. Function calls and arithmetic expressions can be nested inside each other without restriction.

Expression conditions

The equality condition is a special form of expression condition in which expressions can be evaluated and compared. When = is used in a sentence or query its use signals the fact that its arguments are expressions and that they should be compiled.

The default assumption for all other relations is that their arguments are not expressions, but are ordinary terms. Since this is invariably the case, this default assumption saves the time that would be wasted trying to compile non-expression arguments. However, we can override this default assumption, and cause micro-PROLOG to examine and compile expression arguments to any relation, by signalling their use. We do this by placing a "#" between the name of the relation and its list of expression arguments.

Example

LESS # ((2*x) (5+y))

is a **LESS** condition with arguments the values of the expressions (2*x), (5+y).

Syntax of expression condition

Expression conditions have the form

R # (E1 E2 .. Ek)

where R is the name of a relation and E1 ... Ek are expressions.

The # is the signal that E1 ... Ek are not normal arguments but that some or all of them contain arithmetic operators and function calls. Notice that expressions can only be used as arguments in relation conditions expressed in the prefix simple sentence form.

The equality condition

E1 = E2

is equivalent to the expression condition

EQ # (E1 E2)

Compiled form of expression conditions

Examples

(1) The relational form into which the condition

LESS # ((2*x) (5+y))

is compiled as:

(X LESS Y) # (* (2 x X) and + (5 y Y))

The # in this form should be read as **where**. So this condition
is read as

X LESS Y **where** X **is** 2 * x **and** Y **is** 5 + y

The arguments X, Y in the compiled **LESS** condition are such
that the evaluation of the conjunctive condition

* (2 x X) and + (5 y Y)

will result in their having the values of the expressions (2*x) and
(5+y) as required.

(2) The equality condition

(2*x) = (7%y)

is compiled into the relational form

(X EQ Y) # (* (2 x X) and %(7 y Y))

(3) The equality

x=((y*6) (56 ˜ x) 27)

which makes x a list of three numbers is compiled into

(x EQ (Y Z 27)) # (*(y 6 Y) and -(56 x Z))

More generally, the relational form into which an expression condition

R # (E1 E2 .. Ek)

is compiled is the single # complex condition

(R(t1 t2 .. tk)) # (<conjunctive condition>)

The evaluation of the bracketed conjunctive condition which follows the # will produce values for the variables of the terms t1, t2, .. tk so that they become the values of the original expressions E1, E2, .. Ek.

The expression condition is compiled into a single # condition so that it can be recognized and quickly mapped back into the expression condition when the program is listed or edited.

Special arithmetic relations

The compiled form of an arithmetic expression does not make use of the arithmetic primitives. Instead it uses arithmetic relations which have the names of the arithmetic operators. These +, -, * and % relations are defined within SIMPLE in terms of the arithmetic primitives. Their definitions are:

+(x y z) if SUM(x y z)
-(x y z) if SUM(y z x)
*(x y z) if TIMES(x y z)
%(x y z) if TIMES(y z x)

The auxiliary relations are used instead of the arithmetic primitives so that the compiled expressions can be quickly de-compiled back into expression form. You can of course make direct use of these extra arithmetic relations in your programs.

System note - displaying the compiled form - You can see the compiled relational form of the expression and equality conditions used in your program by simply adding the sentence "rel-form" to your program with an

add(rel-form)

command. Now, when you list or edit your program the expression
conditions will be displayed in the relational form. You can still use
expressions in queries and in other sentences that you add to your
program. The "rel-form" sentence does not prevent expressions from
being compiled. It only prevents them from being de-compiled on
listing or editing. By getting rid of this sentence with a

> kill rel-form

SIMPLE will revert to both compiling and de-compiling expressions in
the normal way.

Adding the "rel-form" sentence is a useful way of checking that
the value you intended to denote when you used an expression will be
the value computed by micro-PROLOG.

Evaluation of expression conditions

When an expression condition is evaluated, the conjunction
of extra conditions that produces the values of the expression
arguments is evaluated first, then the condition is evaluated. On
backtracking, alternative solutions will be sought for the condition
with the computed values of the expression arguments but there
will be no attempt to find alternative values for the expression
arguments.

Example

The condition

> salary # (x (12*157))

in the query

> all(x : salary#(x (12*157))

is compiled into the relational form:

> (x salary X) # (* (12 157 X))

The * condition computes the value of (12*157) and so the
evaluation of the entire # condition will reduce to the evaluation
of

x salary 1884

in order to find an x with recorded salary of **1884**. Backtracking will result in different values for x being sought, but will not result in a recomputation of the value 1884.

The # expression query

You can also use a special kind of query to find the value of an expression. The symbol # followed by an expression has a single answer which is the value of the expression.

&.#(3*5+9)
24
&.

It is a briefer alternative to

which(x : x=(3*5+9))

The general form of the query is

#<expression>

Its single answer is the value of the expression.

Exercises 4-5

1. In Chapter 2 we defined the relation "x factorial y" which held when y was the factorial of positive integer x. Redefine this using equality conditions instead of the **SUM** and **TIMES** primitive relations. Then declare it as a function and use it in expression queries to find:

a.   The value of factorial of 6 divided by 3
b.   The value of the factorial of the "mod" of 27 divided by 4.

2. What is the relational form of the expression conditions:

a.   LESS#((factorial (x*7)) (3+y*9))
b.   (factorial (rem 56 (y ~ 1)))=z

3. Redefine the "x has-length y" relation of the last chapter using an equality condition. This time call the relation "length". Define an

analogous relation "x sum y" which can be used to find the sum y of a list of numbers x. Declare both as functions and use them in queries to find:

a.   The length of the list (2 4 6 -8 23 9)
b.   The average of the same list of numbers.
c.   Define the relation "x average y" : y is the average of a list of numbers x. Use function calls to "sum" and "length".

4. Suppose that you have a set of marks defined by facts of the form

    number mark

e.g 34 mark

records the mark of 34. Suppose that each mark is out of a possible maximum of 60. Give queries that use equality conditions to find:

a.   All the marks expressed as a percentage.
b.   The percentage equivalent of the average mark.

    For b. you also will need to use isall.

4.6   Querying the user using is-told

In the last exercise we assumed that we had a set of marks recorded by facts already added to the program. Let us suppose that we did not want to have a permanent record of these marks stored in the program and that they had been added solely in order to be able to convert them to percentages.

It would be preferable if we did not have to explicitly add the mark facts but could pose the query in such a way that micro-PROLOG asks us to give each mark when it is needed for the conversion to a percentage.

We can do this using the is-told condition. is-told is a special relation which asks the user questions. It has a single argument called the *question pattern*. The question pattern is similar to the answer pattern in which and all queries; except that it forms a question that micro-PROLOG poses the user, rather than an answer that micro-PROLOG displays to a user's query.

System note - "is-told" on small computers - as with expressions it may be necessary for you to load an extension to SIMPLE if you want to use the is-told condition.

In the query

all(mark X is Z percent : (mark X) is-told &
      Z=(X/60*100))

the question pattern of the **is-told** condition is "(mark X)", and the questions will be of that form. This query sets up an interaction between us and micro-PROLOG. With our response emphasized an example interaction is:

mark X ? **ans 20**
mark 20 is 3.3333333E1 percent
mark X ? **ans 15**
mark 15 is 25 percent
mark X ? **just 30**
mark 30 is 50 percent
No (more) answers

The condition "(mark X) is-told" is not solved by matching with any "mark" sentences in the program. It is solved by micro-PROLOG displaying the condition and waiting for us to give a value for the variable in the condition with our "ans ..." response. When we respond

ans 20

it is equivalent to a successful match with the sentence

20 mark

Just as a query that used a normal "X mark" condition would backtrack to find another sentence to match with the condition, so micro-PROLOG will backtrack on the **is-told** condition to allow us another way of answering the question. Each different answer we give represents a different mark that we might have explicitly recorded with a "mark" fact before posing the query.

A normal query will terminate when it has exhausted all the "mark" sentences. We must explicitly say that we are giving the last answer by using the form "just ...". When we do this we are not asked for any more answers to the "(mark X) is-told" condition.

Another example of its use is the query

which(Smith sells electrical x : Smith sells x
& (x electrical) is-told))

This can be used to find all the goods that Smith sells that are electrical without us having to explicitly record which goods are electrical with sentences in the data base. Suppose the program contains the facts:

Smith sells bacon
Smith sells light-bulbs
Smith sells string

about what Smith sells. The interaction will be:

bacon electrical ? no
light-bulbs electrical ? yes
Smith sells electrical light-bulbs
string electrical ? no
No (more) answers

This time the questions do not contain variables so we must give a "yes" or "no" answer. The "yes" is equivalent to micro-PROLOG making a successful match of the displayed condition with a sentence in the program, the "no" is equivalent to it failing to find a successful match for the displayed condition.

is-told *in rules*

Like any query condition the is-told condition can also be used in rules. Let us return to the BICYCLE parts data that we used in Chapter 2 in which direct parts are recorded by "part-of" facts and the "indirect-part-of" relation is recursively defined using "part-of". Let us suppose that we are interested in using this information to help us to repair a bicycle. Before we can use it we should perhaps get hold of a bicycle repair expert to tell us what observed problem indicates a fault in some part of the bicycle by giving us some facts of the form:

problem indicates (fault in part)

e.g.

flat-tyre indicates (puncture in wheel)
flat-tyre indicates (faulty-valve in wheel)

wheel-wobble indicates (loose-spokes in wheel)
slack-chain indicates (too-many-links in chain)
no-lights indicates (loose-connection in electrical-system)
no-lights indicates (fault in dynamo)

Notice that where an observed problem indicates more than one
possible fault we have separate "indicates" facts.
Consider the pair of rules:

x possible-fault-in y if z indirect-part-of y and
                                X indicates (x in z) and
                                X is-reported

X is-reported if (X a problem) is-told

which can be read

x is a possible fault in y if x is a fault in some indirect
    part of y indicated by a reported problem

X is reported if we are told that X is a problem

To help us overhaul a bicycle, we can use the query

all(x : x possible-fault-with bicycle)

The evaluation will use the "z indirect-part-of bicycle" condition of
the rule to walk over the structure of the bicycle as recorded in
the "part-of" facts. For each part z, the "X indicates (x in z)"
condition will be used to find possible faults and the problems
associated with them. For each such symptomatic problem we will
be asked if we can report the presence of the problem with a
question such as

flat-tyre a problem ?

For each "YES" response we give we will be given a possible
fault answer to the query.
There is a slight drawback with this query. Answers to is-
told conditions are not remembered. Because we have associated
two possible faults with the same flat-tyre problem we will be
asked about this problem twice. A solution that we will return to
later in the book is to define "is-reported" in such a way that our
answers are remembered.

An alternative way of using the trouble-shooting data makes use of a set of "problem" facts to generate the names of the problems about which we are queried. If we recorded each problem once with a sentence such as

flat-tyre problem

we could use the query

all(x possible fault : y problem &
    y is-reported &
    y indicates (x in z))

to find all the possible faults with our bicycle. Now the "problem" data is used to generate the names of the problems about which we are questioned. Since each one is recorded by only one "problem" fact, we will only be asked once.

Yet another use, that requires us to know the names of the problems, is to let us volunteer the observed problems. The query

all(x possible fault : y is-reported &
                        y indicates (x in z))

sets up an interaction of the form

X a problem ? ans flat-tyre
puncture possible fault
faulty-valve possible fault
X a problem ? just slack-chain
too-many-links possible fault
No (more) answers

The above example is the bare bones of a very simple expert system in micro-PROLOG. The above queries access the expert's data in a particular systematic way and ask us to supply information about observed problems.

We can also get at the expert's knowledge by directly querying the "indicates" data.

all(x : z indirect-part-of electrical-system &
        y indicates (x in z))

will tell us all the possible faults with the electrical system.

General form of **is-told** conditions

An **is-told** condition has the form

<question-pattern> is-told

When evaluated, the sequence of elements in the question pattern (which should be a list) are displayed followed by a ? indicating that we must provide an answer for the condition. The answers and their effects are:

answer   effect

yes   The **is-told** condition is assumed to be true. Backtracking will not cause the question to be posed again.

no   The **is-told** condition is assumed false (the condition fails).

ans ..   The .. is a sequence of values, one for each **different** variable in the question pattern. The **is-told** condition is solved for values of the variables given in the response. The i'th value in the response sequence becomes the value for the i'th variable in the question pattern in the left to right order of the text.
           Example, if the **is-told** condition was "(X likes Y) is-told" the response

X likes Y ? **ans tom bill**

makes X=tom and Y=bill. Backtracking will result in the message being redisplayed when an alternative solution can be given. This repeated prompting for new solutions on backtracking continues until you enter **no** or **just**.

just ..   The same as **ans** except that on backtracking you are not asked for another solution. It is assumed to be the last solution to the **is-told** condition.

Exercises 4-6

1. Give a query that will enable you to find the sum and average of several **lists** of numbers that are given as different user replies to an is-told condition "(X a list) is-told". A sample reply might be

ans (23 -45 98 34.6 -5)

2. Give a query that will prompt you to enter three numbers X, Y, Z and which will display these three numbers as an answer to the query only if $Z = (X*Y)$. This is a query that you can use to test your mental arithmetic capabilities.

3. Suppose that we have a family relations data base which does not record who is male or female. Give rules for these relations such that you will be queried when a "male" or "female" condition needs to be solved.

What will be the difference between the interactions that result from the two queries
a.   all(x : Tom father-of x & x male)
b.   all(x : x male & Tom father-of x)

Top-down development of programs

is-told can be used to help with the top-down development of a program. As an example, in Section 4.3 we gave the following definition of "ordered"

X ordered if (forall (x y) adjacent-on X then x lesseq y)

which was to be used in conjunction with auxiliary definitions of "adjacent-on" and "lesseq". We can test out this definition, before giving the proper definitions of these relations, by adding the following pair of definitions:

(x y) adjacent-on X if ((x y) adjacent-on X) is-told

x lesseq y if (x lesseq y) is-told

If we pose the query

is((3 5 5 6) ordered)

the interaction will be

> (X Y) adjacent-on (3 5 5 6) ? ans **3 5**
> 3 lesseq 5 ? **yes**
> (X Y) adjacent-on (3 5 5 6) ? ans **5 5**
> 5 lesseq 5 ? **yes**
> (X Y) adjacent-on (3 5 5 6) ? just **5 6**
> 5 lesseq 6 ? **yes**
> YES

Our series of answers to the "(X Y) adjacent-on (3 5 5 6)" question gives all the pairs of adjacent elements. Note that the last pair is signalled by the "just".

4.7   Comment conditions

With a judicious choice of relation names micro-PROLOG programs entered using SIMPLE can be self-documenting. Even so, comments are sometimes needed to remind us of certain restrictions on the use of programs or to remind us of the role of certain of the arguments. This is especially the case when we use relations with more than two arguments and the infix form is not sufficient to indicate the role of each argument. There are two ways in which we can associate comments with a micro-PROLOG program. We can add sentences about some "comment" relation, or we can add ignored comment conditions using a micro-PROLOG primitive relation /*.

The /* comment condition

The relation name /* is specially treated by micro-PROLOG. Any condition which uses this relation name is ignored during an evaluation. Another way of looking at it is that every /* condition is always true. We can therefore use /* to add comment conditions to rules.

Example

function factorial

1 factorial 1 if /*(can only be used to find factorials and is
                      declared a function)

x factorial y if /*(vars (x int) (y val)) &
                1 LESS x & y＝(x*(factorial(x ˜ 1)))

is a commented version of the "factorial" program which reminds
us of the restrictions on its use and which reminds us of the role
of the arguments with a comment about the variables of the
recursive rule. (Notice the use of the "factorial" function call in
the recursive rule. This is possible because of the pre-declaration
that "factorial" is a function.)

The use of the commented program will be slightly slower
because micro-PROLOG will momentary look at the comment
conditions before it ignores them.

The comment relation **vars**

In some implementations of micro-PROLOG you can use
constants as variables in a sentence that you enter using **add** or
edit providing you include a special **vars** comment as the last
condition of the sentence. The **vars** comment relation has a single
argument which is the list of all the constants you have used in
place of variables.

Example

int factorial val if
        1 LESS int &
        val = (int*(factorial(int ˜ 1)))) &
        (int val) vars

The last condition

(int val) vars

is picked up by the **add** command and before the sentence is
added to your program all occurences of each constant given in
the **vars** list is replaced by a variable throughout the sentence,
different constants being replaced by different variables. The
sentence is actually added to the list of sentences for factorial in
the form

```
x factorial y if
    /*(vars (x int) (y val)) &
    1 LESS x  &  y=(x*(fact(x ~ 1)))
```

with an /* comment condition as the first condition linking the variables of the rule with the constants that you used in place of the variables when you added the rule.

When you edit or list the program the /* comment is used to find these constants and to substitute them back into the sentence before it is displayed. You will see the sentence in the form

```
int factorial val if
    1 LESS int &
    val = (int*(factorial(int ~ 1)))) &
    (int val) vars
```

with your constants instead of the variables that the **add** introduced. If you are editing the sentence the **vars** constants will again be replaced by variables when you exit the edit. To see it in the actual stored form you have to use the special listing command described in Chapter 9 which enables you to see the fully compiled form of every added sentence. However, if you trace the evaluation of a "factorial" query you will see the /* comment when the rule is applied.

Warning

If you do use constants in place of variables, having a **vars** condition as the **last** condition of the rule which gives **all** the constants used in place of variables is **essential**. If you forget to add the **vars** condition or you do not include all the constants you have used as variables these constants will be left as constants. You can recover from this by editing the sentence and adding or editing the **vars** condition.

Comment sentences

As an alternative or an addition to comment conditions we can add sentences for some "comment" relation. Thus, instead of having the restrictions of use comment embedded in the "factorial" program we can use the following "comment" fact.

factorial comment
    (can only be used to find factorial values and
    is declared a function)

The disadvantage of having a separate "comment" fact is that we do not automatically see the comment when we list the "factorial" program. The advantage is that we can kill the "comment" relation in order to get rid of all the comments at one go. (The comments do take up space.) To access the comment for some relation we query "comment".

which(y : factorial comment y)
(can only be used to find factorial values and is declared
a function)
No (more) answers

Such a "comment" relation is a simple minded description of a program. By adding rules, we can make our "comment" program as sophisticated as we like. For example, we might add facts describing which relations are directly used in the definition of another relation, itself a useful form of program comment.

factorial uses (factorial LESS * ~)

Then, the rule

x comment (x is recursively defined) if
    x uses Y and
    x belongs-to Y

automatically gives us an extra answer to a "comment" query about a recursively defined relation.

By using such auxiliary programs you can use the full power of micro-PROLOG to provide a very sophisticated 'active' documentation of a program.

5.   List Processing

We have seen that we can access the components of lists and construct new lists out of existing lists by defining relations with lists as arguments. When we query these relations we are processing lists. In this chapter we look at some more list relations and their uses.

5.1   The append relation

We begin by examining a very powerful little list program for the relation "append". This has many uses apart from the 'normal' one of appending two lists together; as we shall see, it can be used to find all the ways of splitting a list, to remove an initial or tail segment of a list, even to split a list on a given element.

The condition

append(x y z)

holds when z is the result of appending the list x to the front of the list y.

An example of this is:

append((A B) (C D E) (A B C D E))

Note that z is not simply the list (x|y). For the above example, (x|y) is the list

((A B) C D E)

which begins with a sublist which is the list x. This is quite different from the list

(A B C D E)

which begins with the first element of the list x.

Before defining "append", let us consider an example to illustrate its use. I am trying to remember what I ate for lunch today. It was served in two courses. Each course can be described by a list of its ingredients. Thus

(fish chips) served-in first-course
(rhubarb custard) served-in second-course

What I ate altogether was the list of things I ate in the first course appended to the list of things I ate in the second course. So

Z served-in dinner if
        x served-in first-course &
        y served-in second-course &
        append(x y Z)

which(x : x served-in dinner)
(fish chips rhubarb custard)
No (more) answers

Notice the difference between this answer, which is one list, and the answer to:

which(x y : x served-in first-course &
            y served-in second-course)
(fish chips) (rhubarb custard)
No(more) answers

The answer to this is a pair of lists. The two lists are not 'glued' together in a single list. This is the rôle of "append".

To develop our program for "append(x y z)" we must make statements about the relation that together completely define the relation. As a rule of thumb, when defining relations over lists, we should pick one of the arguments of the relation and give sentences for different *cases* for that argument. The cases should together cover all the different types of lists that might appear in that argument of the relation.

For the "append(x y z)" relation, let us pick the first argument x. We will completely define the relation by having a sentence about all instances of the relation when x is the empty list (), and another sentence about all instances of the relation when x is a non-empty list represented by the pattern (x|X).

When x is (), it is always the case that y and z are the same. (Glueing no elements to the front of y leaves it unchanged.) This is expressed by the unconditional rule

append(() y y)   (1)

which we read as,

> for all y,
>   empty list () and y append to y.

Notice that we do not have to have an explicit condition that says that y and z are the same. We express this implicitly by having the same variable in each argument position.

When x is a non-empty list of the form (x|X) we know that z must also begin with x. So z must be of the form (x|Z) for some Z. We cannot unconditionally state

append((x|X) y (x|Z))

because this does not hold for all X, y and Z. The X, y and Z cannot be arbitrary lists. However, whenever

append(X y Z)

holds, then we can be sure that

append((x|X) y (x|Z))

also holds. This is illustrated by the picture:

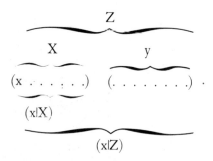

This gives us the conditional rule

append((x|X) y (x|Z)) if append(X y Z)   (2)

(1) and (2) are a pair of sentences that together completely define the "append" relation. They are a logic program for the relation.

Using append to split a list

Queries to the "append" relation in which x and y are given will return a z that is the concatenation of x and y. To use it to split a list, we give the z and leave x and y as variables.

which(x y : append(x y (2 3 4)))
() (2 3 4)
(2) (3 4)
(2 3) (4)
(2 3 4) ()
No (more) answers

In the answers that we got, two were a pair consisting of the empty list and the original list. To exclude these answers we simply replace x and y by patterns that denote non-empty lists.

which((x|X)(y|Y) : append((x|Y) (y|Y) (2 3 4)))
(2) (3 4)
(2 3) (4)
No (more) answers

By describing the second list with the pattern (x|Y) we can insist that the split is at a point where the first element of the list recurs:

which((x|X) (x|Y) : append((x|X) (x|Y) (2 4 2 5 1 2 3)))
(2 4) (2 5 1 2 3)
(2 4 2 5 1) (2 3)
No (more) answers

Alternatively, we can insist that the second list begins with some particular element, say 3. We do this by denoting it by the pattern (3|Y).

which(x (3|Y) : append(x (3|Y) (2 3 5 3 1)))
(2) (3 5 3 1)

(2 3 5) (3 1)
No (more) answers

This finds all the splittings of the list that start at the given number 3.

As a last (but by no means exhaustive) example of the use of "append", consider the query

which(x : append(y (x|X) (2 3 4)))

What will the answers be?

Exercises 5-1

Answer these micro-PROLOG queries:

1. which(x : append((J U M) (B O) x))

2. which(x y : append(x y (J O H N)))

3. which(x y : append(x (R|y) (C Y R I L)))

4. which(x y : append((D A M) (S O N) x) & x has-length y)

5. Try the query
          one(x y z : append(x y z))
Hand evaluate it to the point where you get 4 answers if you have not got a computer.

6. Give the query that checks that the list (2 3 4 2 3 4) is the result of appending some list to itself and which returns that list.

7. Give the query that returns the second list of all the splittings of the list of words
       (the man closed the door of the house)
at the word "the".

8. Use the "belongs-to" relation to pose a query that finds all the second halves of the splittings of
       (Sam threw a ball into the lake)
that start with one of the words in the list (a the).

9. Using "append" pose the query to find the last element of the list (2 3 4).

10. Give an alternative recursive definition of the relation "x ordered" that was defined in Section 4.3. Treat the four cases:
a.   x the empty list
b.   x a list with one element
c.   x a list with at least two elements y & z the same
d.   x a list with at least two elements y,z with y LESS z

11. Give a recursive definition of the relation
remove-all(x X Y): Y is the list X with all occurrences of x removed.
Hint: treat the three cases
a.   X the empty list
b.   X a non-empty list that begins with x
c.   X a non-empty list that begins with a y different from x.

12. Give a recursive definition of the relation
X compacts-to Y:Y is the list X with all but the first occurrence of any duplicated elements removed. Define it using the "remove-all" relation of Exercise 11.
Hint: if X is a non-empty list beginning with x then Y must also begin with x but the tail of Y will be a compacted version of the tail of X after all recurrences of x have been removed. Now say this in micro-PROLOG using list patterns and a conditional rule. Do not forget the case when X is empty.

   Notice that this relation can be used for removing duplicates from a list of answers given by an isall condition. We use a conjunctive condition of the form:

   X isall (A : Q) & X compacts-to Y

However, "compacts-to" is a time-consuming operation.

5.2   Rules that use append

(1) The rule:

   front(x y z) if append(y y1 z) & y has-length x   (A)

defines the relation front(x y z) which holds when y comprises the first x elements of z. It can be used for finding the first x elements of a list as in:

   which(x : front(3 x (A B C D E F))   (B)
   (A B C)
   No (more) answers

In answering this query the condition "append(y y1 z)" of the rule is used to generate candidate splittings of the list (A B C D E F). micro-PROLOG will test every splitting with the "y has-length x" condition.

Notice that we can also define the relation using "length-of":

front(x y z) if x length-of y & append(y y1 z)   (C)

Used to answer the same query, the condition "x length-of y" will be used to construct a list of three variables (x1 x2 x3) as the value of y that is passed on to "append(y y1 z)". The evaluation of this condition then finds values for x1, x2 and x3. In other words, in answering query (B), after the first condition of the derived query

3 length-of x & append(x y1 (A B C D E F)))

has been solved the evaluation is reduced to solving the condition

append((x1 x2 x3) y1 (A B C D E F))

Here we have a powerful use of partial answers that are list patterns. The evaluation of (B) using definition (C) does not involve the generation of candidate splittings of the given list. In consequence, the evaluation using definition (C) is much more efficient than the evaluation that uses definition (A). The one drawback of the second definition is that it can only be used if the length of the front list is given. This is because of the restriction on the use of "length-of" that we noted in Chapter 3.

(2) The rules:

(x|X) initial-segment-of z if append((x|X) y z)
(y|Y) back-segment-of z if append(x (y|Y) z)

define the relations suggested by the relation names. Notice the requirement that the initial and back segments be non-empty lists.

We can use these relations to define the relation "x segment-of z" which holds when x is a non-empty segment of contiguous elements on the list z. Such a list x is an initial segment of a back segment of z.

x segment-of z if y back-segment-of z &
        x initial-segment-of y

which(x : x segment-of (A B C))
(A)
(A B)
(A B C)
(B)
(B C)
(C)
No(more) answers

(3) The rules:

(x) reverse (x)
(x y|X) reverse z if (y|X) reverse Y & append(Y (x) z)

define the relation "z reverse-of x" that holds when z is the non-
empty list x in reverse order. They can be used for checking the
relation or for finding the reverse of a list with a query in which
the first argument is given and the second is to be found.

which(z : (A B C D E) reverse z)
(E D C B A)
No (more) answers

Why should it not be used with the first argument given and the
second to be found? Follow through the evaluation to see what
happens in this case.

(4) The rule:

delete(x X Y) if append(X1 (x|X2) X) & append(X1 X2 Y)

defines the relation which holds when Y is the list X with some
single occurrence of x removed.
        We can use this relation to give a recursive definition of
the relation

Y permutation-of X: Y is some re-ordering of the list X

It is defined by the pair of rules:

() permutation-of ()

(y|Y) permutation-of X if
      delete(y X Z) & Y permutation-of Z

The second rule tells us that the list (y|Y) is a permutation
of the list X if the first element y appears somewhere on X and
the remainder Y is a permutation of the list X when y has been
removed. This diagram illustrates this relationship between (y|Y)
and X.

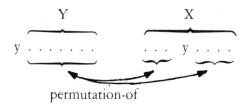

permutation-of

Remember that in Chapter 4 we defined the relation "X same-
elements-as Y" which was true of a pair of lists if every element
of X appeared on Y and vice versa. This is equivalent to
"Y permutation-of X" when X and Y have the same length.
However, because "same-elements-as" was indirectly defined using
forall it can only be used for testing. Our recursive definition of
"Y permutation-of X" can be used for testing or generating. To
generate all the permutations of a list we give X and ask for Y.

    which(Y : Y permutation-of (5 3 7))
    (5 3 7)
    (5 7 3)
    (3 5 7)
    (3 7 5)
    (7 5 3)
    (7 3 5)
    No (more) answers

To find an ordered permutation we pose the query:

    which(Y : Y permutation-of (5 3 7) & Y ordered)
    (3 5 7)
    No (more) answers

Here, "ordered" is the relation defined using forall in Chapter 4.
    Finally, we can give a definition of the sort relation

x sorts-to y: y is a sorted version of the list x

It is:

x sorts-to y if y permutation-of x & y ordered

This can be used, somewhat inefficiently, to sort a list with a query condition in which x is given and y is to be found. It sorts the x by generating successive permutations until one is found that is ordered. In the next section we shall give an alternative recursive definition of the sort relation which is a much more efficient micro-PROLOG program.

Exercises 5-2

1. Using the relations defined above, answer:
a.   which(x : front(4 x (J K L M N P Q))
b.   which(x : x segment-of (F R E D A))
c.   which(x : (E R I C) reverse x)

2. Define the relation "last-of" of Exercise 3-7(3) in terms of "append". Notice that this is a non-recursive definition of "last-of" in terms of the recursively defined "append".

3. Define the list membership relation "belongs-to" in terms of "append".

4. The 'power list' of a list is directly analogous to the power set concept in set theory: i.e. the power-list of a list is the list of all sub-lists of the list. Define the relation "x power-list y" which holds when y is the power list of x.
   Try your program on the following query:

which(x : (A B C D) power-list x)

(Hint: remember that the empty list is also a sublist, but only once. Don't forget about **isall**.)

5. Define the relation: palindrome(x) which holds when x is a list that reads the same forwards or backwards. Thus, (M A D A M) is a palindrome list of letters, (1 2 2 1) is a palindrome list of numbers. Define it in terms of "reverse". Use your definition to test the above two palindromes.

6. Define the relation "adjacent-on" of Exercise 3-7(4) but this time give a non-recursive definition by using "append".

7. Give an alternative recursive definition of the relation delete(x X Y) which was defined above using "append".
Hint: treat the two cases:
i.   the deleted x is the first element of X.
ii. the deleted x is not the first element of X.

8. Consider the relation
split-on(y X X1 X2): X1 X2 is a splitting of the list X such that X1 is of length y.
a.   Define it using "append" and "has-length".
b.   Define it using "length-of" and "append".
c.   Give an alternative recursive definition.
    Compare the programs with respect to efficiency for splitting a list given the length.

5.3   Recursive definition of the sort relation

Next, we develop a recursive description of the sort relation between lists that will provide us with a much more efficient sort program than the one defined above using "permutation-of". We start by making one or two simple observations about the relation.

First we know that a singleton list is already sorted, i.e. a list with one element in it is already in the right order. Similarly the empty list is sorted by default. These two facts about the sort relation are expressed by:

$$() \text{ sort } () \qquad\qquad\qquad (1)$$
$$(x) \text{ sort } (x) \qquad\qquad\qquad (2)$$

However, most lists are neither empty, nor singleton; so we have to be able to sort these too. One way of dealing with bigger lists is to make them small ones; i.e. use some kind of divide and conquer strategy. This would involve splitting the list (which has at least two elements) into two smaller ones, sorting each of the bits and putting them back together again. This means that we must look for a recursive description of the "sort" relation for lists of at least two elements.

Merge sort

The method of splitting that we shall use merely involves dividing the list into two nearly equal halves: i.e. they are within one element of each other in length. We can do this by taking a front segment and a back segment such that when appended together again they make up the original list; making sure at the same time that the lengths are nearly equal.

Let us call this relation split. Thus,

split((x1 x2|x) X1 X2)

holds when

append(X1 X2 (x1 x2|x))

holds and the length of X1 is the length of X2, plus or minus 1.

Now, if X1, X2 are such a splitting of (x1 x2|x), and y1, y2 are sorted versions of X1, X2 respectively, then the sort of (x1 x2|x) is some y which is an order preserving interleaving of y1 and y2. Let us call this relation between y1, y2 and y, merge(y1 y2 y). The following rule gives us a recursive description of the "sort" relation that corresponds to this method of sorting:

$$(x1 \ x2|x) \text{ sort } y \text{ if split}((x1 \ x2|x) \ X1 \ X2) \ \& \qquad (3)$$
$$X1 \text{ sort } y1 \ \& \ X2 \text{ sort } y2 \ \& \ \text{merge}(y1 \ y2 \ y)$$

Rule (3) fairly naturally encodes the English statement of sorting using the divide and conquer method. The merge program we shall look at in a moment is clearly the 'guts' of the sort program, it has to be able to take two ordered lists, and merge them into one. This job is easier than sorting a list since we can make use of the knowledge that the two 'input' lists are already ordered.

In defining the "merge" relation we shall need to treat several cases. The first two are when either y1 or y2 is the empty list:

merge(() x x)   (4)
merge(x () x)   (5)

The remaining case is where both y1 and y2 are non-empty.

In this case we have three possibilities: either the first element of each list is equal, the first element of y1 is less than the the first element of y2 or vice-versa.

Notice that it is here that we have to start discussing what it means for an element of a list to be less than or greater than another element. Up until now we have not actually needed to define what criteria we use to sort lists.

We can define our own notion of order amongst elements which will allow us to sort different types of list. Let us call this relation "less". If we want to sort numbers or constants we simply define "less" as the pre-defined **LESS** relation by adding the definition

x less y if x LESS y

to the sort program. Alternatively, we could define it as

x less y if (x less y) is-told

using the **is-told** relation described in Chapter 4. By interactively supplying the answers to the "less" conditions we can sort to any criterion of order.

Returning to the problem of merging two lists together, having decided that the first element of one is less than the first element of the other we put that element as the first element of the merged list. Assuming that we are supposed to be sorting into increasing order, the smaller of the two elements must form the first element of the merged list.

First the rule for when both the first elements of Y1 and Y2 are identical:

merge((x|y1) (x|y2) (x x|y)) if merge(y1 y2 y)   (6)

This rule states that the merge of the two lists with identical first elements starts with two of that element, and the tail is obtained by merging the tails of Y1 and Y2.

The next rule deals with the case when the first element of Y1 is less than the first element of Y2. In this case the first element of the merged list is the first element of Y1. The tail of the merged list is found by merging the tail of Y1 and the **whole** of Y2:

merge((x1|y1) (x2|y2) (x1|y)) if   (7)
    x1 less x2 &

merge(y1 (x2|y2) y)

In a similar way we get the last rule for merge, which is symmetric to (7):

merge((x1|y1) (x2|y2) (x2|y)) if   (8)
    x2 less x1 &
    merge((x1|y1) y2 y)

Finally, we need to define the split relation. We can say that split(X X1 X2) holds if y1 is approximately half the length of (x1 x2|x) and X1 X2 are a splitting of X such that X1 has y1 elements. This gives us the rule:

split(X X1 X2) if split-on#((div (length X) 2) X X1 X2)

Here, "split-on" is the relation defined in Exercise 5-2(8). The functional relation "div" was defined in Section 4.5 and "length" defined in Exercise 4-5(3).

The complete merge-sort program is as follows:

```
() sort ()
(x) sort (x)
(x1 x2|x) sort y if
        split((x1 x2)|x) X1 X2) &
        X1 sort y1 & X2 sort y2 &
        merge(y1 y2 y)

merge(() x x)
merge(x () x)
merge((x|y1) (x|y2) (x x|y)) if merge(y1 y2 y)
merge((x1|y1) (x2|y2) (x1|y)) if
        x1 less x2 &
        merge(y1 (x2|y2) y)
merge((x1|y1) (x2|y2) (x2|y)) if
        x2 less x1 &
        merge((x1|y1) y2 y)

split(X X1 X2) if split-on#((div (length X) 2) X X1 X2)

split-on(0 X () X)
split-on(y (x|X) (x|X1) X2) if
        0 LESS y &
        split-on#((y ˜ 1) X X1 X2)
```

And, just to make sure it works, let us try sorting a list of numbers. We add the definition

x less y if x LESS y

and pose the query:

which(x : (4 3 6 100 -5 3) sort x)
(-5 3 3 4 6 100)
No (more) answers

Quick sort

The same basic strategy for divide and conquer can lead to completely different sort programs if we choose slightly different methods of 'dividing'. For example, in our split, we simply chopped the list into a front and a back half. If instead we had chosen to partition the list in such a way that all the elements of one list were less than all the elements in the other we get a quite different recursive description of the sort relation.

The first thing to notice about this scheme for splitting is that when we are merging the two lists back together again we can take advantage of the fact that one list is entirely less than the other. In other words each element of one partitioned list (and hence its sorted variety) is less than **all** the elements of the other list. This enables us to replace the "merge" part of the sort- is program by a simple "append".

On the other hand the partitioning of the lists is more complicated; *it* has to do the main work of the sort.

Exercises 5-3

1. Assume that you have some suitable definition of the relation partition(x y z1 z2): each element of the list x which is less than y appears on the list z1, all the other elements of x appear on z2. Give a definition of the sort relation that makes use of "partition". Call the relation "quick-sort". Add the definition

partition(x y z1 z2) if (partition x y z1 z2) is-told

to your program and test it by sorting some small lists. You supply the answers to the "partition" condition when they are required. Make sure each answer you give is a "just .." answer so that micro-PROLOG does not ask you for an alternative partitioning.

2. Give a recursive definition for "partition", and delete its is-told definition. How does the complete quick-sort program compare with the merge-sort program for speed of sorting?

3. Inefficiency in the merge sort program results from the need to continually recompute the length of a list on each recursive call. This is not necessary since the split relation effectively finds the lengths of the lists X1 and X2 that are recursively sorted. Change the definition of the "sort" relation so that it is a relation between a pair (x X) and a list Y where Y is the sorted version of X and x is the length of X. You will need to change the recursive rule for "sort" and the rule that defines "split". Call the new sort relation "merge-sort", and the new split relation, "merge-split". Do not forget the base cases for "merge-sort". Compare the speed of this program with that for "sort" and "quick-sort".

5.4   List functions

We can declare some of our list relations as functions and then use them in expressions. For example, we can declare "append" a function with

function append

because the last argument of "append(x y z)" is uniquely determined by the first two arguments. Now, each appending use of the relation can be expressed as a function call.

The expression query

#(append (1 2) (append (3 4) (5 6)))

gives the value (1 2 3 4 5 6). The rule

(x|X) reverse z if X reverse Y & z=(append Y (x))

uses a function call to "append" instead of an appending relation condition.

We can also declare "sort" a function and use "sort" function calls to sort lists.

#(sort (3 2 4 1))

(1 2 3 4)

using | in expressions

The expression query

#(2 3 | (append (4 5) (6 7))

will give you the answer

(2 3 append (4 5) (6 7))

not the answer

(2 3 4 5 6 7)

which is 2 followed by 3 followed by the result of appending (4 5) to (6 7).

The reason is that expressions are just special forms of list, and the list pattern

(2 3 | (append (4 5) (6 7))

is just another way of writing the list

(2 3 append (4 5) (6 7))

in which the function call sublist has disappeared. If you follow a | in a list pattern with a list micro-PROLOG automatically simplifies the pattern absorbing the sublist following the | into the main list. This means that when the expression parser is passed the above list to parse as an expression it does not see the sublist function call to "append". It sees a list of four elements and leaves it unchanged.

The moral is you can never use | in an expression followed by a function call sublist. When you do want to denote the rest of a list by a function call you must use an explicit CONS function call which adds an element to the front of a list. The above expression query must be re-expressed as

#(CONS 2 (CONS 3 (append (4 5) (6 7))))

CONS is defined in the SIMPLE front-end program. It is

automatically recognized as a function in expressions. Its definition
is

CONS(X Y (X|Y))

System note - other predefined list relations - SIMPLE also contains
definitions of the relations APPEND and ON. APPEND is exactly the
same as the "append" relation we have defined in this chapter. Like
CONS it can be used as a function in expressions without your having
to declare it a function. ON is exactly the same as the "belongs-to"
relation we defined in Chapter 3. The definitions of these relations are
embedded in SIMPLE because they are so frequently used. Whilst you
are using SIMPLE you can use them as though they were built-in
relations of micro-PROLOG. From now on we shall use APPEND and
ON instead of "append" and "belongs-to".

6. Introduction to Parsing

One of the more impressive application areas for logic programming has been in natural language understanding. We introduce this application area by looking at a very simple example of parsing. Parsing involves splitting up a list of words or symbols into sublists that satisfy certain syntactic constraints.

Our first program will make use of the **APPEND** relation to do the splitting. It will parse very simple sentences of English. Although the program is not very efficient, it is very close to a specification of the grammar of the English sentences that it recognizes.

We shall then rewrite the program so that the splitting of the list is done implicitly rather than explictly with an **APPEND** condition. This will give us a very efficient parsing program. It will also introduce us to the important logic programming concept of *difference pairs of lists*.

6.1   Parsing sentences expressed as lists of words

The English sentence to be parsed is represented as a list of words. The various ways that this list of words can be broken up represent the various possible 'parsings' of the sentence. For example the sentence "the boy kicked the ball" is represented by the list:

(the boy kicked the ball)

By re-organizing this list into a list of nested sub-lists we can see some of the grammatical structure of the sentence:

((the (boy)) (kicked (the (ball))))

We can then augment the list with *labels* which describe the various parts of speech:

```
(SENTENCE (NOUN-PHRASE (DETERMINER the)
                       (NOUN boy))
          (VERB-PHRASE (VERB kicked)
                       (NOUN-PHRASE (DETERMINER the)
                                    (NOUN ball))))
```

This nested list structure represents the *grammatical structure* of our sentence, except of course that it is highly simplified: there is no tense to the verb, and there is no representation of plurality in the noun phrases. Still, this kind of grammar is a suitable base for further development.

The program which recognizes sentences like this is composed of rules and facts which are organized around the parts of speech found in sentences. For example the rule for "is-sentence" can recognize a sentence, and the rules for "is-noun-phrase" can recognize a noun phrase. The most simple rule for recognizing sentences is:

```
x is-sentence (S X Y) if
     APPEND(x1 x2 x) and
     x1 is-noun-phrase X and
     x2 is-verb-phrase Y
```

In other words, if we can split the list of words x into two sub-lists x1 and x2 which form a noun phrase and verb phrase respectively then x is a sentence. The grammatical structure of the sentence is represented by the structure: (S X Y) where X and Y are the grammatical structures of the noun phrase and verb phrase respectively. (For the sake of brevity we use abbreviations such as "S" to stand for SENTENCE)

One definition of a noun phrase is that it is a determiner followed by a noun expression, i.e. a word like "the" or "a" followed by a word like "boy" or a phrase such as "big silly boy":

```
x is-noun-phrase (NP X Y) if
     APPEND(x1 x2 x) and
     x1 is-determiner X and
     x2 is-noun-expression Y
```

"NP" stands for noun phrase. The program for "is-determiner" must recognize a list which contains just one word, which is one of the known determiners:

> (x) is-determiner (DT x) if
>   x dictionary DET

The program for "dictionary" represents the vocabulary of the recognized sentences and it records the type of each word. Only those words which are in the dictionary are known to the program, if we try to parse a sentence with a word *not* in the dictionary it will simply fail. The part of the dictionary program concerned with determiners is:

> the dictionary DET
> a dictionary DET
> an dictionary DET

The simplest kind of noun expression is just a noun. This is expressed by the rule:

> (x) is-noun-expression (N x) if
>   x dictionary NOUN

i.e. a singleton list is a noun expression if the dictionary has that word recorded as a noun. Some nouns are:

> boy dictionary NOUN
> ball dictionary NOUN
> girl dictionary NOUN
> apple dictionary NOUN
>   etc.

Going back to our rule for sentences we have yet to describe what a verb phrase is. A very simple kind of verb phrase is a verb expression (i.e. a verb or a verb with associated adverbs) followed by a noun phrase, this being the object of the sentence. This rule is expressed by:

> x is-verb-phrase (VP X Y) if
>   APPEND(x1 x2 x) and
>   x1 is-verb-expression X and
>   x2 is-noun-phrase Y

By ignoring problems regarding tense we can get a rule for verb expressions which is similar to our noun expressions rule.

The simplest form of verb expression is a verb.

> (x) is-verb-expression (V x) if
>   x dictionary VERB

and we extend our knowledge of the dictionary with

> kicked dictionary VERB
> likes dictionary VERB
> etc.

This more or less completes our first approximation to English syntax. We can now parse some very simple sentences:

> which(x : (the boy kicked the ball) is-sentence x)
> (S (NP (DT the) (N boy))
>   (VP (V kicked) (NP (DT the) (N ball)))))
> No (more) answers

One simple extension would be to add adjectival phrases. That is, to allow noun expressions to comprise an adjective followed by a noun expression. Some example noun expressions involving adjectives are:

> silly boy
> sad girl
> big fat bouncy ball etc.

We can extend the program so that it recognizes such noun expressions by adding an extra rule for "is-noun-expression":

> x is-noun-expression (NE X Y) if
>   APPEND(x1 x2 x) and
>   x1 is-adjective X and
>   x2 is-noun-expression Y

This recursive description allows an arbitrary number of adjectives to precede the noun, and the parse structure returned tells us the adjectives used. Of course we now need to define what an adjective is and we need to extend the dictionary to include some adjectives:

> (x) is-adjective (A x) if x dictionary ADJ

big dictionary ADJ
silly dictionary ADJ
fat dictionary ADJ
etc.

We can now parse sentences such as:

which(x : (the sad boy likes the bouncy ball) is-sentence x)
(S (NP (DT the) (NE (A sad) (N boy)))
          (VP (V likes)
              (NP (DT the) (NE (A bouncy)
                              (N (ball))))))
No (more) answers

Finding sentences

We can use the program, somewhat inefficiently, to find all sentences of a given length. A query such as

which(x : 6 length-of x & x is-sentence y)

will give us all the six-word sentences recognized by the program. If you have been following the development of the program on a computer try the query.

We can be more precise. We can insist that x1 is "the" and x5 is "a" with the query:

which((the x2 x3 x4 a x6) : (the x2 x3 x4 a x6) is-sentence X)

Finally it can be used, very inefficiently, to generate a sentence from a parse structure. The query:

one(x : (the boy kicked the girl) is-sentence X and
              x is-sentence X)

will parse the given sentence and then convert the parse structure back to the same sentence. Try it!

The inefficiency results from the fact that the **APPEND** condition of each grammar rule should really appear as the last condition of the rule when we want to use them to generate sentences. Placed as it is, the APPEND condition will generate larger and larger lists of variables until one is generated that is long enough to hold the sentence whose parse structure is given. (Remember Exercise 5-1(5).)

This use of the **APPEND** condition as a generator makes the use of the **one** form of query essential. The evaluation of the analogous **which** query would never terminate because the backtracking would cause the **APPEND** to generate larger and larger lists of variables as candidate sentence lists.

Exercises 6-1

1. Find the parses of the following sentences (possibly involving an extension of the vocabulary):

a.   the sad boy likes a happy girl
b.   the ball kicked the boy
c.   a lonely man wandered the hills
d.   a piper plays a tune

2. Extend the grammar program so that it can cope with verb expressions that are verbs preceded by a conjunction of adverbs. The new program should cope with sentences such as:

a man **slowly and deliberately climbed** the mountain

The extension required is analogous to that which copes with adjectives. Just add a new rule for "is-verb-expression" and give rules and dictionary entries describing adverbs. Use your new grammar to parse the above sentence. Hint: you could treat an adverb followed by "and" as an adverb.

3. Inefficiency in the grammar program results from the use of **APPEND** to generate candidate splittings of a sentence or sentence fragment which are then tested to see if they have a given form. The first splitting returned by **APPEND** is the empty list paired with the given list of words, which for our grammar never results in a successful parse.

We can speed up the execution of the program by constraining the form of the splittings that **APPEND** generates in a particular grammar rule. Thus, in the fragment of English that we are treating, noun phrases always have at least two words and verb phrases at least three words.

Modify the program along these lines. In particular, change the rules for "is-noun-phrase" and "is-noun-expression" to exploit the fact that determiners and adjectives are always single words.

6.2   An alternative parsing program

The last exercise was an attempt to improve the efficiency of the parsing program by constraining the candidate splittings produced by the **APPEND** condition of a grammar rule. There is a far more radical way of rewriting the program that will make it very efficient. Consider the top-level rule:

    x is-sentence (S X Y) if
        APPEND(x1 x2 x) and
        x1 is-noun-phrase X and
        x2 is-verb-phrase Y

Instead of explicitly stating that x1 and x2 are some splitting of the sentence list x with an **APPEND** condition we can implicitly state this by changing the x1 of the "is-noun-phrase" condition to the pair of lists "(x x2)". Here, x2 is a the tail sublist of x that is the verb phrase and the pair "(x x2)" is implicitly representing the noun phrase initial segment of x as the *difference* between x and x2. Our new version of the rule is:

    x is-sentence (S X Y) if
        (x x2) is-noun-phrase X and
        x2 is-verb-phrase Y

The logical reading of the rule is:

    x is a sentence with parse (S X Y)
        if the difference between x and
        its tail end sublist x2 is a noun phrase X and
        x2 is a verb phrase Y

The pair of lists

    ((the boy kicked the ball) (kicked the ball))

represents the initial sublist

    (the boy)

because this is the difference between

(the boy kicked the ball)

and the tail end sublist

(kicked the ball)

Our rules for "is-noun-phrase" must now relate a difference pair of lists to a parse structure. The rewrite of the first rule is:

(x z) is-noun-phrase (N X Y) if
        (x y) is-determiner X and
        (y z) is-noun-expression Y

Again we have removed the explicit **APPEND** condition. The fact that the list which is the difference between x and z is split into the lists that comprise the determiner and the noun expression is now implicit in the representation of these sublists as the difference between x and y and the difference between y and z for some y. The logical reading of the rule is:

The difference between x and tail end sublist z
        is a noun phrase of the form (N X Y)
    if there is some y such that the difference between x
        and tail end sublist y is a determiner X and the
        difference between y and tail end sublist z is a noun
        expression Y

Of course, y must be a larger tail sublist of x than z. The following diagram illustrates the rule:

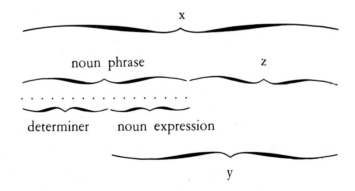

Our rule for determiner must now recognize a difference pair that represents a list containing a single determiner. Any pair of lists of the form "((x|X) X)" represents a list of one word x because the difference between (x|X) and the tail X is the single element list (x).

((x|X) X) is-determiner (DT x) if
    x dictionary DET

Our two rules for "is-noun-expression", which must also relate a difference pair to a parse structure, become:

((x|X) X) is-noun-expression (N x) if
    x dictionary NOUN

(x z) is-noun-expression (NE X Y) if
    (x y) is-adjective X and
    (y z) is-noun-expression Y

Finally the single rule for "is-adjective", like the single rule for "is-determiner" must recognize any pair of lists representing a list of one adjective.

((x|X) X) is-adjective (A x) if
    x dictionary ADJ

Exercises 6-2

1. Rewrite the rules for "is-verb-phrase", "is-verb-expression" and "is-adverb" using difference pairs of lists.

2. Trace through the evaluation of some parse query using the new grammar program. Notice how when a condition is attempted that involves a difference pair of lists that the tail end sublist is always a variable that is given a value when the condition is solved. So, when the rule

    x is-sentence (S X Y) if
        (x x2) is-noun-phrase X and
        x2 is-verb-phrase Y

is used to parse the sentence (the boy kicked the ball) the first condition becomes

    ((the boy kicked the ball) x2) is-noun-phrase X

When the condition is solved both x2 and X have values. X is (NP (DT the) (N boy)) and x2 is (kicked the ball). Thus the evaluation of the "is-noun-expression" condition passes on to the "is-verb-phrase" condition the tail end sublist representing the point where its parsing finished.

Finding sentences

The new program is just as efficient at generating sentences from parse structures as it is at generating parse structures from sentences. It is instructive to examine the behaviour of this inverted use.

Consider the rule

    x is-sentence (S X Y) if
        (x x2) is-noun-phrase X and
        x2 is-verb-phrase Y

For the use to generate a sentence list from a parse structure it has the control reading:

    To find a sentence list x from a parse structure (S X Y)
    find a most general difference list of the form (x x2)
        which represents the list of words that is parsed into X
    then make x2 the list of words parsed into Y

If you try the query

    which(x : x is-sentence (S (NP (DT the) (N boy))
                    (VP (V kicked) (NP (DT the) (N ball)))))

it will first reduce the query to the evaluation of the condition

    (x x2) is-noun-phrase (NP (DT the) (N boy)))

which will have the solution

    x=(the boy|X), x2=X

This makes (x x2) the most general difference list

    ((the boy|X) X)

representing the noun phrase (the boy). When the variable X of such an answer is passed over to the "is-verb-phrase" condition it is given the value (kicked the ball) and the most general answer to the "is-noun-phrase" condition becomes the specific answer

x=(the boy kicked the ball), x2=(kicked the ball))

When X is given the value (kicked the ball), the list pattern

(the boy|X)

is transformed into the list

(the boy kicked the ball)

and there is therefore an implicit appending of the list of words (the boy) with the list of words (kicked the ball) .

Our new program is a very efficient program for generating sentences from parse structures. If you have a computer try again the query

which(x : 6 length-of x & x is-sentence y)

using the new program. It should be very much faster than before.

6.3   General use of difference pairs

Difference pairs can be used in any program in which an APPEND condition is being used to generate all candidate splittings of a list or to append a pair of lists generated by other conditions. We must of course alter the other conditions so that they are relations with difference pairs as arguments. But if we do this, we can remove the APPEND condition.

As an example let us consider the definition of the list reverse relation:

(x) reverse (x)
(x|y) reverse z if y reverse z1 & APPEND(z1 (x) z)

In the normal use of this program the APPEND is used to append the result of reversing the tail y of the given list to the

single element list (x) comprising the head of the given list.
The definition

(x) D-reverse ((x|X) X)
(x|y) D-reverse (z z1) if y D-reverse (z (x|z1))

defines a reverse relation that relates a list to a difference pair
representing the reverse of the list. The recursive rule has the
logical reading:

(x|y) has a reverse represented by a difference pair (z z1)
    if y has a reverse represented by a difference pair (z
    (x|z1))

The rule records a true statement because the difference between
z and z1 is the difference between z and (x|z1) with the single
element x added as a new last element.
    As an example, suppose that (z (x|z1)) is ((3 2 1 0) (1 0))
representing the list (3 2). Then (z z1) is ((3 2 1 0) (0))
representing the list (3 2 1).
    If you query "D-reverse" you will find that you will always
get back a most general difference pair represention of the reverse
of the list.

which(z : (1 2 3) D-reverse z)
((3 2 1|X) X))
No (more) answers

Finally, we can define "reverse" in terms of "D-reverse". If
the "D-reverse" of a list x is of the form (z ()), with an empty
tail list to 'subtract' from z, then z is the normal reverse of x.

x reverse y if x D-reverse (y ())

This is a very efficient program for reversing lists. Trace through
its evaluation for some query using **all-trace** or by hand. You will
be surprised at its behaviour.
    A further property of the "D-reverse" program is that it can
be used in 'reverse' as efficiently as forward. Compare the speed
of evaluating the query:

one(z : z D-reverse ((1 2 3 4 5 6 7 8 9 0) ())
(0 9 8 7 6 5 4 3 2 1) more(y/n)?n

with the query:

> one(z : z reverse (1 2 3 4 5 6 7 8 9 0))
> (0 9 8 7 6 5 4 3 2 1) more(y/n)?n

(You have to use the "one" query because otherwise micro-PROLOG goes off into a bottomless pit after finding the first and only solution (why?).)

Exercises 6-3

1. Rewrite the "quick-sort" program of Exercise 5-3 so that it is a program for a "D-quick-sort" relation from lists to difference pairs of lists. Then define the old relation "quick-sort" over lists in terms of "D-quick-sort". This will give you a very fast program for sorting lists.

2. Extend the grammar program so that it checks that the determiner matches the noun regarding the singular/plural case and that the singular/plural case of the noun phrase that begins the sentence matches the singular/plural case of the verb phrase. To do this, you will need to extend the dictionary to record the case of each word, e.g.

> boy dictionary (N SI)
> boys dictionary (N PL)
> a dictionary (DT SI)
> the dictionary (DT x)

The variable representing the case for "the" means that it can be any case, that is both singular and plural.

The main rule must now be something like:

> x is-sentence (S (X case y) (Y case y))
>   if (x x2) is-noun-phrase (X case y) &
>   x2 is-verb-phrase (Y case y)

where the common y of the noun phrase and verb phrase parse structures means that they have the same case. Rewrite all the other rules to take into account the extra case component of the parse structure.

7. Some pragmatic considerations

In this chapter we examine some more issues related to the time required and the space needed for the evaluation of queries. We introduce two control primitives that can be used to eliminate redundant search during the backtracking evaluation of a query. This speeds up the evaluation of queries. We also briefly describe micro-PROLOG's use of memory space to keep track of the nested sequence of queries that are generated when rules are used. We shall see that the primitives that help to eliminate redundant search also help to minimize the use of space during an evaluation, an important consideration when using micro-PROLOG on small memory machines.

Related to this minimal use of memory space, we examine a special form of recursive definition, called *tail recursive*. The evaluation of a tail recursive definition uses a fixed amount of memory no matter how many times the recursive rule is applied. Normally, the evaluation of a recursive definition requires an amount of free memory space proportional to the number of uses of a recursive rule. Tail recursive definitions of list relations are particularly useful. They have the property that keeping track of their recursive evaluation requires the same small amount of memory space no matter how large the list argument.

Finally, we show how a collection of relation definitions can be wrapped up and protected from accidental modification as a named program *module*. Modules *export* certain relation names. Exported relations can be used in other programs but their definitions cannot be modified using the **add**, **delete** or **edit** commands. The use of modules also helps with respect to space management. This is because an entire module, containing definitions of many relations, can be deleted with a single **kill** command. So, if the exported relations of a module are not required for some query evaluation the module can be deleted to free space for the evaluation. The module can then be reloaded as and when required.

7.1   Limiting a condition to a single solution

Let us consider the evaluation of the query:

which(y : Tom father-is x & y brother-of x)   (A)

to find the uncles of Tom. In the evaluation of the query the
first condition will be solved by scanning all the sentences about
"father-is" until the one giving the father of Tom is found. This
gives a value for x which is then passed on to the second
condition.

When all the solutions to this second condition have been
found micro-PROLOG will return to its scan of sentences for
"father-is". This is because it does not know that there will be no
more matching sentences for the first condition and it is trying to
find all the solutions to the conjunctive condition. We know that
this search for a second solution to the condition

Tom father-is x

is pointless, because a person only has one father. There are two
ways that we can tell micro-PROLOG not to bother searching for
a second solution. For now we shall deal with the first method.
We. shall give the second method in Section 7.2.

The first and more elegant way is to make the "x father-is
Tom" condition of the first query a *single solution condition*. We
express the query as

which(y : father-is!(Tom x) & y brother-of x)   (B)

The "!" tells micro-PROLOG to look for only one way of solving
the first condition and not to backtrack to look for alternative
ways of solving the condition once it has been solved.

The query (B) should be read

which are the y's such that y is a brother of
the only father of Tom

General form of single solution condition

The form of a single solution condition is

R!(t1 t2 .. tk)

It is the prefix simple sentence form with a "!" placed between the relation name R and the list of arguments.

When a single solution condition is solved backtracking does not result in a search for other ways of solving the condition.

Single solution test conditions

Consider the query

all(x: x father-is Bill & x male)

This time we do not want to restrict the "father-is" condition to a single solution because it is being used to find all the children of Bill but we will improve the efficiency of the evaluation if we make the "male" condition a single solution condition. This is because, as micro-PROLOG finds each child x of Bill it passes this on the "x male" condition and looks for *all* ways of solving this condition. That is, even after it has found a match for some given x with a "male" sentence, it will continue scanning the list of sentences to see if there is a second match. If there is, because we have accidentally recorded some "male" fact twice, we would get a repeated answer to the query.

micro-PROLOG redundantly looks for a second way of confirming the test condition because it does not know that it is a test. To check each condition as it is being evaluated to see if it is a test condition because all its variables have already been given values would considerably slow down the evaluation of queries. The onus is upon us to tell micro-PROLOG that it is a test condition that should be confirmed once. For the most efficient evaluation we must pose the query in the form

all(x : x father-is Bill & male!(x))

Another example of the utility of making a test a single solution condition is the query all(x : x ON (R O B E R T) & x ON (B O B))

which is the same as that given in Exercise 3-4(2) except that it uses the **ON** relation defined in SIMPLE. You may remember that this gives the answer "B" twice because it can be confirmed as being on the list (B O B) in two different ways. We can make sure that each letter on (R O B E R T) is only checked once for being on the second list by making the second condition a single solution condition. We pose the query in the form:

all(x : x ON (R O B E R T) & ON!(x (B O B)))

Single solution conditions in rules

We can, of course, also use single solution conditions in rules. The rule

x is-male-with-son y if y father-is x & male!(y)

is a rule that can be used to find sons of fathers or to find all father/son pairs. It is more efficient as a program because in checking the condition "male!(y)" micro-PROLOG will stop scanning the "male" sentences as soon as it is confirmed that the y value is male.

Test versions of relations

The rules

x male-test if male!(x)

x on-test y if ON!(x y)

define variants of the "male" and "ON" relations that should only be used for testing. For the test use they are efficient programs. Using the "male-test" and "on-test" relations is an alternative to using single solution conditions involving the "male" and "ON" relations.

Exercises 7-1

1. Re-express the following queries using single solution conditions to speed up the evaluation:
a.   all(x : John likes y & y female & y mother x)
b.   which(y : Oliver-Twist written-by x & y written-by x
                      y published z & z LESS 1860)

7.2   Controlling the backtracking with a / condition

Let us return to query (A). The second way of preventing micro-PROLOG from searching for further solutions to the "Tom father-is x" condition is to insert a / after the condition in the query. We express it as

all(y : Tom father-is x & / & y brother-of x)   (C)

The / is a primitive of micro-PROLOG which should be read as "true" or just ignored in the logical reading of the query. A / condition is always immediately solved when encountered during a query evaluation. However, when it has been solved it prevents micro-PROLOG from backtracking to find alternative ways of solving *any* conditions that precede it in the query. In this case, it prevents the evaluation of (C) from backtracking to look for alternative ways of solving the single condition "Tom father-is x" that precedes the /.

/ in rules

In queries single solution conditions can always be used instead of /. However, / is more powerful when used in rules. When a rule is invoked to solve some condition C and a / is evaluated in the rule, the evaluation of the / not only prevents the backtracking to look for alternative solutions to the conditions that precede it in the rule, it also tells micro-PROLOG to treat the rule as the *last* rule that can be used to find a solution to C even if there are other as yet untried rules. It is primarily because of this second effect of telling micro-PROLOG to ignore the untried rules that / is used.

Example use of / in rules

When we defined the "sort" relation in Chapter 5 we gave the following definition of the "merge" relation:

```
merge(() x x)
merge(x () x)
merge((x|y1) (x|y2) (x x|y)) if
      merge(y1 y2 y)
merge((x1|y1) (x2|y2) (x1|y)) if
      x1 less x2 &
      merge(y1 (x2|y2) y)
merge((x1|y1) (x2|y2) (x2|y)) if
      x2 less x1 &
      merge((x1|y1) y2 y)
```

The only sensible use of this definition is the way it is used within the "sort" program to achieve an order preserving merge of two given ordered lists. When it is used in this way only one rule ever applies to a given merge condition. Consider the query:

which(z : merge((2 3 6) (2 4 5 9) z))

Only the third rule applies to the condition of the query but micro-PROLOG does not know this. Even when it has solved the condition by applying the third rule micro-PROLOG will try to apply the fourth and fifth rules to see if they result in an alternative solution. Moreover, this fruitless search for other "merge" rules that might result in a different solution will take place when each of the recursively generated "merge" conditions have been solved. Thus, when rule 3 is applied to the condition of the query its application reduces it to the new "merge" condition

merge((3 6) (4 5 9) z1)

to which only the fourth rule can be successfully applied because 3 is less than 4. However, on backtracking to find an alternative solution to the original query micro-PROLOG will try to solve this derived "merge" condition using the fifth rule. The rule matches the condition but it will not lead to a solution because the "less" test will fail.

System note - tracing merge - if you are using a computer, trace the evaluation of this query using **all-trace**. You will see micro-PROLOG trying to use the untried sentences for each recursively generated "merge" condition even when it has found a solution.

We can prevent all this fruitless backtracking search by always using "merge" in a single solution condition. That is, we re-express our query as

which(z : merge!((2 3 6)(2 4 5 9) z))

and we can rewrite the recursive "sort" rule that uses "merge" as

```
(x1  x2lx) sort y if
          split((x1  x2lx) X1 X2) &
          X1 sort y1 & X2 sort Y2 &
          merge!(Y1Y2 y)
```

There is another remedy: by putting / conditions in the rules, we can instruct micro-PROLOG only to use a single rule to solve a "merge" condition irrespective of whether it is specified as a single solution condition. We rewrite the program as

```
merge(() x x) if /
merge(x () x) if /
merge((xly1) (xly2) (x xly)) if
        / & merge(y1 y2 y)
merge((x1ly1) (x2ly2) (x1ly)) if
        x1 less x2 & /&
        merge(y1 (x2ly2) y)
merge((x1ly1) (x2ly2) (x2ly)) if
        x2 less x1&
        merge((x1ly1) y2 y)
```

In each rule, the / is ignored when giving a logical reading. The / conditions only have a control effect. When a rule is applied in order to find a solution to some "merge" condition M, as soon as the left to right evaluation of the conditions of the rule reaches the /, micro-PROLOG will treat the rule as though it was the last "merge" rule.

This treating of the rule as the last rule only applies to the attempt to solve the condition M. It does not prevent the other rules from being applied to any other "merge" condition, even one that is recursively derived from M.

Let us see what this means. Since the / is the first

condition in the first three rules a successful match between a "merge" condition and any of these rules instructs micro-PROLOG to ignore the other rules for that condition because no other rule can lead to a solution. In the case of the fourth rule the / comes after the test "x1 less x2". It is therefore only after a successful match *and* the confirmation of this condition that the / is evaluated and the option to use the fifth rule is cut off.

The / cannot come before the test. If it did the fifth rule would never be applied because any "merge" condition to which it might apply will always also match the fourth rule. There is no need to place a / in the last rule as there are no other rules that need to be ignored when the "x2 less x1" condition is confirmed.

Actually, the / conditions in the two non-recursive rules can also be dropped without too much loss since these are only applied once at the end of the evaluation. The / conditions in the first two recursive rules bring the greatest benefit since they cut out all the useless backtracking search at the many intermediary points in the evaluation at which the rules will be applied.

Using / to define test relations

We can use a / instead of a single solution condition to define test versions of relations.

x male-test if x male & /

x on-test y if x ON y & /

are alternative definitions to the ones we gave above. Now, the / is not preventing the use of any other rule, it is preventing backtracking on the evaluation of the condition that precedes it in the rule. These rules are behaviourally equivalent to the earlier rules that used the single solution conditions.

Query the user defaults for test relations

Consider the pair of rules

x male-test if x male & /
x male-test if (x male) is-told

They give us two ways of confirming the "male-test" relation for some given argument. They are read

> x male-test is true if
> > either x can be confirmed as a male
> > or micro-PROLOG is told that x is male

Because of the / at the end of the first rule the second rule will not be applied if the use of the first rule confirms that the given x is male. The second rule is a *default* 'query the user' rule that checks with us before concluding that someone really is not a male. It gives a safety net for "male-test" conditions. In the next chapter we shall see how we can modify the rule so that it also automatically adds a "male" sentence whenever we have told micro-PROLOG that someone is male even though they are not recorded as male by some "male" sentence.

7.3   Query stack and space saving

This section and Section 7.4 can be skipped on a first reading.

When micro-PROLOG is trying to solve a query it generates a nested sequence of derived queries as it applies rules to solve conditions in the query.

Suppose that it is trying to solve some condition C of a current query Q. If it applies a rule to C a new query Q' is generated which micro-PROLOG must solve before continuing with the remaining conditions of the current query Q. Q' becomes the new current query. In solving Q' further derived queries may be generated, resulting in a nested sequence of derived queries.

micro-PROLOG keeps track of this sequence of queries by constructing a stack of queries, rather like a stack of plates. Each time it applies a rule which generates a new query it puts the new query on top of the query stack. The stack starts out with only one query on it, the initial query. As the evaluation proceeds the stack grows. Each time a new query is generated it is put on top of the stack of queries and it becomes the current query.

When a solution has been found to the current query, unless it is the initial query, it means that a solution has been found to a condition C in a query Q lower down the query stack. (Each query on the stack refers back to the query condition lower down the stack that it will solve.) So, on solving the current query, micro-PROLOG returns to its task of solving the query Q which again becomes the current query.

micro-PROLOG will not necessarily remove the query at the top of the query stack that it has just solved. If there are untried sentences for any of the conditions in this top of stack query micro-PROLOG will leave it on the stack in order to return to its evaluation should it be necessary to seek an alternative solution to the condition C.

A query is removed from the top of the stack only when micro-PROLOG knows, **or is told**, that there is no need to seek other solutions to the query. This can mean that the current query, the query for which micro-PROLOG is trying to solve some new condition C', is not always the query at the top of the stack.

The construction of the stack takes up memory that is shared with your program and any modules that you are using. Sometimes micro-PROLOG will run out of space and be unable to add a new query to its stack of queries. When this happens you will get the evaluation error message "No space left" and the evaluation of the current query will be aborted. On micro-computers with very little memory this means that you may have to kill relation definitions that are not being used and kill any module that is not needed and try again.

Getting rid of unnecessary definitions and modules is one way of increasing the space for query evaluation. The other way is to write the program in such a way that the growth of the stack is minimized. In the next section we describe a form of recursive definition that minimizes the growth of the query stack. The use of single solution conditions and / also help in this matter.

For example, the top query of the stack is always removed when the condition C that it has solved is a single solution condition. There is no need to leave it on the query stack because micro-PROLOG never needs to backtrack to that query to find an alternative solution to C.

The use of / similarly reduces the size of the stack. This is because, whenever a / condition is evaluated in some current query Q in the stack all the queries on the stack which are above Q are immediately removed.

They can be removed because they are always the derived queries that were put onto the stack by the attempts to solve the conditions that precede the / in the query Q. (Do not worry if you do not understand why this is the case. Just accept it as a property of the query stack.)

The queries were left on the stack because each had at least one condition with an untried sentence. The evaluation of the /

tells micro-PROLOG that it need not bother to keep a record of these previously solved queries because it does not need to look for alternative solutions to the conditions that they solved.

Finally, if the / is the last condition of the query Q, Q is also removed from the query stack. In this case the / also tells micro-PROLOG not to bother looking for alternative solutions to Q.

7.4   Tail recursive definitions

When recursive definitions of relations are evaluated there is nearly always a rapid growth of the query stack as the recursive rules are applied. However, there is a form of recursive definition that does not result in a growth of the stack. It is a form of definition in which there is a single recursive rule which is the last rule for the relation and in that rule the recursive condition is the last condition. This *last* rule, *last* condition constraint is the reason for the name: *tail recursive definition*.

A classic example of a tail recursive definition is the "append" program:

append(() x x)
append((x|y) z (x|y1)) if append(y z y1)

When micro-PROLOG is using this program to solve some "append" condition it does not need to grow the stack of queries when it re-applies the recursive rule to a recursively derived "append" condition, that is when it applies the recursive rule in order to try to solve the "append" condition of the recursive rule.

We shall not go into the reasons why this is the case. We ask the reader to accept that it is the case. It means that no matter how large the list arguments of the "append" condition there is only ever one new query added to the query stack when the condition is being solved.

General form of a tail recursive definition

A tail recursive definition is a sequence of rules defining a relation R in which the only recursive rule is the last rule which has the form

R(t1 t2 .. tn) if C1 & ... & Ck & R(t'1 ... t'n)

where only the last condition refers to R. The conditions C1 ..
Ck that precede it in the rule must be such that when they are
solved micro-PROLOG will know that there are no more
solutions to be found to any of the conditions.

   This extra condition is always satisfied if there are no C
conditions as in the above "append" program, or if each of the
C's is a single solution condition or a condition involving one of
the primitive relations of micro-PROLOG that only have one
solution, such as the arithmetic primitives. It is also satisfied if
the last condition Ck is a /.

Other tail recursive definitions

   The "D-reverse" program that we gave in Chapter 6 is
another example of a tail recursive program:

   () D-reverse (X X)
   (x|y) D-reverse (Y Z) if y D-reverse (Y (x|Z))

whereas the original "reverse" program is not:

   () reverse ()
   (x|y) reverse Z if y reverse Z1 & append(y (x) Z)

This is not tail recursive because the "reverse" condition is not the
last condition of the rule. The definition of "reverse" in terms of
"D-reverse":

   X reverse Y if X D-reverse (Y ())

is therefore a more efficient program for two reasons. It does not
involve any evaluations of **append** conditions and its evaluation
will not result in a recursive growth of the query stack no matter
how long the list being reversed.

   The definition of "split-on" that we gave in Chapter 5 is
also tail recursive.

   split-on(0 X () X)
   split-on(y (x|X) (x|X1) X2) if
            0 LESS y & SUM(y1 1 y) &
            split-on(y1 X X1 X2)

Here **LESS** and **SUM** are primitive relations so micro-PROLOG knows that they only have one solution.

Changing into tail recursive form

The definition of the "merge" relation that we considered in Section 7.2 is not tail recursive because it has more than one recursive rule. An alternative tail recursive form, which is not as readable, is:

    merge(() x x)
    merge(x () x)
    merge((x1ly1) (x2ly2) (xly)) if
            choose!((x1ly1) (x2ly2) x Y1 Y2)
            & merge(Y1 Y2 y)

    choose((x1ly1) (x2ly2) x1 y1 (x2ly2)) if
            x1 less x2
    choose((x1ly1) (x2ly2) x2 (x1ly1) y2) if
            not x1 less x2

The auxiliary relation "choose" is used to select the minimum of the x1 x2 values and to give the Y1 Y2 forms of the two lists when this minimum has been removed from one of the lists. The use of "choose" in the single recursive rule is a single solution condition so that micro-PROLOG knows there are no alternative solutions to be found.

Alternatively, the "choose" condition could have been followed by a /, or we could have put / conditions at the end of the first of the two rules defining "choose".

The example illustrates a general method for trying to transform a definition in which there are several recursive rules, each of which has a single recursive condition at the end of the rule, into a tail recursive definition.

First, absorb all the recursive rules into one general rule. (Unfortunately, as we saw in Chapter 4 with the use of **either ..** **or** conditions, this absorbing into a single rule can often make the program much less readable.)

Then, providing only one solution to each of the non-recursive conditions of this general rule needs to be found for the intended uses of the program, make each of them a single solution condition or put a / before the recursive condition. You are left with a tail recursive definition.

Generalizing relations

We can sometimes transform recursive definitions in which the recursive condition is not the last condition into tail recursive form by defining a more general relation.

The following is a non-tail recursive definition of the maximum of a non-empty list:

```
x max-of (x)
x max-of (y|Z) if x1 max-of Z & x greater-of (y x1)

x greater-of (x x)
x greater-of (x y) if y less x
y greater-of (x y) if x less y
```

To get a tail recursive definition we must define a more general relation

```
x Max-of (Z y) :
          x is the greater of y and the maximum of list Z
```

This has a tail recursive definition:

```
y Max-of (() y)
z Max-of ((y1|Z) y) if
          y2 greater-of (y1 y) & / & z Max-of (Z y2)
```

The second rule of this definition tells us that the greater of y and the maximum of (y1|Z) is the greater of the maximum of Z and whichever is the greater of y and y1.

The / condition after the "greater-than" condition ensures that micro-PROLOG knows that this condition in the recursive rule will only have one solution. This is the case for the intended use of the program to find the maximum of a list.

We can define the original "max-of" relation in terms of "Max-of". The definition is:

```
x max-of (y|Z) if x Max-of (Z y)
```

i.e. x is the maximum of (y|Z) if it is the greater of y and the maximum of Z. The evaluation of a "max-of" condition using the tail recursive "Max-of" definition will only result in one new query being placed on the query stack no matter how long the list for which the maximum is to be found.

Semi-tail recursive definitions

Consider the following rules for "quick-sort" which make use of difference pairs to represent the sorted list.

```
() quick-sort (x  x)
(x) quick-sort ((x|y) y)
(x  y|X) quick-sort (z1  z3) if
          partition((y|X) x  X1  X2) &
          X1 quick-sort (z1  (x|z2)) & / &
          X2 quick-sort (z2  z3)
```

In this case there are two recursive conditions but we still have one of these as the last condition of the last rule. micro-PROLOG will have to grow the query stack as it applies the recursive rule to the first recursive condition, but it will not grow the stack as it applies the recursive rule to the second recursive condition.

The / before this condition tells micro-PROLOG that there are no further solutions to the preceding conditions so it applies the same optimization as it does when the last condition is the only recursive condition. It removes the top of stack query put there on the last application of the rule before it puts on the query that records the new application of the rule. This means that for this program the query stack will on average need to grow to only half as much during the evaluation of each recursive condition.

The optimization whereby micro-PROLOG does not grow the query stack when it is applying a rule to the last condition of the last rule of a program actually applies irrespective of whether the last condition is a recursive condition. Providing micro-PROLOG knows that there are no other solutions to the conditions preceding the last condition, and providing the rule being applied is the *last* rule for the relation of the last condition, micro-PROLOG does not grow the query stack. The tail recursive and semi-tail recursive forms are just special cases of these constraints in which the *same* last rule is being re-applied.

Exercises 7-2

1. Define the "min-of" relation for a non-empty list using a tail recursive "Min-of" definition.

2. Use "min-of" to give an alternative tail recursive definition of the "sort" relation for lists.

3. Give an alternative definition of the "factorial" relation defined in Chapter 2 which makes use of an auxiliary relation that has a tail recursive definition.
Hint: use the auxiliary relation "tail-fact(x y z)" which holds when z is the product of x and the factorial of y. Then define "factorial" in terms of "tail-fact".

4. Redefine the "partition" relation of Exercise 5-3(2) so that it is tail recursive.

7.5   Use of modules

Modules are named collections of relation definitions with two associated lists of names: an *export* list and an *import* list.
In the export list we must put all the names of relations defined inside the module that we want to use in queries or in rules outside the module.
In the import name list we must put all the names of relations that will be defined outside the module but which are used by some definition inside the module. We must also put in the import list all the names of individuals used inside the module that we want to use in queries to its exported relations.
When we have wrapped up a collection of definitions as a module the definitions for its exported relations are protected. We cannot **add** to or **delete** or **kill** any of the sentences of the exported relations of the module. We can only use the exported relations.
Moreover, all the names that are not in the export or import name lists are *local* (and private) to the module. If a local name of a module is used in a workspace program or in some other module micro-PROLOG treats it as a quite different name. (micro-PROLOG does this by keeping separate dictionaries for the local names of each module and a separate dictionary for the names of our workspace program. The dictionaries hold all the

constants used in a program. The program is compiled so that all uses of the constant become references to the dictionary entry.)

This means that the definitions of the non-exported relations of a module are invisible outside the module because each of these will be named by a local name of the module. Finally, when a module program is loaded its sentences are not added to the sentences of our existing program as with the load of a normally saved program.

As we mentioned in Section 1.2, sentences that we enter using the **add** or **accept** commands, or which are brought in when we load a non-module program, are held in a special area called the *workspace*. When we use the **list** command we only ever see relation definitions in this workspace area. Loaded modules do not enter the workspace. Even if we do a **list all** we will not see any of the sentences of a loaded module. (However they still take up space within the computer's memory.)

These properties of modules make them the appropriate program structure for finished programs, for example, the "sort" program that we developed in Chapter 5. With some added refinements which minimize the space needed during an evaluation, the program is:

```
() sort ()
(x) sort (x)
(x1 x2|x) sort y if
        split((x1 x2|x) X1 X2) &
        X1 sort y1 & X2 sort y2 & / &
        merge(y1 y2 y)

merge(() x x)
merge(x () x)
merge((x1|y1) (x2|y2) (x|y)) if
        choose!((x1|y1) (x2|y2) x Y1 Y2)&
        merge(Y1 Y2 y)

choose((x1|y1) (x2|y2) x1 y1 (x2|y2)) if
        x1 less x2
choose((x1|y1) (x2|y2) x2 (x1|y1) y2) if
        not x1 less x2

split(X X1 X2) if
        split-on#((div (length X) 2) X X1 X2)
```

```
split-on(0  X  ()  X)
split-on(y  (x|X)  (x|X1)  X2) if
        0 LESS  y  &
        SUM(y1  1  y)  &
        split-on(y1  X  X1  X2)
```

The / in the recursive "sort" rule tells micro-PROLOG that there will be no alternative ways of solving the preceding conditions and so the 'record' of their evaluations is removed from the query stack before the tail recursive evaluation of the "merge".

The relation "sort" is the main relation, the other relations are auxiliary relations that we shall usually not use in queries and other definitions. If we wrap up this program as a module we only need to export the relation name "sort".

When we use the program we must supply an appropriate definition of the "less" relation. So, "less" must be an imported name. It is a relation that we shall define outside the module but which is used inside the module.

We must also either import the names "div" and "length", or we must include the definitions of these relations in the module. We will take the latter option. Unlike "less" the definitions of these relations will not change with different uses of the "sort" program and including them in the module means that we do not need to define them each time we want to use the module.

We do not need to import the names of the primitive relations **LESS** and **SUM**. The micro-PROLOG primitive relations are available to every program whether or not it is wrapped up as a module.

However, we do need to import the name "#". This is actually the name of a relation defined in and exported from one of the three modules that comprise the SIMPLE front end program that we are using. It is not a primitive relation of micro-PROLOG. To link the definition of a relation exported from one module with its use inside another module we must *import* its name to the other module.

There are no names of individuals in the sentences of the program so we do not need to import any other names.

Constructing a module

We shall describe one way in which a module can be constructed using the "sort" program as an example. For this section we assume the reader has access to a computer with micro-PROLOG.

First, all and only the relation definitions that are to be included in the module must be put into the workspace area. To do this, we must **add** all the definitions or load them from various other files. We should then **kill** the definitions of any relations that are not to be included in the module so that when we do a **list all** only the definitions we want in the module are displayed. In the case of the "sort" program this should be the above definitions together with the definitions:

() length 0
(x|y) length z if y length z1 & SUM(1 z1 z)

div(x y z) if TIMES(y z1 x) & INT(z1 z)

We must now load a utility program, which is itself a module, which is in the file "MODULES" supplied with the micro-PROLOG system. We do this with a

load MODULES

command. This program enables us to construct and save a module. The next step is to **add** a sentence to the program that describes the module we want to construct from the workspace program. We must add the sentence

Module(sort-mod (sort) (less #))

for the relation name "Module". The relation has three arguments:

the name of the module, sort-mod
the export name list, (sort)
the import name list, (less #)

We now enter the command

wrap SORT

The entire sort program will now be wrapped up as a module and saved, in a special module format, in the file "SORT" and the workspace area will be cleared.

It is a useful convention to give the module the name "name-mod" where the file in which it is saved is called "NAME".

The name of the file must be different from the name given to the module and each of these must be different from the names of the relations of the module.

The **wrap** command uses the "Module" sentence of the workspace program in order to discover the name of the module and its export and import name lists. It does not save this sentence in the module.

Whenever we want to use the "sort" program we load it with a

    load SORT

command. (On disk-based systems the **wrap** command automatically re-loads the module after it has been saved so an explicit **load** after the **wrap** is not required. An explicit **load** is required for tape-based systems.) Because the program in the file is a module it does not enter the workspace area and a **list all** command will now not display the program. To check that it is present we can ask if "sort" is defined with a

    is(sort defined)

query. If you try to load the module and you already have a definition for the relation "sort" that it exports you will get the evaluation error "Illegal use of modules" and the load will be aborted. If you try to **add** a sentence about the "sort" relation after the module has been loaded you will get the error "Cannot add sentences for sort". Both error messages are a result of the fact that the definitions of the exported relations of a module are protected.

Before we use the "sort" relation we must **add** an appropriate definition of "less" to the workspace, for example,

    x less y if x LESS y

We can then query "sort" with

    which(x : (2 4 6 3 9 -4) sort x)

When we have finished using the module we can remove it with a

> kill sort-mod

command which uses the name of the module. All the relation definitions of the module will be deleted freeing the memory space that the module occupied.

To change a module program once it has been created we must first unwrap it and put it back into the workspace area using the **unwrap** command of the MODULES utility. For details we refer the reader to the section of the micro-PROLOG Reference Manual that documents this utility program.

Exercises 7-3

1. Take one of your programs and convert it into a module. Do not forget to import the names of all the individuals used in your program that you want to use in queries to the exported relations.

8.   Metalogical programming

In this chapter we introduce a style of logic programming which is best described as *metalogical* programming. micro-PROLOG is highly suited to this style of programming which we shall more fully explore in Part III. The prefix "meta" means "about" and it is used because the rules and queries of a metalogical program talk 'about' and manipulate the relation names and rules of other logic programs.

8.1 Relation names and argument lists
as variables

Consider the situation where we have a data base describing several relations and that what we want to know is what the data base records about some individual "Tom". An unsatisfactory solution is to do a list all. It is unsatisfactory because we may have many facts and rules and the information about "Tom" will not be isolated and specially displayed in the way that an answer to a query is. An alternative is to find out what the names of the relations are with a

   all(x : x dict)

query and then to pose a query about each relation.
   Providing we know how many arguments each relation has we can use a series of queries of the form

   all(x1 ... xk : R(x1 ... xk) & Tom ON (x1 ... xk))

in order to discover everything in the data base about "Tom". We pose the query for each relation R. For example, if there is a binary relation "likes" in the dict relation we can use the query

   all(x y : likes(x y) & Tom ON (x y))

to find out all the "likes" information about "Tom".

Variable as the list of arguments

If we cannot remember how many arguments a relation has this strategy will not work. The ideal solution would be if we could pose the query without specifying how many arguments the relation has. This we can do:

all(Y : likes true-of Y & Tom ON Y)

is an alternative to the above query. The "true-of" is a meta-relation; the condition "likes true-of Y" is read: the list of terms Y is true of the likes relation. The Y represents *any* list of arguments.

Relation name as a variable

We can also use "true-of" to pose a single query in which the relation name is not given but is generated by a **dict** condition:

all(X Y : X dict & X true-of Y & Tom ON Y)

will find each relation name, find each list of arguments for which the relation can be confirmed, and display the relation name and the list of arguments if "Tom" is one of the arguments.

true-of meta-condition

The **true-of** meta-condition has the form

<variable or relation name> true-of <variable or list pattern>

If the first argument is a variable then this must have been given a value which is the name of a relation by the time that the **true-of** condition is solved. If it does not have a value the evaluation error message "Too many variables" will be displayed together with a condition which has a variable in the position of the relation name.

If the second argument is a variable it represents any list of arguments of the relation, otherwise it is a list pattern that will be matched against the argument list of each sentence of the relation. A variable appearing as the first argument is a *meta-variable* standing for a relation name. A variable appearing as the second argument is a meta-variable standing for a list of arguments.

Examples

X true-of (x y)	checks if x and y satisfy some given relation X
gives true-of (Tom IY)	checks if Tom is in the "gives" relation to some unknown remaining list of arguments Y
likes true-of X	finds an argument list X that satisfies the "likes" relation

Exercises 8-1

1. Pose the query to find all the instances of the "employee" relation without knowing how many arguments the relation has.

2. Pose the query to find out the information given in the "employee" relation about "Jones". Assume that "Jones" will be the second argument but that you do not know how many other arguments there are.

Generalized programs

The **true-of** relation enables us to generalize certain programs with respect to some of the relations that they use. It allows the name of one or more relations to be given in the condition that will 'invoke' the program. The "sort" program of Chapter 5 is an excellent candidate for such generalization.

You may remember that we deliberately used the relation name "less" rather than the micro-PROLOG primitive **LESS** so that the element comparison relation could be redefined for different uses of the program. Then, when we transformed the program into a module in the last chapter, the name "less" was made an imported name of the module which had the effect of generalizing the module so that the "sort" program could still be used with different definitions of "less".

The program is not completely general because at any one

time it can only be used with a single definition of the "less" relation. A better generalization is to make the name of the comparison relation an argument to the "sort" relation. When we use the program we tell it which comparison relation to use by passing it as an argument. We re-write the "sort" program in the form:

```
sort(() () X)
sort((x) (x) X)
sort((x1 x2|x) y X) if
        split((x1 x2|x) X1 X2) &
        sort(X1 y1 X) &
        sort(X2 y2 X) & / &
        merge(y1 y2 y X)

merge(() x x X)
merge(x () x X)
merge((x1|y1) (x2|y2) (x|y) X) if
        choose!((x1|y1) (x2|y2) x Y1 Y2 X) &
        merge(Y1 Y2 y X)

choose((x1|X1) (y1|Y1) x1 X1 (y1|Y1) X) if
        X true-of (x1 y1)
choose((x1|X1) (y1|Y1) y1 (x1|X1) Y1 X) if
        not X true-of (x1 y1)
```

The extra X argument of both "sort" and "merge" is the name of the comparison relation. This is then used in "choose" in a "true-of" condition to actually compare the elements of the two lists. A use of the new "sort" is

which(x : sort((3 -5 7 2 8 4) x LESS))

in which we give the comparison relation as the primitive **LESS** relation. If we convert the new program into a module there is no need to import the name "less" which is no longer used in the program. We can also have several different comparison relations "less1", "less2" etc. defined at the same time in our own program. When we want to sort we pass the name of the appropriate comparison relation to the "sort" program by giving it as the last argument.

Another example of a generalized program is the following program for the relation "reduce". "reduce(X y x)" holds when x is the result of 'reducing' list y using the relation X. For example, "reduce($+$ (2 3 4) 9)" holds because 9 is the addition reduction of the list (2 3 4), it is the result of cumulatively applying $+$ to all the elements of the list.

The program defining the "reduce" relation is:

```
reduce(X (x) x)
reduce(X (x y|Z) z) if
        X true-of (x y x1) & reduce(X (x1|Z) z)
```

When the program is used the X argument, which is the name of the reduction relation, must be given.

If we also assume that the second list argument will also always be given and that the **true-of** condition will only have one solution, as when we reduce a list using $+$, we can ensure that the program is tail recursive by putting a / before the recursive condition of the second rule.

Exercises 8-2

1. Give a generalized definition of the program for the relation "ordered" so that the comparison relation is given as an argument.

2. Give a recursive definition of maplist(X x y) : each top-level element of the list x is in the X binary relation to the corresponding element of the list y. Give queries using "maplist" to
a.   Find a list of numbers that are the doubles of the numbers on the list (3 -5 9 5).
b.   Find a list of the fathers of (Tom Bill Mary).
c.   Check that each element of the list (John Jill Frank) is in the "parent-of" relation to the list (Jim Mary Sally).

In the case of (a) define the auxiliary relation that you need.

3. Give queries that use the "reduce" relation and which find
a.   the product of the list (3 6 -5 8)
b.   the number of elements in the list (2 4 -5 7 78)

In the case of (b) define the auxiliary relation that you need.

A general list mapping relation

The relation "maplist" of the above exercise relates the pair of lists only at the top level, if the elements of the lists are sublists it is the sublists that are related by the mapping relation not the elements of these sublists. A different type of "maplist" relation would relate two lists of arbitrary structure but insist that the two lists have the same structure with corresponding non-list elements related by the given relation. Its definition is:

Maplist(X () ())
Maplist(X (x|y) (x1|y1)) if
   not x LST & X true-of (x x1) &
   Maplist(X y y1)
Maplist(X (x|y) (x1|y1)) if
   x LST & Maplist(X x x1) &
   Maplist(X y y1)

Remember that **LST** is the micro-PROLOG primitive relation for testing if something is an empty list or a term of the form (z|Z). So the condition "not x LST" is confirmed if x is not a sublist element of "(x|y)". Notice that because we have tested the element of the first list rather than the second list there is an implicit assumption that the program will be used to solve conditions in which this first list argument is always given. (There was no such assumption in the program for "maplist" given as the answer to the above exercise. In that program either or both list arguments could be given.)

8.2   Metaprograms that check conditions of use

If the above "Maplist" program is used without the relation name argument X being given we will get the evaluation error "Too many variables" when the **true-of** condition is evaluated. To avoid this, we could add the explicit condition "X CON" to each rule. **CON** is another micro-PROLOG primitive relation for confirming that a value is a constant. Then, the attempt to solve some "Maplist" condition with X not given as a constant will fail rather than result in an error. To make sure that we also have a definition for the given relation we could also add the condition "X defined". This would transform the first rule into

Maplist(X () ()) if X CON & X defined

"defined" is a relation exported from the SIMPLE front-end that we met in Chapter 1. "defined" is a metalogical relation because it tests if there is a program for a given name.

 A better solution is to define an auxiliary relation

"MAPLIST" which we use instead of "Maplist". The program for this auxiliary relation is a metalogical program that tests if the conditions of use for the "Maplist" program are satisfied. If they are, it reduces to the evaluation of the corresponding "Maplist" condition. Its definition is:

MAPLIST(X Y Z) if
    X CON &
    X defined &
    Maplist(X Y Z)

Now the tests for applicability are only done once, not each time a rule for "Maplist" is used. Later we shall see how we can augment this metalogical program by adding a second default rule which causes a message to be displayed when the "Maplist" conditions for use are not satisfied.

Selecting a definition for a given use

In Chapter 2 when we discussed the "ancestor-of" relation we found that the definition that was an appropriate program for finding ancestors was not appropriate for finding descendants. We were forced to define a program for the inverse relation "descendant-of" which was much more suited to the task of finding descendants. We then had to remember to use the one relation for finding ancestors and the other for finding descendants. An alternative is to give a metalogical program for an auxiliary relation "Ancestor-of" which tests for conditions of use for each relation and which uses one or other relation as appropriate. Its definition is:

x Ancestor-of y if y CON & / & x ancestor-of y
x Ancestor-of y if not y CON & y descendant-of x

We can now use "Ancestor-of" both for finding ancestors and for finding descendants without loss of efficiency. If the y argument is given the "ancestor-of" program is used and the / prevents any attempt to use "descendant-of" program on backtracking. The "descendant-of" program is used if the y argument is not given. This is because the "y CON" condition of the first rule will fail to be confirmed if the y argument does not have a value.

An equivalent program for this relation is

x Ancestor-of y if y VAR & / & y descendant-of x
x Ancestor-of y if not y VAR & x ancestor-of y

This uses another primitive test relation of micro-PROLOG, the VAR relation. A VAR condition is confirmed only if its single argument is a variable which has not yet been assigned a value. VAR is one of the metalogical primitives of micro-PROLOG.

Exercises 8-3

1. In Chapter 3 we needed to give two definitions of the relation between a list and its length. The one for the relation name "has-length" was to be used to find the length of a given list, the other for the relation name "length-of" was to be used to find a list of variables of a given length. Either program could be used for checking. Give a metalogical program for the relation "length-is" which can be used in any way.

8.3   Programs that manipulate other programs

In Section 4.6 we introduced a simple bicycle fault finder program which contained the following two rules:

x possible-fault-in y if
    z indirect-part-of y and
    X indicates (x in z) and
    X is-reported

X is-reported if (X a problem) is-told

together with facts such as:

flat-tyre indicates (puncture in wheel)
flat-tyre indicates (faulty-valve in wheel)

To help in finding faults with a bicycle we could use a query such as

all(x : x possible-fault-with bicycle)

and we would be asked to report on the various problems, such

as "flat-tyre", given in the "indicates" facts. We will be asked
questions such as

> flat-tyre a problem ?

The drawback which we noted in Chapter 4 is that the reported
problems are not remembered. Whatever we answer to this
question we will be asked the same question again when the next
"indicates" fact is used. The program for "is-reported" is actually a
metalogical program because it switches the problem of solving
an "is-reported" condition to a query to an external data base in
our heads. It would be a much more sophisticated metalogical
program if it also remembered the results of these external queries
by storing them as facts in the internal data base of micro-
PROLOG.

At the end of an interaction in which we are prompted to
report on the presence or otherwise of certain problems we can
always **add** sentences, such as

> flat-tyre was-present
> wheel-wobble was-absent

to the fault finder data base which explicitly records our answers.
Ideally, the "is-reported" program should **add** these facts
automatically as we give the answers to the **is-told** prompts.

As a first step we can put an **add** condition at the end of
the single "is-reported" rule.

> x is-reported if (x a problem) is-told &
> (x was-present) add

Notice that this is making use of the command **add** as a
unary relation. We simply switch the order of the command name
and its bracketed sentence argument. The bracketed sentence is,
of course, just a list of terms satisfying certain syntactical
constraints. (It is a general rule of micro-PROLOG that all
command names can also be used as relations in rules and
queries. A one-argument use of the command becomes a unary
relation, a two-argument use becomes a binary relation. We shall
discuss this correspondence between relations and commands more
fully in the next section.) The effect of the **add** condition is that
a "was-present" fact will be added to the data base for each
problem which gets a "yes" response to the **is-told** condition. To
remember the "no" responses we need to use two rules and a /.

```
x is-reported if
     (x a problem) is-told & / &
     (x was-present) add
x is-reported if (x was-absent) add & FAIL
```

The second rule will only be used if our answer to the "x a problem" prompt is "no", which is interpreted as a failure to solve the is-told condition of the first rule The second rule will then add the appropriate "was-absent" fact **and then fail.** (FAIL is a built-in primitive that is never satisfied, logically it can read as "false".) If the answer to the question is "yes" the is-told condition of the first rule is confirmed and the evaluation of the / then prevents the use of the second rule. This is an essential use of the /. The alternative, of having an explicit negated condition

```
not (x a problem) is-told
```

would result in each question being asked at least twice as micro-PROLOG checks for applicability of the second rule.

If we now pose the query

```
all(x : x possible-fault-with  bicycle)
```

at the end of the query evaluation all our answers will be recorded by facts in the data base. However, we will still be asked about the "flat-tyre" problem twice because our "is-reported" program does not make use of the "was-present" or "was-absent" facts that it is itself adding to the data base. We must define "is-reported" so that it looks for a "was-present" or a "was-absent" fact *before* it uses the default 'query the user' rule. The complete metalogical program is:

```
x is-reported if
     x was-present & /
x is-reported if
     not x was-absent &
     (x a problem) is-told & / &
     (x was-present) add
x is-reported if not x was-absent &
     (x was-absent) add & FAIL
```

The first rule checks if the problem was already reported as present and hence recorded by a "was-present" fact. If it was, the / prevents the use of the other rules.

The second rule first checks if the problem is recorded by a "was-absent" fact. If it is, the user has already been queried about this problem and has answered "no". Only if there is no "was-present" or "was-absent" fact for the problem will the user be queried about the problem.

If the response is "yes", a "was-present" fact is added and the / prevents the use of the third rule. If the response is "no", the third rule is used which adds a "was-absent" fact providing there is not already such a fact for that particular problem.

The "not x was-absent" condition in the last rule is needed because the backtracking evaluation will try to use the third rule when the second rule does not apply because the problem is already recorded by a "was-absent" fact. So without this extra check, the "was-absent" fact might be added a second time.

Our metalogical program for "is-reported" is now highly imperative, it uses command relations that change the data base and the program can only be understood in terms of the query evaluation mechanism of micro-PROLOG. It also depends crucially on the effect of the backtracking control primitive /. None the less, the net effect of the program is logically defensible. It progressively transfers facts from an external data base in some user's head to the micro-PROLOG internal data base and it makes use of this incrementally constructed extension to the internal data base whenever it can. It is an example of an imperative program used to achieve a logically sound effect.

There is one final thing that must be done before the program is used. Remember that micro-PROLOG normally treats the attempt to solve a condition for a relation name for which there are no defining sentences as an error condition. The first time the above rules are used to solve an "is-reported" condition there will be no "was-present" (or "was-absent") sentences in the data base. So the attempt to use the first rule will result in an error. There is a way of preventing the error. We tell micro-PROLOG that both "was-present" and "was-absent" are special relations for which the absence of defining sentences is to be treated as a normal failure to solve the condition, not as an error. We do this by adding the sentences

    was-present data-rel
    was-absent data-rel

to our program. The "data-rel" facts tell micro-PROLOG that

these are data relations - relations whose programs are manipulated by other programs. Having no defining sentences for a data relation is not an error condition. The SIMPLE error handler, which is described in the Reference Manual, checks to see if a relation is a "data-rel" relation before it gives the error message. If it is, it allows the evaluation to continue with the condition assumed to have no solution. This is analogous to the way that the evaluation is resumed when we give a "no" response to an is-told question.

Exercises 8-4

1. In Section 7.2 we gave the following program for the "male-test" relation

> x male-test if x male & /
> x male-test if (x male) is-told

a. Give an alternative program which
>   (i)   records each "yes" answer by adding a new "male" fact
>   (ii)   records each "no" answer by adding a "female" fact
>   (iii) only asks about names not recorded as "male" or "female".
b. Further modify the program so that it only adds a new "female" fact if the answer to the "x male" question is "no" and the answer to a supplementary "x female" question is "yes".

Saving the answers to a query as facts

We can use **add** in a query to save all the answers to a query as facts. Instead of the query:

> all((x parent-of-son y) : x parent-of y & y male)

we can use:

> all((x parent-of-son y) : x parent-of y & y male &
>   (x parent-of-son y) add)

At the end of the evaluation each "(x parent-of-son y)" answer is recorded is a "parent-of-son" fact in the data base. We can see the answers again by listing the "parent-of-son" relation, and we can use the relation in subsequent queries without the need to define it with a rule.

If we do not want to see the answers to the query

immediately we can pose the is query

    is((forall x parent-of y & y male
            then (x parent-of-son y)add))

The answer to this query will be the uninformative "YES". However, its evaluation will have the imperative effect of adding all the solutions to the **forall** generator condition as facts about the "parent-of-son" relation. This use of **add** together with **forall** is analogous to the use of **isall**. While **isall** records all the answers to some condition in a list the **forall/add** combination records them as data base facts.

Use of **delete**

        The **delete** command can be used in rules and queries to delete sentences from the data bases. As with **add**, it can be used either as a unary relation or as a binary relation. In the unary form the sentence to be deleted must be given as the single argument. In the binary form the sentence is specified by its relation name and position in the listing of sentences for the relation as in its two argument command use. (In the binary use of **add** the two arguments are the position of the new sentence and the sentence, in that order. Again this corresponds to its command use.)

Data base as scratch pad memory

        add and **delete** used in combination enable us to use the data base as a scratch pad memory. As an example, suppose that we wanted to keep track of the number of times a rule is used during some query evaluation. Suppose that we wanted to record how many times the parsing rule

    (x x2) is-noun-expression (NE X Y) if
        (x x1) is-adjective X & (x1 x2) is-noun-expression Y

is used in parsing some sentence. First we need to name the rule in some way. Let us call it "Rule-NE". Before we start to parse the sentence, we should add the fact

    Rule-NE count 0

to the data base, recording 0 uses of the rule. We then add an extra condition to the rule which will update this recorded number of uses each time the rule is successfully used. The transformed rule is

> (x x2) is-noun-expression (NE X Y) if
>   (x x1) is-adjective X &
>   (x1 x2) is-noun-expression Y &
>   Rule-NE count-up

where "count-up" is defined by the program

> x count-up if
>   (x count y) delete &
>   SUM(y 1 y1) &
>   (x count y1) add

Each time the rule is successfully applied the old "count" fact for the rule is deleted and a new "count" fact, with the count increased by 1, is added.

If we do this monitoring of the use for several rules the set of "count" facts is behaving as a table of information that is being continually updated during the query evaluation. It behaves like an array in a conventional programming language.

Notice that when the **delete** condition of the above rule is solved the variable y will not have a value. The **delete** will match the fact pattern

> Rule-NE count y

against the "count" sentences. It will delete the first one which matches, and in so doing will give y the value of the old count. This use of **delete** does not normally arise when the relation is used as a command. However, we can leave arguments unspecified when we use it as a command.

> delete (Tom father-of x)

will delete the first "father-of" fact about "Tom".

Another use of the data base as a scratch pad memory is illustrated by the following alternative program to find the sum of a list of numbers. It is an alternative to the "sum" program of Exercise 4-5(3).

X Sum y if (total 0) add &
    (forall x ON X then x update-total) &
    (total y) delete

x update-total if
    (total y) delete & SUM(y x y1) & (total y1) add

In this program, the data base is used as a temporary scratch pad to keep a running total of the numbers in the list. As each one is retrieved, by the "x ON X" condition, its value is added to the current total as recorded in the "total" fact which is updated.

The advantage of this use of the data base as a scratch pad memory is that it can be used to sum a sequence of numbers given as data sentences about some unary relation without the need to construct a list of the numbers. If we make the name of the relation an argument to the condition we have the program

X Sum-is y if (total 0) add &
    (forall X true-of (x) then x update-total) &
    (total y) delete

Suppose now that we have a set of "num" facts such as

4 num
-3 num

and so on. We can find the sum of all these numbers with the query

which(y : num Sum-is y)   (A)

If we want to use the earlier recursive "sum" program we need to first construct a list of all the numbers. We need to use the query

which(y : x isall (z : z num) & x sum y)   (B)

However, query (B) coupled with the recursive "sum" program is much easier to understand than query (A) coupled with the "Sum-is" program. Moreover, with most implementations of micro-PROLOG the evaluation of (B) will be faster than the evaluation of (A) because isall conditions are solved so quickly. The manipulation of the data base using add and delete is a relatively slow operation.

Exercises 8-5

1. Use **is-told** together with either Sum-is or sum to pose a query that will repeatedly prompt you with

   X ?

to enable you to enter the list of numbers whose sum is to be found.

2. Give the query which will give you the names of all the mothers referred to in some "mother-of" fact in the data base that are not recorded as female by some "female" fact. At the end of the query a "female" fact should have been added for each answer given.

Variables in sentences

   Both **add** and **delete** when used as imperative relations accept any micro-PROLOG sentences as arguments, they are not restricted to unconditional sentences. The arguments are in fact sentence lists, lists of terms that satisfy the syntactic constraints of a valid sentence when the **add** or **delete** condition is solved. Any variable in the list argument of an **add** condition, that has not been given a value by the time that the condition is solved, becomes a variable in the added sentence. As with the negated condition, this means that the position of the **add** in a rule is crucial. It must come after any condition that is intended to give a value to a variable in the sentence pattern before it is added. Thus, an evaluation of the pair of conditions

   x EQ Algernon & (x male) add

adds the fact, "Algernon male". An evaluation of

   (x male) add & x EQ Algernon

adds the rule

   x male

which says that every one is male. It does this because x does not have a value when the **add** condition is solved.
   The pair of conditions

x EQ likes & (Tom x Mary) add

will add the fact "Tom likes Mary". However,

(Tom x Mary) add & x EQ likes

will result in a syntax error message when the **add** is evaluated. This is because the list will still be "(Tom x Mary)" which is not a valid sentence list. **add** and **delete** used as relations check that their list arguments are valid sentences just as they do when used as commands.

When using **add** or **delete** in rules you must beware! You have to pay great attention to the way that micro-PROLOG will use the rule. You must be especially careful when using **delete**. Theoretically you can have a **delete** condition in a rule which has the effect of *deleting the rule* when the rule is used. But if you try to do this micro-PROLOG may get hopelessly confused. It will probably get into an error state from which it cannot recover. Only use **delete** in programs to **delete** sentences for *other* programs.

8.4   Unary relations as commands

We have seen that we can use the commands **add** and **delete** as relations. We can also use any of our own unary relations as commands. We will of course not observe any 'effect' of the evaluation of such a command unless the relation is defined in terms of other command relations that cause micro-PROLOG to do something.

A simple example of this is provided by the following pair of rules which define synonyms for the command names **all** and **is**.

x find if x all
x check if x is

If we add these rules to our program we can immediately use "find" instead of **all** and "check" instead of **is**. We can of course still use the predefined **all** and **is** commands.

For a more sophisticated example of the definition of a new query command let us return to the example of the **all** query of the last section which remembered the answers by adding sentences to the data base. The query was

all((x parent-of-son y) : x parent-of y & y male &
                                (x parent-of-son y) add)

The query has the form

all(<sentence list to be added>:
        <query condition> &
        <sentence list to be added> add)

Its relationship to a non-remembering query of the form

all(<sentence list that could be added>:<query condition>)

is just that it has an extra condition at the end that adds the sentence list given as the answer pattern to the data base just before each such answer is displayed. The following rule defines a new command relation "all-rem" which takes a query of this second form and appends the extra condition to the end of the list of terms given as the query pattern before using the predefined all.

(X : | Y) all-rem if
        append((X : |Y) (& X add) Z) &
        Z all

The predefined all is a unary relation whose argument is a list of terms which comprises a sequence of terms which is the answer pattern followed by the colon followed by a sequence of terms which is the conjunctive condition comprising the query pattern. Our "all-rem" insists that the answer pattern is a single term which is also a list giving the form of a sentence to be added to the data base each time a solution to the query is found.
      When we use "all-rem" as a command, for example

all-rem ((x parent-of-son y): x parent-of y & y male)

the X of the rule becomes

(x parent-of-son y)

and the Y of the rule becomes

(x parent-of y & y male)

The "append" condition makes Z the list

((x parent-of-son y) : x parent-of y & y male &
     (x parent-of y) add)

which is the single list argument passed over to all. The new command relation automatically remembers each answer providing the answer is a valid sentence list. If it is not, the evaluation of the add condition will give a syntax error message and the evaluation of the query will be aborted.

The read/write imperative relations

The query commands defined in SIMPLE and the is-told relation are all defined by micro-PROLOG programs. They all display messages and is-told also reads in responses. They can do this because they make use of two primitive relations of micro-PROLOG for reading from the keyboard and for writing terms to the display.

As an example, a simplified version of the is-told relation can be defined by the following program.

x Is-told if P true-of x & P(?) & R(y) & y EQ yes

The primitive relation P takes any number of terms as arguments, displays them as a sequence on the screen, and leaves the cursor at the end of the displayed sequence. Thus, if the "Is-told" condition is

(Tom a male) Is-told

the first P condition of the rule is equivalent to

P (Tom a male)

and the sequence

Tom a male

is displayed. The next "P(?)" condition of the rule then displays a "?" leaving the cursor immediately after the "?":

Tom a male?

The **R** relation is the read primitive. It has a single argument which must be a variable which does not have a value when the condition is solved. It displays a read prompt which is a "." and waits for a term to be entered. That is it waits for a term to be typed at the keyboard followed by a RETURN or ENTER. The variable is then given the value of the entered term. So, if we respond with a "no" as in

Tom a male?.no

then the y of the rule will have the value "no" after the **R** condition is solved. The last condition of the rule checks if the entered response is "yes". If it is not, the test fails and the "Is-told" condition is not confirmed. If it is "yes", the "Is-told" condition is confirmed.

*The **R** primitive*

micro-PROLOG solves an **R** condition by reading in the *next term* typed in at the console and making this term the value of the variable given as the argument to **R**.

The closest we can get to a logical reading of the relation is:

R(x) holds if and only if x is a term.

The control reading is:

To solve a condition of the form R(x)
    check that x is a variable not yet given a value,
    read in the next term t entered at the keyboard,
    make R(t) the only solution to the condition.

The logical reading suggests that **R** can be used to check if something is a term, or to find a term. The control reading tells us it can only be used to find a term and that this term is always the next one to be typed at the terminal. It is the non-logical, entirely behavioural aspect that is crucial to the use of **R**. We do not use it to find an arbitrary term, we use it to read terms from the terminal.

An attempt to use **R** in a checking mode results in an error message. If we want to check that the entered response is some particular term, we use an "R(x)" condition followed by an equality test as in the above rule for "Is-told".

Another example use

We can use R directly as a rudimentary form of is-told condition to query us during the evaluation of one of our queries. Consider the rule:

    x average-of-entered-list if
        P(enter a number list) &
        R(y) & y average x

If we query this relation with

    which(x : x average-of-entered-list)

we will get the following interaction

    enter a number list.**(34 -5 89 66)**
    46
    No (more) answers

We are only asked once to enter a number list because micro-PROLOG only allows one solution to be given to a R condition. It is not like the is-told relation that allows us to give several answers.

The R primitive will read in any term. It may be a number, a constant, a list or a variable. Any variables read in are immediately converted into internal form: in particular the name of the variable is **not** remembered. This has its advantages and disadvantages, it is beyond the scope of this book to go into them.

System note - inputting terms - when the read prompt "." is given you can enter more than one term. That is, before hitting the RETURN or ENTER key you can type several different terms separated by spaces and you can edit what you have typed. When you hit the ENTER, micro-PROLOG will only use the first entered term to solve the current R condition. However, when the next R condition needs to be solved it will use the second term that you entered and will not display the read prompt. It will continue using up your sequence of entered terms until it has used the last term. Then when it needs to solve an R condition again it will re-display the read prompt. Entering several terms for one prompt is only sensible when we know that micro-PROLOG will want to read in several terms.

A large list term as input does not have to be completed before we hit ENTER. Just as we can add a sentence over several lines when we use the **add** command we can also enter a list to be read in by the R primitive over several lines. micro-PROLOG displays a special prompt after each RETURN or ENTER until the whole list has been read in. The prompt is the number of right brackets that need to be entered to complete the list.

The arguments of the **add** command are actually read in using R so it is not surprising that the same rules apply for the entering of sentence lists and the entering of any list.

Finally, to enter constants which contain special characters we quote the constant with double quotes. Thus, if s is a sequence of any characters other than the quote sign itself, "s" is a constant. The sequence s can contain spaces. This means that

> "any old answer"

is a single constant that can be entered in response to a read prompt. For more details on the syntax of quoted constants and on the rules for entering terms we refer the reader to the Reference Manual.

The **P** and **PP** primitives

As we have seen the read term relation is most often used in combination with the write term relation, **P**. This relation is unusual in that it can have any number of arguments, it is a multi-argument relation. An approximate logical reading is:

> P(t1 t2 ... tn) is true iff t1 .. tn are terms.

The control reading is:

> To solve a condition of the form P(t1 .. tn),
>   check that t1,..,tn are terms, and (if they are)
>   display the terms as a sequence on the screen.

Again, the crucial property is not that it checks that its arguments are terms but that it displays these terms on the console. It is used for its non-logical *side-effect*, the side-effect of displaying a sequence of terms.

The **PP** primitive also takes any number of arguments and displays them as a sequence. The main difference is that it always positions the cursor at the beginning of a new line after it has displayed the terms.

If we had used **PP** instead of **P** in the above definition of "average-of-entered-list" the interaction would be

enter a list
.(34 -5 89 66)
46
No (more) answers

with the read prompt positioned at the beginning of the next line waiting for us to enter the number list. The other difference is the **PP** quotes any constant it displays if the constant would need to be quoted on input.

PP ("an output")

displays

"an output"

whereas

P ("an output")

displays

an output

The print imperatives are useful for displaying messages during the evaluation of a query about error conditions. (All the error messages displayed by micro-PROLOG when we have a syntax error or an evaluation error are actually displayed by micro-PROLOG programs that use these relations.) The odd print scattered around the rules of a program does not effect its declarative reading but can give useful information during an evaluation, especially when we are developing a program.

As an example of this use of a print, consider the extended metalogical program for the relation "MAPLIST" defined in Section 8.2.

> MAPLIST(X Y Z) if
> > X CON & X defined & / & Maplist(X Y Z)
>
> MAPLIST(X Y Z) if
> > PP(Maplist cannot be applied to Y Z because
> > > relation argument is not given)
> >
> > & FAIL

The second rule which displays the message is only used if the tests for the conditions of use of "Maplist" fail. This is because when the conditions are satisfied the / of the first rule prevents the use of the second rule. We could drop the / but we would then have to have the explicit negated condition

> not(X CON & X defined)

at the beginning of the second rule. The effect of **FAIL** in the second rule is to ensure that the "MAPLIST" condition which does not satisfy the conditions of use of the "Maplist" program fails to be solved. Without the **FAIL** condition the successful conclusion of the **PP** condition would be interpreted as a solution of the condition for the given arguments.

Printing variables

Since variables in read-in terms are converted into an internal form, and their original names are lost, it is not possible to display them using their original names. The first variable printed by "P" or "PP" is displayed as "X", the next as "Y" and so on in the sequence

> X, Y ,Z, x, y, z, X1, Y1, ..

In other words, exactly the same rules apply to the display of variables in printed terms as when program rules are listed. This is not surprising as the list command of SIMPLE is defined by a program that displays the sentences using **P**. Each time "P" or "PP" is called the name sequence is started afresh. This can lead to a situation where two apparently different variables have the same **print name**:

> is(PP(x) & PP(y))
> X
> X
> YES

Reading and writing to files

The above **R** and **PP** primitives are just special cases of more general **READ** and **WRITE** primitives for transfering terms to and from files. The **save** and **load** commands of SIMPLE are ultimately defined in terms of these file transfer primitives.

A more elaborate "Is-told" definition

Let us look at a slightly more elaborate definition of the "Is-told" relation which is still not as general as the **is-told** described in Chapter 4. This version can display a question pattern which is a list of constants and variables and will respond to "ans" answers in the same way as **is-told**. That is, on backtracking it will prompt us for another answer until an answer other than "ans" is given. It does not handle "yes" and "just" responses.

x Is-told if P true-of x & P(?) & R(y) & x answered-with y

x answered-with ans if x variables-given-values
x answered-with ans if x Is-told

(x|y) variables-given-values if
            x VAR & / & R(x) &
            y variables-given-values

(x|y) variables-given-values if
            y variables-given-values

The "Is-told" rule displays the prompt sequence followed by a "?" and then reads in the first term typed in. The "answered-with" condition deals with the response.

If the response is "ans" the variables of the question pattern are given the values of the sequence of terms entered after the "ans". The program for "variables-given-values" recurses down the message list and each time it finds a variable it reads in the next term making it the value of the variable.

Note the use of the metalogical primitive **VAR** to pick up the variables of the question pattern that do not yet have values. Once a variable has been given a read-in value, subsequent occurences of the variable in the message list will not be picked up by the **VAR** test. The second rule for "variables-given-values" skips over each item in the message list which is not a variable.

When backtracking to the "Is-told" condition an attempt is made to find an alternative way of handling the last response using the second rule for "answered-by". This second rule, reduces to a new "Is-told" condition for the same message list which can be answered with another "ans" response. The prompts will continue until something other than an "ans" is entered.

Using the read/write primitives to define new commands

The following program defines a more general version of the accept command described in Chapter 1 which can be used to enter a series of arbitrary sentences defining some relation until "end" is entered. It is not restricted to the entry of the arguments of fact sentences like accept.

    x Accept if P(Sentence for x) & x R & x respond

    end respond
    x respond if x LST & x add & x Accept

An example use as a command is

    Accept last-of
    Sentence for last-of.(x last-of (x))
    Sentence for last-of.(x last-of (y|z) if x last-of z)
    Sentence for last-of.end

Before you edit some sentence for a relation you probably first list the relation to find the position of the sentence to edit. The following program defines a new command "Edit" using the predefined list and edit commands as relations. It has a single argument that is the name of the relation to edit. It lists the relation and then prompts for the number of the sentence to edit before using edit as a two argument relation.

    x Edit if x list & P(Sentence number) & y R & x edit y

The built-in supervisor program

Any user defined unary relation can be used as a command because the top level interaction between you and micro-PROLOG is controlled by a special built-in program called the supervisor.

The supervisor is actually a micro-PROLOG program for a no-argument relation that is automatically invoked when you enter the micro-PROLOG system and which never terminates. It is this program that prints out the "&" which is part of the "&." top-level prompt that you get when you can enter a new command.

The "." is the read prompt that you get because the supervisor program immediately attempts to read in two terms which are the name of some unary relation followed by its single argument. It then 'applies' the relation to the argument before cycling back to read in the next unary relation name and its argument.

The following is a simplified form of the supervisor program.

    SUPERVISOR if
        P(&) and R(x) and R(y) and
        (either x true-of y or P(?)) and / and
        SUPERVISOR

The "x true-of y" condition is the application of the command x to its single argument y. If the condition is not solved the response "?" is displayed. The / before the recursive condition ensures that the program is tail recursive. This is absolutely essential since the program only terminates when you exit micro-PROLOG or switch off the computer. If it was not tail recursive it would very quickly fill up the available space for the query stack.

Defining two argument relations

The supervisor only allows us to use unary relations directly as commands. We can use relations with more than one argument as commands only if we add an extra one argument rule for the relation that reads in the extra arguments using explicit R conditions.

For example, the **edit** command of SIMPLE is defined by

the following form of program

    x edit if y R and x edit y
    x edit y if ......

The rules defining **edit** as a two argument relation are the main rules. These are the rules that are used when we use **edit** as a two-argument command relation in our programs. The first rule is the one used to solve the supervisor **true-of** condition when we use **edit** as a command since it is the only one for a single argument condition. The application of the rule causes the second argument of the command line to be read in and given as the second argument to a two argument **edit** condition.

    The **add** command that has both a single and two argument command form is defined by a program of the form

    x add if x NUM & / & y R & x add y
    x add if x LST & / & 32767 add x
    x add y if .....

If the single argument to the command is a number, giving the position at which to add the sentence, the sentence list follows the number and it is read in before the two argument form of the relation is used. If the single argument is a list, it is the sentence. The two argument form of **add** is then used with the position to add the sentence given as 32767 to ensure that it is added at the end of the sentences for its relation.

Exercises 8-6

1. Extend the second program for the "Is-told" relation given above so that it will cope with "yes", "no" and "just" answers. You need to extend the definition of "answered-with".

2. Extend the definition of the "Edit" command relation so that it will re-list the program after the selected sentence has been edited and prompt for the number of another sentence to edit. It should continue doing this until you enter "no".

3. Define a new command "List" which can be followed by a sequence of any number of relation names terminated by "end" and which will list the programs for each relation. An example use is

    List father-of mother-of male end

4. Define a new supervisor program which makes use of an auxiliary relation "command" which defines which relations are commands which can be invoked and which also states how many arguments the command takes. For example, we might have:

add command 1
edit command 2
quit command 0

The supervisor checks each command to see if it is a valid command, and automatically reads in the required number of arguments before applying the command.

Remember to make sure it is a tail recursive program.

Part III
Core micro-PROLOG

9. The standard syntax of micro-PROLOG

The programs and queries that we have used so far have been written in a special easy to read syntax. There is another *standard* syntax for programs and queries which has a simpler structure but which is less readable. The standard syntax is the only syntax directly understood by micro-PROLOG.

Programs written in the SIMPLE sentence syntax (i.e. the syntax used in Chapters 1 to 8) are compiled sentence by sentence into the standard syntax as they are entered. Similarly, queries are converted to their standard syntax equivalents before they can be answered. All this is accomplished by the SIMPLE front-end program which is itself written in the standard syntax.

For example, the **add** command of SIMPLE takes a sentence list as argument and converts it into another list that is the standard syntax form of the sentence and stores the added sentence in this standard syntax form. When you **list** or **edit** a program these commands convert back from the standard syntax to sentence syntax before displaying the sentence.

SIMPLE is a program development system that provides us with a range of facilities for building and querying programs using a particular user friendly syntax. As we shall see, we can bypass the facilities of SIMPLE and even dispense with them altogether.

In this chapter we introduce the standard syntax by describing the compiled form of SIMPLE sentences and queries. We then introduce some primitives of micro-PROLOG that can be used for entering, listing and querying programs in the standard syntax. We show how these can be used to quickly define more elaborate program manipulation and query commands for the standard syntax programs. The way in which sentences are compiled into the standard syntax is also briefly described.

We then examine the meta-variable features of standard syntax. These are much more extensive than the **true-of** condition of the sentence syntax described in the last Chapter. They enable us to write very elegant and powerful metalogical programs, programs that can *only* be written in the standard syntax.

Finally, we describe a micro-PROLOG primitive that can be used for accessing the rules that define a relation. Using this primitive we can define our own query evaluator as a metalogical program. For example, we can define an evaluator that is not constrained to use the rules defining a relation in the order in which they are stored but can use them in an order determined by some other metalogical program.

9.1 Atoms and Clauses

We adopt a slightly different terminology when talking about programs and queries written in the standard syntax. This helps to avoid confusion when we are discussing the differences between the two forms of syntax.

A *sentence* becomes a **clause** in the standard syntax. A condition or conclusion of a sentence becomes an **atom.**

In a simple sentence condition, or a conclusion of a sentence there is a relation name and a number of arguments. In the atom equivalent, the relation name becomes the first element of a list with the arguments comprising the tail of the list. In an atom the relation name will also be referred to as the *predicate symbol*

Example simple sentence atoms

simple sentence	*Atom*
John likes Mary	(likes John Mary)
SUM(1 2 3)	(SUM 1 2 3)
x male	(male x)

In general, the infix form

t1 R t2 becomes the atom	(R t1 t2)

the postfix form

t R becomes the atom	(R t)

the prefix form

P(t1...tk) becomes the atom   (P t1...tk)

and the single name condition

N becomes the atom   (N)

There are *no* differences between the standard syntax and sentence syntax form of the *arguments* which are in both cases any micro-PROLOG term.

Definition: An **atom** is a list which begins with a constant called the **predicate symbol** which is the name of a relation.

Remember that the SIMPLE **add** command accepts a sentence list, a list of terms that satisfy the syntax conditions of a sentence. The **add** command converts this list of terms into a list of atoms. The first atom of the list of atoms is the atom corresponding to the conclusion of the sentence, the remaining atoms correspond to the conditions of the sentence if there are any. Thus, an unconditional sentence becomes a list of one atom, a conditional sentence becomes a list of more than one atom.

Definition: A **clause** is a list of atoms the first atom being the conclusion of the clause. The relation name of the head atom is the relation that the clause is about.

There are no connective words such as "if" and "and" between the atoms of a clause.

Example sentences as clauses

sentence	*clause*
John likes Mary	((likes John Mary))
x member-of (x|y)	((member-of x (x|y)))
append (() x x)	((append () x x))

x friend-of y if
    x likes y and
    y likes x
	((friend-of x y)
	(likes x y)
	(likes y x))

x belongs-to (y|z) if	

x belongs-to z   ((belongs-to x (y|z))
                                  (belongs-to x z))

append((x|X) Y (x|Z)) if   ((append(x|X) Y (x|Z))
   append(X Y Z))   (append X Y Z))

Complex conditions in a sentence nearly all become atoms with lists of atoms as arguments.

Example complex conditions as atoms

complex condition	*atom*
not x male	(NOT male x)
not(x likes y & y male)	(NOT ? ((likes x y) (male y)))
z isall (x y : x likes y & y male)	(ISALL z (x y) ((likes x y) (male y)))
(forall Tom father-of x & x male then x married)	(FORALL ((Tom father-of x) (male x)) ((married x)))
(either x male or not x married)	(OR ((male x)) ((NOT married x)))
X=((Z * 4) + y) recall that this has relational form: (X EQ Y)#(*(Z 4 x) & +(x y Y))	(# (EQ X Y) ((* Z 4 x)(+ x y Y)))
father-of!(x Joe)	(! father-of x Joe)

As you can see there is quite a straightforward correspondence between conditions and atoms and between sentence lists and clauses. The **NOT, ?, !, ISALL, FORALL** and **OR** are primitive meta-relations of micro-PROLOG. All except **ISALL** are defined by micro-PROLOG metalogical programs using the meta-variable facilities of the standard syntax. In Section 9.4 we shall give their definitions.

The programs for these meta-relations, although written in micro-PROLOG, are part of the interpreter. They are automatically loaded when you enter micro-PROLOG and cannot be deleted. In this respect they are like the. supervisor program that was introduced in the last chapter which controls the interaction between the user and the system. **#** is a meta-relation defined in SIMPLE.

9.2   Programming in the standard syntax

When you enter micro-PROLOG and then bring in the SIMPLE front end with a

LOAD SIMPLE

command you are using the primitive **LOAD** command of micro-PROLOG to load a standard syntax program. The **load** command that we can subsequently use is defined within SIMPLE in terms of **LOAD**.

The primitive command and relation names of micro-PROLOG are either symbols such as **?** or they have entirely upper case letter names. Remember that all the command names of SIMPLE are lower case. This should help you to remember what command is defined in SIMPLE and can only be used when it has been **LOAD**ed and what commands are primitive.

Entering clauses

We enter sentences using the **add** or **accept** commands of SIMPLE. We can directly enter a clause by typing the clause. Instead of

&.add(Tom likes Mary)

we can use

&.((likes Tom Mary))

This represents another role of the supervisor program. It either accepts the name of a command followed by its argument as when we use **add** or it accepts a clause. It can tell when we have entered a clause rather than a command name because the clause is a list.

&.((likes Joe Mary))
&.((belongs-to x (x|y))
&.((likes Bill Joe))
&.((belongs-to x (y|z))
1. (belongs-to x z))
&.

As when we use **add**, we can interleave the clauses for different relations, and each new clause is put at the end of the current list of clauses for its relation.

There are two primitive relations **ADDCL** and **DELCL** that can be used to add and delete clauses. Used as commands each must have a single argument which is a clause.

&.ADDCL ((likes Bill Mary))

is equivalent to just entering the clause.

&.DELCL ((likes Bill Mary))

will delete the clause. As with **delete** we can use **DELCL** to delete a clause matching a given pattern:

&.DELCL ((likes Bill X))

will delete the first clause about whom Bill likes.

Both **ADDCL** and **DELCL** can be used in programs and queries to manipulate the clauses of other programs. Like **add** and **delete** they have both single and two argument forms but only the single argument form can be used directly as a command.

The two argument use of **ADDCL** is an atom of the form

(ADDCL X y)

where X is a clause and y is the clause position *after* which the clause should be added. This is different from the two argument use of **add**. With **add** the position is the position *before* which to add the sentence. The following program defines a command relation "addcl" that is the clause equivalent of **add**.

```
((addcl  y)
   (INT  y)
   (R  X)
   (addcl  X  y))
((addcl  X)
   (LST  X)
   (ADDCL  X  32767))
((addcl  X  y)
   (SUM  y1  1  y)
   (ADDCL  X  y1))
```

The command

    addcl 1 ((likes John Keith))

will add the clause as a new first clause for its relation. Defining
a similar command relation that is the clause equivalent of the
delete command is left as an exercise below (Exercise 9-1(3)).

Listing clauses

    We can see the clauses we have entered using the primitive
LIST command.

    LIST ALL

(with the "ALL" in uppercase) will list all the workspace program
in clause form. It does not matter whether we have entered a
clause directly or as a sentence using **add**. The **LIST** command
will still list it.

    Incidentally, if you have used **add** the "LIST ALL"
command will also list clauses for the "dict" relation. You will
see a

    ((dict R))

clause for each relation name for which you have entered at least
one sentence using **add**. This is because the **add** command
automatically puts a "dict" clause into your workspace program
each time you **add** a sentence for a new relation. That is why,
when you are only using **add** to construct a program, you can
find out all the relation names you have used by querying the
"dict" relation or listing it.

    There is a similar relation to "dict" for directly entered

clauses. It is the primitive **DICT** relation which is maintained by the micro-PROLOG interpreter. If you do

> LIST DICT

the answer will be a single clause of the form

> ((DICT & () (.....) likes Joe Mary belongs-to Bill ..))

The **DICT** relation is a multi-argument relation. After the third argument comes a sequence of all the constants that you have used so far in your program. It includes the names of all the relations as well as the names of all the individuals such as "Joe" and "Mary". The third argument is the list of all the names exported by currently loaded modules. If you are using SIMPLE it will include the names of all the SIMPLE commands and relations that we have been using. This third argument of **DICT** is accessed when you do a

> which(x : x reserved)

query. In fact **reserved** is defined by the clause

> ((reserved (dict func data-rel |Z))
>   (DICT X Y Z |x))

in SIMPLE. It picks up the list of imported names and adds **dict**, **func** and **data-rel** to the front.

For an explanation of the first two arguments of the **DICT** relation we refer the reader to the section on modules in the Reference Manual. Essentially they are there because the workspace and each module has its own distinct **DICT** relation. The "&" as the first argument tells us that this is the workspace dictionary that is being displayed.

We can also use **LIST** to list the programs for individual relations.

> &.LIST belongs-to
> ((belongs-to X (X|Y))
> ((belongs-to X (Y|Z))
>   belongs-to X Z))
> &.

or a list of relations

&.LIST (likes belongs-to)

In this respect it is more general than the SIMPLE list command. Indeed, LIST allows you to list the exported relations of the loaded modules as well as your own relations.

Normally, we cannot use the the SIMPLE command list to display a relation which has been entered as clauses. However, if we also directly enter a dict clause for the relation then we can use the list command. This is because the list command of SIMPLE will only allow you to list programs for relations recorded by a dict clause. Remember that the "list all" command also only lists relations recorded by dict. So, to list our "belongs-to" program we must first enter the appropriate dict clause.

```
&.((dict belongs-to))
list belongs-to
X belongs-to (X|Y)
X belongs-to (Y|Z) if
    X belongs-to Z
&.
```

(What would happen if we used the command:

add(belongs-to dict)

to add the dict clause?) The clauses are now displayed as sentences even though they were not entered as sentences.

We suggest that you load in some previously saved program and LIST its various relations to see what the definitions look like in clause form. This will help you to become familiar with the clause notation.

Exercises 9-1

1. Give the clauses that correspond to the "has-length" program of Chapter 3.

2. Give the clauses that correspond to the sentences of the geography data base of Exercise 1-1(2) and Exercise 1-4(1).

3. The two argument use of DELCL is an atom of the form

(DELCL X y)

where X is the name of a relation and y is a positive integer. It deletes the y'th clause for X. Define a command relation "delcl" that can be used in exactly the same way as delete.

The query primitive ?

There is no primitive command relation that is the equivalent of the SIMPLE which query command. ? is the primitive query relation and it roughly corresponds to is.

? is a unary relation which takes a list of atoms as its argument. The evaluation is a backtracking search to find a solution to the conjunction of conditions represented by this list of atoms. The search for a solution is exactly the same as the search for a solution to the conjunctive condition of an is query.

&.?((likes Bill X)(likes X Mary))
&.

The query is solved.

&.?((belongs-to 6 (4 5 7)))
?
&.

The query is not solved.

When ? is used as a command it does not display any answer. If the query is confirmed we simply get the next supervisor "&." prompt and if it is not confirmed we get the "?" response which the supervisor displays whenever a command fails.

To see the values assigned to the variables of a solved ? query we can use PP to display the values.

&.?((likes Bill X)(likes X Mary)(PP X))
Joe
&.

System note - tracing programs using ?? - You can trace programs in the standard syntax by using the ?? command. To access this trace program you have to load the TRACE program:-

LOAD TRACE

For details of how to use this trace see the reference manual.

? is the primitive query relation in terms of which all other query relations are defined. The other query relations use **PP** to display answers.

The following metalogical program defines the exact equivalent of is for queries that are lists of atoms.

((IS X) (? X) / (PP YES))
((IS X) (PP NO))

The / condition of the first clause ensures that the second clause is used only when the query condition "(? X)" fails. Single name atoms are normally expressed in the form (name) and we could have expressed the / condition as "(/)". However, / and **FAIL** are specially recognized single name atoms that do not need to be entered as a list.

The program

((WHICH (X I Y))
  (FORALL Y ((PP X)))
  (PP No (more) answers))

defines a command relation similar to which. Its single argument is a list comprising an answer pattern X followed by a tail list of query atoms Y. The primitive **FORALL** condition has two arguments both of which are query lists of atoms. For each solution S to the first query list it checks that it can confirm the second query list with the variable values of solution S. In this case the effect is to display the answer pattern X for each solution to the query pattern Y.

&.WHICH(X (Bill likes X)(X likes Joe))
Mary
No (more) answers

&.WHICH((X Y) (X likes Z)(Z likes Y))
(Bill Joe)
No (more) answers

9.3   Parsing sentences into clauses

In this section we shall briefly describe a simplified form of the parsing program in SIMPLE that converts sentences to clauses and back again. The main parsing relations are exported from SIMPLE and so are available for use in your programs. Most of them make use of the difference list representation which was described in Chapter 6.

Parse-of-SS relation

(Parse-of-SS x y z)

holds when the simple sentence which is represented by the difference between the lists y and z forms the atom x.

(Parse-of-SS (likes Tom Mary) (Tom likes Mary) ())
(Parse-of-SS (belongs-to X (Y|Z))
        (X belongs-to (Y|Z) if X belongs-to Z)
                    (if X belongs-to Z))

are both instances of the relation. Sample clauses from the definition of the relation are:

((Parse-of-SS (X Y Z) (Y X Z |x) x)
        (CON X)/)
((Parse-of-SS (X Y) (Y X|Z) Z)
        (CON X)/)

which deal with the infix from of simple sentence and the postfix form respectively. The / conditions tell micro-PROLOG that only one rule applies.

The relation can be used for parsing simple sentences into clauses or vice versa.

WHICH((x y) (Parse-of-SS x (X likes Y if Y likes X) y))
((likes X Y) (if Y likes X))
No (more) answers

WHICH(x (Parse-of-SS (male Bill) x ()))
(Bill male)
No (more) answers

The Parse-of-ConjC relation

(Parse-of-ConjC x y)

holds when the list of terms y is a conjunctive condition corresponding to the list of atoms x.

(Parse-of-ConjC ((father-of x y)(NOT male y))
                        (x father-of y & not y male))

(Parse-of-ConjC ((ISALL x (y z) (likes y z))
                        (x isall (y z : y likes z)))

both hold. Again this can be used for converting atom lists to conjunctive conditions or vice versa.

The Parse-of-S relation

(Parse-of-S x y)

holds when x is the clause corresponding to the sentence list y. For example:

(Parse-of-S ((likes Bill Joe)) (Bill likes Joe))
(Parse-of-S ((likes X Y)(likes Y X))
                    (X likes Y if Y likes X))

It too can be used for parsing or generating sentences.
    The definition of **Parse-of-S** in SIMPLE is more complex than the following definition. In fact, the whole program contains meta-logical conditions to determine whether it is being used to parse or generate so that the syntax error messages can be given for the parsing use. The following definition gives the flavour of the parsing program.

((Parse-of-S (X) Z)
   (Parse-of-SS X Z ()) /)
((Parse-of-S (X|Y) Z)
   (Parse-of-SS X Z (if|Z1))
   (Parse-of-ConjC Y Z1))

The / at the end of the first rule is purely for efficiency to tell micro-PROLOG that when the rule is successfully used either for parsing or generating the second rule will not apply.

Using **Parse-of-ConjC** you can define your own query commands that use the sentence syntax. As an example:

```
((a  (x  :  | y))
     (Parse-of-ConjC  Y  y)
     (?  Y)  /
     (PP  x))
```

defines a query command similar to **which** but it only ever gives one answer to the query, the first one found. Another difference is that the answer pattern must be a single term - the x of the pattern "(x : | y)" which becomes the argument of the **PP** condition.

```
&.a((x  y):APPEND(x  y  (2  3  4)))
(()  (2  3  4))
&.
```

```
&.a(x:  Bill  likes  x  &  y  male)
Joe
&.
```

9.4   Meta-variables in standard syntax programs

What we have seen so far of the standard syntax of micro-PROLOG corresponds quite closely to the sentence syntax. But, just as we can use meta-variables in **true-of** conditions in sentences, so we can use meta-variables in clauses and query lists of atoms.

The main principle behind the meta-variable is that *during the evaluation* the meta-variable will be given a value before micro-PROLOG comes to evaluate the part of the clause in which it appears. This value must be such that it is syntactically correct for the part of the clause represented by the meta-variable. The clause is then used as though it had been written with the value in place of the variable.

There are four different forms of use of a meta-variable in standard syntax programs. These arise naturally from the list structure of clauses. These various uses also have parallels in more conventional programming languages, notably Pascal, ALGOL and

"C". We will point out these analogies where it is appropriate. Readers not familiar with these languages should ignore these comments.

Incidentally, do not try to list a clause that uses one of these forms of meta-variables. You can only list clause programs that are of the form that would be produced by parsing a sentence. If you have used a meta-variable in a clause the reverse parsing of the clause into a sentence will fail or it will produce an incorrect representation of the clause as a sentence.

Meta-variable replacing the predicate symbol of an atom

In this first case, the predicate symbol of an atom in a query or the body of a clause is given as a variable. Recall that an atom is a list, the first element of which is the predicate symbol. If this is a variable, the variable must have a value which is a relation name before the atom is evaluated. In practice this means that the variable must appear in an earlier atom of the query or clause.

The one constraint on this use of a meta-variable is that the predicate symbol of the head atom of a clause can never be a variable, it must always be a constant.

In SIMPLE queries we have to use **true-of** to achieve the same effect as the predicate symbol meta-variable.

WHICH(x (dict x)(x Bill Joe))
likes
No(more) answers

What this query asks is:

What relationships are known to hold between "Bill" and "Joe"?

As a SIMPLE query this must be expressed

which(x : x dict & x true-of (Bill Joe))

Suppose we view a collection of facts about binary relations as the description of a graph in which the nodes are labelled by the individuals and the arcs by the relation names as in:

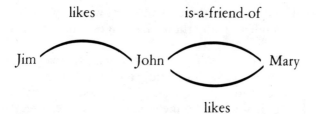

Used with **dict** the meta-variable enables us to find the names on the arcs between particular nodes, as in the above query. It also enables us to find all the nodes connected to a given node together with the name of the connection:

&.WHICH((x z) (dict x) (x John z))
(likes Mary)
(is-a-friend-of Mary)
(likes Jim)
No (more) answers

The clause

((connects x y z) (dict x) (x y z))

is a rule that can be used to walk over this graph.

Just as we can use **true-of** to write generalized programs so we can use the predicate symbol meta-variable. The program for "maplist" given as the answer to Exercise 8-1(2) can be written in clause form as:

((maplist x () ()))
((maplist x (y|Y) (z|Z))
    (x y z)
    (maplist x Y Z))

The "reduce" relation of Section 8.1 can be written:

((reduce x (y) y))
((reduce x (y1 y2|Y) z)
    (x y1 y2 y3)
    (reduce x (y3|Y) z))

This use of predicate meta-variable has an analogy in many conventional programming languages: the passing of procedures as parameters. For example in Pascal it is possible to have a procedure or function name as the parameter of another procedure or function (or even the same one). The 'host' procedure supplies the actual parameters to the 'guest' procedure whose name has been passed. However in Pascal, as in many other similar languages, the name of a procedure is not a 'first class' object: it cannot become the value of a variable or be stored in a data structure.

In micro-PROLOG the predicate symbol is such a first class object; it is a constant and as such can be stored, passed around and retrieved with total flexibility.

Exercises 9-2

1. Write a program, in clause form, which takes a pair of lists and returns a list of pairs: each pair coming from successive elements of the two lists. For example:

WHICH(x (pair (1 2 3) (a b c) x))
((1 a) (2 b) (3 c))

2. Use this program, together with "maplist" and "reduce" to write the program "dot" which performs the dot product of a pair of lists of numbers. The dot product is the sum of the pair-wise products of the elements of the lists. For example, given the two lists (2 5 8) and (2 4 3) then the dot product is $4+20+24$ which is 48.

3. The meta-variable can be used to implement a very simple arithmetic expression evaluator. Such arithmetic expressions can have two shapes; either the expression to evaluate is already a number, in which case the value is the number, or it is a list of the form ."(leftarg operator rightarg)". In this case the value is obtained by evaluating the left and right hand arguments and applying the relation given as the operator to their values. Each operator must therefore be defined as a three argument relation, with, say, the last argument being the result of 'applying' the operator to the first and second arguments.

Write a program in clause form for the relation "has-val" such that "x has-val y" holds when x is a valid expression as defined above and y is its value.

Test your program with a query such as

which(x : ((2 * 3) / (-3 + 5)) has-val x)

or

WHICH(x (has-val ((2 * 3) / (-3 + 5)) x))

This is quite different from the use of expressions that we described in Chapter 4. There the expressions were compiled into a conjunction of conditions that would evaluate the expressions. Here they are left as lists that are evaluated by recursing down the expression list when the value is needed.

Meta-variable as an atom

A whole atom can be named by a variable. This variable must have a value which is a atom list when the condition represented by the variable is evaluated. This form of meta-variable is very commonly used in clause programs.

A very simple use is in the clause:

((Holds x) x)

The "Holds" relation is true of a term if and only if that term is an atom that is solved. A negated condition is the opposite of a "Holds" condition. It can be defined by the meta-logical program.

((not x) x / FAIL)
((not x))

When used to try to establish (not A), where A is some atom, the first rule of this program is invoked. It reduces (not A) to A. If A can be solved, the / prevents use of the second rule and the FAIL ensures failure of the (not A) condition. Only if A cannot be established will the second rule be used to confirm (not A). But this is exactly the circumstance in which (not A) holds.

This definition of "not" restricts x to a single atom. The "not" of the sentence syntax can be applied to a conjunction of conditions which corresponds to a list of atoms. The following clauses define a "not" that has a list of atoms as its argument:

((not x) (? x) / FAIL)
((not x))

The difference is that here the query primitive "?" is used to check if all the atoms on the list x can be solved.

The atom meta-variable has no obvious counterpart in conventional programming languages (apart from LISP). There is a link with ALGOL 60 and its close counterparts through the 'call-by-NAME' parameter passing mechanism.

We saw above that the meta-variable as a predicate symbol

was close to the procedure name passing mechanism of Pascal: the name of the procedure was passed and the actual arguments are given by the host procedure. In the atom form of meta-variable the whole 'procedure call' is passed, an operation akin to passing an *unevaluated expression* to a procedure. The time that the expression is evaluated is determined by where the meta-variable appears; this is exactly analogous to call-by-NAME. A value passed by call-by-NAME in ALGOL 60 is actually passed as a special unevaluated expression (called a "thunk" for the technically curious) which is then evaluated as the corresponding formal parameter appears in the text.

Meta-variable as the remainder of a clause

Another variant of the meta-variable is the meta-variable as the remainder of the list of atoms of a clause. The simplest example of this is the metalogical program for ? which is the standard syntax equivalent of is:

$$((?\ X) \mid X) \tag{1}$$

The variable "X" must be matched against a list of atoms when the rule is used and this list of atoms becomes the list of conditions of the clause when the clause is 'entered'. You will see this program if you do a "LIST ?".

Below is the program for the **OR** meta-relation.

```
((OR  x  y) | x)
((OR  x  y) | y)
```

Yet another use is the definition of the **IF** relation, another primitive meta-level relation of micro-PROLOG which does not have a sentence form equivalent.

IF has three arguments, an atom which is the conditional test and two 'arms' which are lists of atoms and correspond to the 'then' and 'else' branches. Thus (IF x y z) is solved if x and y are solved or if x is not solved and z is solved. It is defined by:

```
((IF  x  y  z)  x  /  |  y)
((IF  x  y  z) | z)
```

Notice that we have two types of meta-variable in the first clause.

The x stands for an atom, the y for the remainder of the clause following the |.

Exercises 9-3

The following program is an alternative definition of the "WHICH" relation.

```
((WHICH (X|Y))
  (? Y)
  (PP X)
  FAIL)
((WHICH (X|Y)
  (PP No (more) answers))
```

In this program it is the **FAIL** of the first clause that causes micro-PROLOG to backtrack to find an alternative solution to (? Y). For each different solution the answer term X is displayed.

Using this program as a model, define a "ONE" form of query which corresponds to the SIMPLE **one** query in the way that "WHICH" corresponds to **which**. The program for the relation must prompt after each solution is found. If the response is "yes" then use "FAIL" to force the micro-PROLOG to look for the next solution, otherwise do nothing.

Meta-variable as the remainder of the argument list

The pattern (x|y) is a list with head x and tail y. When this pattern is used in place of an atom, y is a meta-variable standing for the list of arguments of the atom. This form of meta-variable is used when the number of arguments is unknown.

Example use

&.WHICH((x|z) (dict x) (x Tom|z))

is the generalization of the query

&.WHICH((x z) (dict x) (x Tom z))

that we encountered above. The generalization removes the restriction to binary relations. It gives all the *tuples* of individuals related to Tom by any relation. This is because the pattern (x Tom|z) denotes an atom of any number of arguments providing the first argument is "Tom". To achieve the effect of this in the sentence syntax we must use **true-of**. Moreover, **true-of** is itself defined as a clause program which makes use of both this form of meta-variable and the predicate symbol meta-variable:

((true-of X Y) (X|Y))

A meta-variable standing for a list of arguments can appear in the head atom of a clause. The head of a clause can be an atom (R|x) where R is the constant which is the predicate symbol. This use enables us to define relations with a variable number of arguments.

A simple example is a "Sum-up" relation which has n + 1 arguments: the first is the sum of all the others. It is defined by the single clause:

((Sum-up x|y)
    (reduce SUM y x))

This makes use of the "reduce" relation defined above. A typical use would be "(Sum-up x 3 4 5)" which makes x the SUM of the three number arguments.

This form of meta-variable doesn't normally have an equivalent in conventional programming languages. However systems programming languages such as "C" and BCPL do allow you access to the arguments of a call as a list or array of items as opposed to individual named parameters.

In practical terms multi-argument relations enable us to drop brackets. We could have defined "Sum-up" as a binary relation between a number and a list of numbers. Its definition would then be

((Sum-up x y) (reduce SUM y x))

But to use the program we would now have to write the multi-argument atom "(Sum-up x 3 4 5)" as the two argument atom "(Sum-up x (3 4 5))" in which we wrap-up all but the first argument as a list.

Earlier we gave a definition of a "not" relation that had a *list* of atoms as its argument. An example use is

(not ((Tall Tom) (Fat Tom)))

The *single* argument for "not" is the list of atoms

((Tall Tom) (Fat Tom))

It is more convenient to have "not" as a multi-argument relation, able to take any number of atom arguments. We could then write the condition

(not (Tall Tom) (Fat Tom))

The clauses defining such a multi-argument "not" are:

((not|x) (? x) / FAIL)
((not|x))

An analogous modification of the earlier "not" definition

((not x) x / FAIL)
((not x))

that has a single atom argument gives us the definition

((NOT|x) x / FAIL)
((NOT|x))

This enables us to write single atom negations as

(NOT Male Tom) instead of (not (Male Tom)).

This is the definition of the primitive **NOT** meta-relation that is embedded in the micro-PROLOG interpreter.

The primitive ! which restricts an atom to a single solution has the definition

((! | X)
   X /)

The / restricts the atom X to a single solution. An example use is

(! father-of x Tom)

which is the atom form of the complex condition

father-of!(x Tom)

of the sentence syntax.

To apply **NOT** to several atoms we use **?** as the relation with the list of atoms as the argument.

(NOT ? ((Tall Tom)(Fat Tom)))

is confirmed if and only if the query condition

(? ((Tall Tom)(Fat Tom)))

fails.

The primitive **FORALL** is defined in terms of **NOT** and **?**. Remember that in sentence syntax

(forall C then C')

is equivalent to

not(C and not (C'))

This equivalence is embedded in the definition of **FORALL**.

((FORALL X Y)
    (NOT ? ((? X)(NOT ? Y))))

(FORALL X Y) is confirmed providing the query atom list

((? X)(NOT ? Y))

fails. This fails providing there is no solution to the query list X, or every solution is such that it is also a solution to query list Y.

9.5   The clause accessing primitive CL

ADDCL and **DELCL** are micro-PROLOG program manipulation primitives. There is another very useful primitive that enables us to access the clauses for a relation and then to manipulate them as list terms. The program listing commands make use of this relation to retrieve the clauses before displaying them and it is used by the edit and save commands. It is the relation **CL**.

The relation has a single argument and a three argument

form. We shall just describe the single argument form. The three argument form is fully described in the Reference Manual. An example use of the single argument form is

WHICH(((likes|X) y |Y) (CL ((likes|X) y |Y)))

which displays all the conditional clauses about likes - all the clauses that have at least one condition y.

The argument to **CL** is any clause pattern in which at least the relation name of the head atom is given. **CL** can only retrieve clauses for specified relations. A use such as

WHICH((x) (CL (x)))

to try to retrieve all the single atom clauses will result in an error. We must specify the relation that the clause is about.

WHICH(((likes|x)) (CL ((likes|x))))

will retrieve all the single atom clauses for "likes". The most general use of **CL** is

(CL ((namely)|Y))

This matches and can be used to generate as answers each clause for the relation "name". The answers are generated in the order that the clauses are listed. On each match with a "name" clause y becomes the argument list of the head atom and Y becomes the list of condition atoms. The condition fails if there are no clauses for "name". So as a test, it tests if the relation is defined. The **defined** relation of SIMPLE has the definition

((defined x)
 (CON x)
 (CL ((x|y)|Y)))

Defining new query relations

Perhaps one of the most important uses of **CL** is in the definition of new query evaluation relations. The trace commands such as **all-trace**, **is-trace** and **??** are defined using **CL**.
The clauses

```
((confirmed ())
((confirmed ((x|y)|Y))
   (CL ((x|y)|Y1))
   (confirmed Y1)
   (confirmed Y))
```

define a relation that is almost equivalent to ?. It is not exactly equivalent because it does not handle / conditions.

The CL condition will retrieve the clauses for the relation x of the first atom in the list of atom conditions ((x|y)|Y) in the order in which they are stored; so its backtracking behaviour in the search for a solution is exactly the same as ?.

We can alter the way in which the clauses are tried by first constructing a list of all the clauses that match (x|y). We can then select the clauses from the list in any order we choose.

```
((confirmed ((x|y)|Y))
   (ISALL X ((x|y)|Y1) (CL ((x|y)|Y1)))
   (select ((x|y)|Z) X)
   (confirmed Z)
   (confirmed Y))
```

ISALL is the micro-PROLOG primitive into which isall conditions are mapped. Its atom use is

(ISALL X Y | Z)

where X is a variable or list pattern, Y the answer term and Z the sequence of atoms defining the query condition. When the ISALL is solved X becomes a list of copies of the values of the answer term Y for each solution to query list Z. In the above definition of "confirmed" it will give X the value of a list of copies of all the clauses that match the condition (x|y).

The "select" relation must be defined so that each clause copy on the list Z can be retrieved by a new match with the condition (x|y).

If we define "select" as ON then, since ISALL constructs the list of copies of the answer term in the reverse of the order in which the answers are found, queries will be evaluated by trying clauses for each condition in their reverse order.

If we define "select" as

```
((select  X  Y)
 (sort  Y  Y1  fewer-atoms)/
 (ON  X  Y1))

((fewer-atoms  x  y)
 (has-length  x  x1)
 (has-length  y  y1)
 (LESS  x1  y1))
```

where "sort" is the generalized merge sort relation of Chapter 8.
The sort condition reorders the list of clauses to be a list of
clauses of increasing numbers of atoms, queries will be evaluated
by always trying single atom clauses first, then two atom clauses
and so on no matter what order they have been entered. Such an
evaluator might be useful for a naive user of micro-PROLOG as
a data base system.

Exercises 9-4

Define a variant of the "confirmed" query evaluator which reorders the atoms of its query list before finding a clause that matches
the first condition. The order relation used is that an atom is 'less than'
another atom if it is for a relation declared to have fewer clauses. The
declaration is a clause for the special relation "number-of-clauses". E.g.

```
((number-of-clauses  likes  3))
```

declares that "likes" has three clauses. Again, such an evaluator might be
useful for a naive user of a micro-PROLOG data base who does not
know anything about the way that queries are normally evaluated.

Part IV
Applications of micro-PROLOG

10. A Critical path analysis program

F. Kriwaczek

Introduction

When writing a computer program it is advisable to start off by producing a careful statement of the problem to be solved. With most computer languages, the next and most difficult stage is the conversion of this specification of objectives into an algorithm. In other words, translating a statement about what is to be done into a sequence of steps which express how the task is to be accomplished.

One of the great strengths of PROLOG is its ability to take the declaration of a problem, and to obtain a solution to it directly. PROLOG achieves this by giving an operational interpretation to the collection of definitions and facts that constitute the problem specification. To be sure, many concepts possess several equivalent definitions, and the choice of a particular definition will often affect the efficiency with which a problem can be solved. Thus, the detailed specification of a problem can often demand a pragmatic approach.

However, it still remains true that the final specification, written in the form of a PROLOG program, deals with the subject area of the problem. A program in PASCAL, BASIC or COBOL, deals with the workings of a machine, however abstract it may be. In this sense, PROLOG can be seen as a further step in the evolution of programming languages from low-level machine orientation to higher-level problem and user orientation.

As software systems grow in complexity, this move towards bringing the program nearer to the user can be seen as having great relevance to areas such as program development, verification and maintenance.

In addition, this approach has great pedagogic value. With

many schools and colleges having small computers that can be taken into the classroom, it is quite possible to teach students a particular topic, and then construct a PROLOG program directly from the definitions that they have just been taught. The computer can then be used by the students to discover further consequences and results of the definitions, or to solve problems that would be tedious to do by hand. This chapter deals with just such an example.

10.1   Statement of the problem

Critical Path Analysis is a technique used by managers in the planning and coordination of complex projects. Its primary aim is to schedule and monitor the progress of a project so that it is completed in the minimum time. Extensions of the basic method can be used to assist in allocating resources such as labour and equipment, so that, by finding the optimum balance between the various costs and times involved, the total cost of the project is reduced to a minimum.

The idea is to split up the project into a number of smaller subtasks or **activities**. In some cases an activity can only commence once another one has been completed, whereas in other cases activities can be carried out concurrently. By carefully analysing the logical/chronological relationship between the different activities one obtains a partial precedence ordering. In addition, an estimate of the duration of each of these activities is made.

For example, a hypothetical stock control system project might yield the following table of activities:

	ACTIVITY	IMMEDIATE PREDECESSORS	DURATION (WEEKS)
A	design stock control model	-	4
B	develop stock control program	A	13
C	design forecasting model	-	4
D	develop forecasting program	C	15
E	collect product data	-	12
F	design product database	A	4
G	set up product database	E, F	2
H	train staff	B, D	2
I	test system	G, H	2

A **network diagram** is constructed from such information, with each activity represented by an arrowed branch. At either end of each activity arrow is a cirular node that represents an **event**, i.e. a stage or milestone in the project's progress. The events are numbered in such a way that each node has a higher number than any preceding node.

The following is a network diagram for the example project:

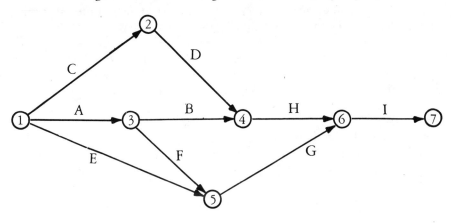

A **critical path** is a path of longest total duration through the network. Its length determines the minimum time within which the project can be completed. **Critical activities** are those activities lying on a critical path. A critical path is a crucial focus for management. For if any critical activity is delayed then the whole project will be held up. Conversely, if it is desired to shorten the duration of the project by the application of extra resources, then it will only pay to "crash" critical activities.

The normal procedure for determining the critical path(s) involves working forwards through the network, calculating the earliest times that the events could possibly be reached. Then working backwards through the network, calculating the latest times that the events could be reached without causing the overall project to be delayed. Those events with equal earliest and latest times lie on the critical path(s).

However, it is quite possible to ignore events altogether when conducting network analysis, and to concentrate instead on the activities. The activity-oriented analysis first involves computing the earliest start time and the earliest finish time of each activity.

The **earliest start time** is the earliest time that an activity could possibly be commenced. The **earliest finish time** is the earliest time by which it could possibly be completed. It is always equal to the earliest start time plus the duration. For those activities with no predecessor (such as A, C and E above) the earliest start time is zero. An activity cannot be started until all the preceding activities have been finished. It follows that, in the general case, the earliest start time is the maximum of the earliest finish times of the preceding activities.

(In the above example, since A has an earliest start time of zero and a duration of four, its earliest finish time is four. Similarly, E has an earliest finish time of twelve. Since the only activity preceding F is A, the earliest start time of F is four and its earliest finish time eight. Now, G has two immediate predecessors - E and F. Their earliest finish times are twelve and eight, the greater of which is twelve. This is thus the earliest start time of G).

It is possible to work systematically through the network calculating the earliest start and earliest finish times of all the activities. At least one activity precedes no others (such as I above). The project cannot be completed until the last of these has been finished. Thus the minimum duration of the overall project is the maximum of the earliest finish times of these "end activities".

The process is now reversed, with latest finish and latest start times being calculated for each activity. The **latest finish time** of an activity is the latest time that an activity could possibly be completed without holding up the whole project. The **latest start time** is the latest possible time that an activity could be commenced without delaying the project. It is always equal to the latest finish time minus the duration. For "end activities" the latest finish time is precisely the minimum project completion time, just calculated. In the general case, the latest finish time of an activity is the minimum of the latest start times of all succeeding activities.

If an activity has equal earliest and latest start times, then its finish times will also be equal, and the implication is that there is no leeway or "float". The activity must be commenced at a particular date and there cannot be any delay in carrying it out. Such an activity is critical, and a path through the network made up of such critical activities is a critical path. (In the case of large networks there may be more than one critical path.) Incidentally, the times calculated for the activities are of interest in their own right, since the project manager will want to know at what time activities can be started and finished.

10.2   Defining the concepts in micro-PROLOG

It is a quite straightforward affair to write down a set of micro-PROLOG rules that define the various concepts introduced above, and hence a micro-PROLOG program for carrying out critical path analysis. As a starting point, there must be a database of facts about the duration and precedence relation of the activities. A database equivalent to the example activity table could be:

design-stock-control-model	duration	4
develop-stock-control-program	duration	13
design-forecasting-model	duration	4
develop-forecasting-program	duration	15
collect-product-data	duration	12
design-product-database	duration	4
set-up-product-database	duration	2
train-staff	duration	2
test-system	duration	2

design-stock-control-model	precedes	develop-stock-control-program
design-forecasting-model	precedes	develop-forecasting-program
design-stock-control-model	precedes	design-product-database
collect-product-data	precedes	set-up-product-database
design-product-database	precedes	set-up-product-database
develop-stock-control-program	precedes	train-staff
develo-forecasting-program	precedes	train-staff
set-up-product-database	precedes	test-system
train-staff	precedes	test-system

It is useful to start off with a definition for "activity". In the context of our database, an activity is anything that has a duration:

        X activity if
                X duration Y

A "begin-activity" is an activity which is not preceded by anything:

            X begin-activity if
                    X activity &
                    not Y precedes X

whereas, an "end-activity" is an activity which does not precede
anything:

            X end-activity if
                    X activity &
                    not X precedes Y

    The latter two definitions are programs that can be used for
finding or testing beginning and ending activities.
    There are two sentences corresponding exactly to the
definition of "earliest start time" given in the previous section:

            X earliest-start 0 if
                    X begin-activity & /
            X earliest-start Y if
                    Z isall (x : y precedes X &
                                    y earliest-finish x) &
                    Y max-of Z

    For efficiency, the first sentence is terminated in a slash,
which ensures that if X is a begin activity and thus the first
sentence succeeds, the system will not try to use the second
sentence to find an alternative way of solving X earliest-start Y.
In this case the second sentence would have failed, since X has
no predecessors, but time and space would still have been wasted
in the attempt.
    In general, if a program is to be used functionally, an
alternative and perhaps neater way of ensuring that only one
solution will be sought is to use "!" in all calls to it. In the
above example, we could have removed the slash at the end of
the first clause, and instead made all calls to earliest-start of the
form: "earliest-start!(X Y)".
    The second sentence of earliest-start can be read as follows:

    X has earliest start time Y if Z is the list of all x, such that
    x is the earliest finish time for some y that precedes X, and
    Y is the maximum of Z

or less formally:

the earliest start time of an activity is the maximum of all the earliest finish times of preceding activities

The **isall** condition makes Z the list of earliest finish times of the predecessors of X. Since X is a global variable of the condition, earliest-start can only be used to find the earliest start time of a given activity X.

Earliest finish time, which was defined operationally as being the sum of the earliest start time and the duration, leads directly to the program:

```
X earliest-finish Y if
      X earliest-start Z &
      X duration x &
      SUM(Z x Y)
```

The program for minimum project completion time is:

```
X project-time if
      Y isall (Z : x end-activity &
                   x earliest-finish Z) &
      X max-of Y
```

Its detailed declarative reading is:

X is the project time if Y is the list of all Z, such that Z is the earliest finish time of some end activity x, and X is the maximum of Y

that is:

The project time is the maximum of the earliest finish times of the end activities

The programs for the latest finish and latest start times are defined in a strictly analogous fashion. (See below for a full listing of the whole program.) In these cases it is necessary to compute the minimum value of a list of times.

Now that programs for the various activity times have been written, critical activities can be defined by:

```
X critical if
     X activity &
     X earliest-start Y &
     X latest-start Y
```

The strategy adopted for finding a critical path is to work backwards through the network, building up a connected path of critical activities. The concept of a "partial critical path" is adopted, which is any connected set of critical activities terminating in a critical end activity. The micro-PROLOG structure for such a path is the list of its component activities. The definition and program for partial critical path is:

```
(X) partial-critical-path if
     X end-activity &
     X critical
(X Y|Z) partial-critical-path if
     X critical &
     X precedes Y &
     (Y|Z) partial-critical-path
```

A proper (i.e. full) critical path is a partial critical path with a critical begin activity at its head viz:

```
(X|Y) critical-path if
     X begin-activity &
     (X|Y) partial-critical-path
```

To find all critical paths, we can now use the *which* query:

```
which(x : x critical-path)
```

A last piece of useful information about activities is their float. As regards critical activities, if their starting time is delayed or their duration drawn out, then the whole project will be delayed. However, other activities are not so rigidly constrained. The **total float** of an activity is the difference between its latest start time and its earliest start time. This is the largest amount by which the activity may be delayed without affecting the completion time of the project. For critical activities the total float is zero. The program for total float is:

```
X total-float Y if
      X earliest-start Z &
      X latest-start x &
      SUM(Z Y x)
```

However, delaying one activity may affect the amount by which subsequent activities can be delayed, since total float is really a characteristic of network segments rather than of individual activities. In other words, the activities along a (non-critical) segment share their total float. The **free float** of an activity is the amount by which it may be delayed without interfering with subsequent activities. For an "end activity" it is the same as the total float, namely the difference between the project completion time and the activity's earliest finish time. In the general case, it is the difference between the minimum of the earliest start times of its successors and the activity's earliest finish time:

```
X free-float Y if
      X end-activity &
      Z project-time &
      X earliest-finish x &
      SUM(x Y Z) & /
X free-float Y if
      Z isall (x : X precedes y &
                      y earliest-start x) &
      z min-of Z &
      X earliest-finish X1 &
      SUM (X1 Y z)
```

As was mentioned near the start of this chapter, the precedence relation between activities imposes a partial ordering on them. One property of such an ordering is transivity, that is:

If X precedes Y and Y precedes Z then X precedes Z.

It was assumed, implicitly, that a database giving the precedence relation between activities would only deal with **immediate predecessors**. All other details about the precedence ordering could be inferred from the facts about immediate predecessors. (A fact, in the example database, stating that activity C precedes activity H, would, for example, be redundant).

Were the database to contain such redundant precedence information, all the above calculations would be correct, with the single exception that extra "phantom" critical paths would be found, in which the critical activities were not connected. This is because of the way that partial critical paths are generated. (In the above example, the only true critical path is C to D to H to I. If the database contained the additional fact "C precedes H", then a query about the critical paths would also give the answer C to H to I.)

In the case of large networks, it may not be easy to eliminate all such redundant precedence information. An easy way of avoiding trouble is to keep a note of the length of partial critical paths as they are being generated. In place of the previous program, a suitable definition for "partial-critical-path" would be:

    (X) partial-critical-path Y if
            X end-activity &
            X critical &
            X duration Y
    (X Y|Z) partial-critical-path x if
            X critical &
            X precedes Y &
            X duration y &
            (Y|Z) partial-critical-path z &
            SUM(y z x)

Here "X partial-critical-path Y" means that X is a partial critical path of length Y.

A critical path can now be defined simply as a partial critical path starting at a beginning activity whose length is equal to the project completion time:

    X critical-path if
            X begin-activity &
            (X|Y) partial-critical-path Z &
            Z project-time

The above complete network analysis program can be used in conjunction with SIMPLE or MICRO to interrogate a database containing the details of a project. Queries such as:

    which(x : train-staff earliest-start x)
    which(x : x critical)
    which(x : x critical-path)
or
    is(collect-product-data total-float x & 4 LESS x)

can be posed. Alternatively, the definitions of "which" and "is" needed for putting such questions, could be included in a critical path analysis package.

10.3   Using lemmas

If the program described above is used, it will be seen to take a considerable time to obtain the results of queries. The reason for this is the fact that in executing almost any query, certain information, in particular the various activity times, are required on many occasions during the same calculation. On each occasion the system works out these values "from basic principles" using the rules. Were the process carried out manually, then on each occasion an activity time was required, it would first be checked to see whether the value had already been calculated. If it had not been, then its value would be computed and noted down for next time.

The micro-PROLOG counterpart of this activity is lemma generation. Immediately after computing a value, a clause or lemma expressing this newly found fact will be added to the database. Whenever a value is required, the program will first search the database to see whether the desired information has already been recorded. Only if it fails to find the necessary lemma will it resort to carrying out the calculation.

The program "earliest-start" with the lemma generation facility is:

```
X earliest-start Y if
      known-earliest-start defined &
      X known-earliest-start Y & /
X earliest-start 0 if
      X begin-activity &
      (X known-earliest-start 0) noted & /
X earliest-start Y if
      Z isall (x : y precedes X &
                  y earliest-finish x) &
      Y max-of Z &
      (X known-earliest-start Y) noted
```

Suppose, for example, that the earliest start time of activity "test-system" is required. The program will search down the "known-earliest-start" lemmas, in accordance with the new first rule for "earliest-start". If it finds a lemma of the form ((known-earliest-start test-system t)), for some number t, it will take the value t given, but will not go on to the subsequent rules for "earliest-start", because of the slash that terminates the first rule. Thus, duplicate solutions are avoided. If a suitable lemma is not found then the program will "drop through" to the following rules and actually calculate the required value, generating a new "known-earliest-start" lemma before returning.

The "defined" condition in the first rule is there to avoid the "No definition for ..." error, that would otherwise arise when the rule is used before there are any lemmas generated. It tests if the "known-earliest-start" relation is defined. (Alternatively, the relation could have been declared a **data-rel** relation as described in Section 8.3.)

The "noted" conditions, that terminate the second and third rules, are responsible for generating "known-earliest-start" lemmas. The program for "noted" is:

```
(X Y) noted if
    ((Y X)) ADDCL
(X Y Z) noted if
    ((Y X Z)) ADDCL
```

"noted" takes a unary or binary simple sentence and adds the corresponding list-based micro-PROLOG clause to the database. Thus, for example, the condition "(test-system known-earliest-start 21) noted" succeeds by adding the clause ((known-earliest-start test-system 21)) to the database. In clauses, the relation name always comes first

The previous programs for the other activity times and for the project time are similarly modified for lemma generation. (Since "known-project-time" is unary, the first rule for "noted" will be invoked whenever such lemmas are generated.)

It would have been possible to use SIMPLE's own "add" program (followed by a slash) in place of "noted". However, because "add" is designed to handle SIMPLE sentences of any degree of complexity, it takes longer than the specially defined "noted" to produce the lemmas required in this application.

Not only is a lemma of use in speeding up the answering of the query during which it is generated, but, because it remains in the database afterwards, it can often be of help in the execution of subsequent queries. It is interesting to note that the query:

which(x : x critical-path)

requires the calculation of all the activity times for the whole
project. If this is the first query posed, it will be responsible for
generating all the possible lemmas. Thereafter other questions are
answered extremely quickly. Thus, this query can be used to force
lemma generation and thereby increase the efficiency of the
remaining session.

A complete summary of the various activities, their duration,
earliest start and other features can be displayed with the query:

which(X Y Z x y z X1 Y1 Z1:   (A)
    X duration Y &
    X earliest-start Z &
    X latest-start x &
    X earliest-finish y &
    X latest-finish z &
    X total-float X1 &
    X free-float Y1 &
    X crit Z1)

the program "crit" being responsible for putting a star alongside
the critical activities:

X crit * if
        X critical & /
X crit -

For the example project, the answers to (A) would be:

design-stock-control-model 4 0 2 6 2 0 0 -
develop-stock-control-program 13 4 6 17 2 2 -
design-forecasting-model 4 0 0 4 4 0 0 *
develop-forecasting-program 15 4 4 19 19 0 0 *
collect-product-data 12 0 7 12 19 7 0 -
design-product-database 4 4 15 8 19 11 4 -
set-up-product-database 2 12 19 14 21 7 7 -
train-staff 2 19 19 21 21 0 0 *
test-system 2 21 21 23 23 0 0 *
No (more) answers

System note - constructing a table of the results - a more tabular display
of this information could be constructed in micro-PROLOG by using

the FWRITE record output facilities available in some versions. However, for our purposes it is not necessary to produce a pretty table.

10.4   The Critical Path Analysis Program

X activity if
        X duration Y

X begin-activity if
        X activity &
        not Y precedes X

X end-activity if
        X activity &
        not X precedes Y

X earliest-start Y if
        known-earliest-start defined &
        X known-earliest-start Y & /
X earliest-start 0 if
        X begin-activity &
        (X known-earliest-start 0) noted & /
X earliest-start Y if
        Z isall (x : y precedes X &
                        y earliest-finish x) &
        Y max-of Z &
        (X known-earliest-start Y) noted

X earliest-finish Y if
        known-earliest-finish defined &
        X known-earliest-finish Y & /
X earliest-finish Y if
        X earliest-start Z &
        X duration x &
        SUM (X x Y) &
        (X known-earliest-finish Y) noted

X project-time if
        known-project-time defined &
        X known-project-time & /
X project-time if
        Y isall (Z : x end-activity &
                        x earliest-finish Z) &
        X max-of Y &
        (X known-project-time) noted

X latest-finish Y if
      known-latest-finish defined &
      X known-latest-finish Y & /
X latest-finish Y if
      X end-activity &
      Y project-time &
      (X known-latest-finish Y) noted & /
X latest-finish Y if
      Z isall (x : X precedes y &
                    y latest-start x) &
      Y min-of Z &
      (X known-latest-finish Y) noted

X latest-start Y if
      known-latest-start defined &
      X known-latest-start Y & /
X latest-start Y if
      X latest-finish Z &
      X duration x &
      SUM (Y x Z) &
      (X known-latest-start Y) noted

(X Y) noted if
      ((Y X)) ADDCL
(X Y Z) noted if
      ((Y X Z)) ADDCL

X critical if
      X activity &
      X earliest-start Y &
      X latest-start Y

(X) partial-critical-path if
      X end-activity &
      X critical
(X Y|Z) partial-critical-path if
      X critical &
      X precedes Y &
      (Y|Z) partial-critical-path

(X|Y) critical-path if
      X begin-activity &
      (X|Y) partial-critical-path

X total-float Y if
        X earliest-start Z &
        X latest-start x &
        SUM (Z Y x)

X free-float Y if
        X end-activity &
        Z project-time &
        X earliest-finish x &
        SUM (x Y Z) & /
X free-float Y if
        Z isall (x : X precedes y &
                      y earliest-start x) &
        z min-of Z &
        X earliest-finish X1 &
        SUM (X1 Y z)

X crit * if
        critical (X) & /
X crit -

11.   micro-PROLOG for Expert Systems

P.Hammond

11.1   Introduction

The unceasing acquisition of technological knowledge inevitably leads to specialisation and to the importance of the expert. The knowledge required for many specialist fields demands years of training and apprenticeship and so expertise is a costly commodity to produce. The frequent shortfall of availability of expertise over demand is commonplace and consequently many experts are able to command substantial financial rewards for their services. Hence, the concept of an *expert system*, computer software which can emulate an expert consultant, is very appealing. Its recent rise in popularity (and possible notoriety) is due to a number of factors:

(i)   the proven success of a number of such computer programs in the world of Artificial Intelligence, particularly in the United States;

(ii)   the financial advantages expert systems would bring to industry both from their direct use and their commercial exploitation;

(iii)   their explicit mention by the Japanese as being an important part of their plans for the "Fifth Generation Computers".

In this chapter we illustrate how some expert system techniques can be implemented in micro-PROLOG and indicate the advantages gained from the flexibility of the micro-PROLOG environment.

11.2   The MYCIN Expert System

In recent years a great deal of attention has been drawn to expert systems some of which has even appeared in the national press. One system which has enjoyed a significant share of the publicity is the expert system MYCIN. MYCIN contains expert knowledge and "rules of thumb" about diagnosing and treating bacterial infections of the blood.

As with many expert systems, MYCIN's knowledge is expressed as a collection of rules. The 500 or so MYCIN rules are in the form "If conditions Then actions". A typical MYCIN rule is

Rule 1

If: 1)   The infection which requires therapy is meningitis, and
    2)   The stain of the organism is known, and
    3)   The morphology of the organism is known, and
    4)   The patient has been seriously burned

Then: There is weakly suggestive evidence (0.3) that pseudomonas-aeruginosa is one of the organisms (other than those seen on cultures or smears) which might be causing the infection.

The number 0.3 is a measure (between -1 and 1) of some medical expert's opinion of how "strong" the connection is between the "conditions" of the rule and its conclusion. This rule strength (each MYCIN rule has one) is used to calculate a numerical measure of confidence in the conclusion. The information relating to a patient's symptoms and circumstances is asked for as it is needed and is supplied by a user during a *consultation* or *interaction* with the MYCIN system. The user can also qualify answers to MYCIN's questions by supplying a number (between -5 and 5) rather than a straight "yes" or "no". MYCIN is able to combine all these *fuzzy* or uncertain measures to supply a final confidence value for each of the conclusions it makes. We do not have enough space in this chapter to discuss such **reasoning with uncertain information.**

Besides the knowledge expressed explicitly as rules MYCIN also has information stored in other forms. For our purposes, though, we need only concentrate on the rules. The term *knowledge base* is used to describe the application-specific information contained in an expert system in whatever form it is represented. MYCIN uses its knowledge base along with knowledge of a particular patient to determine suitable and unsuitable drug treatments for the infections the patient has contracted.

Now, what separates MYCIN from many other medical diagnostic computer programs is its ability to explain to a user **why** it asks particular questions about the patient, **how** it concluded which treatments to give the patient and **why** it did **not** offer other treatments as possible therapies. Obviously, an ability to justify questions and conclusions is essential but not peculiar to medical diagnostic systems. Any knowledge based computer program which is to be considered to be in any way "expert" must be capable of **explaining its behaviour.** Otherwise, the system's judgements and reasoning are unlikely to be accepted by its users and, more importantly, by those human experts in the same field of knowledge.

11.3   Representing Knowledge in micro-PROLOG

An expert system shell

The rules in MYCIN represent a great deal of medical knowledge which has been painstakingly extracted from medical experts. The process of coaxing experts to describe their expertise is known as *knowledge acquisition* whereas *knowledge engineering* describes the moulding of the expert's knowledge into a form suitable for wider use and, in particular, for use in a computer as a knowledge based or expert system. Both knowledge acquisition and knowledge engineering are difficult and time consuming tasks and are the subject of much recent research. We shall avoid these difficult stages in the development of an application specific expert system. Instead, we shall concentrate on implementing an expert system *shell* which can ask the user to supply information (rather like **is-told** in Chapter 4) and explain its reasoning when asking questions and answering queries. A previously defined knowledge base must be added to the shell before it can display or emulate human expertise.

Rule-based representation of knowledge

The rule-based nature of micro-PROLOG suggests that it should be an excellent vehicle for representing knowledge in the form of rules. Moreover, micro-PROLOG's greatest asset for knowledge representation is its facility for expressing relationships in very general terms. This often results in a simpler and more accessible representation of the knowledge. For example, consider the four MYCIN rules

Rule 2

If: 1)   The morphology of the organism is coccus, and
      2)   The stain of the organism is not known
Then: There is suggestive evidence (0.6) that the stain of the organism is Grampos.

Rule 3

If: 1)   The morphology of the organism is rod, and
      2)   The stain of the organism is not known
Then: There is suggestive evidence (0.6) that the stain of the organism is Gramneg.

Rule 4

If: 1)   The stain of the organism is Grampos, and
      2)   The morphology of the organism is not known
Then: There is suggestive evidence (0.6) that the morphology of the organism is coccus.

Rule 5

If: 1)   The stain of the organism is Gramneg, and
      2)   The morphology of the organism is not known
Then: There is suggestive evidence (0.6) that the morphology of the organism is rod.

We could represent these rules in micro-PROLOG as

```
X may-have (gramstain Grampos) if
     X has (morphology coccus)
```

> X may-have (gramstain Gramneg) if
>   X has (morphology rod)
>
> X may-have (morphology coccus) if
>   X has (gramstain Grampos)
>
> X may-have (morphology rod) if
>   X has (gramstain Gramneg)

but then the gramstain-morphology connection is not as explicit as it should be. The representation is much improved if we use a general micro-PROLOG rule (MYCIN is unable to cope with such general rules)

> X may-have Y if
>   X has Z and
>   Z suggests Y

along with an explicit description of the gramstain-morphology connection in terms of four facts

> (gramstain Grampos) suggests (morphology coccus)
> (gramstain Gramneg) suggests (morphology rod)
> (morphology coccus) suggests (gramstain Grampos)
> (morphology rod) suggests (gramstain Gramneg)

We now have a clearer and more compact representation of the knowledge; but more importantly, we have represented the important concept explicitly and also now have greater access to it. By having to use a number of similar rules the MYCIN representation fails to capture the general principle and hides away its specific instances.

Another MYCIN rule which hides information unnecessarily in a rule is the following

Rule 6

If: 1) The site of the culture is urethra, and
     2) The sex of the patient is male, and
     3) It is definite that the identity of the organism is one of:

> corynbacterium-non-diptheriae
> mycoplasma

Then: There is suggestive evidence (0.5) that the organism is
          normally found at this site.

In fact the rule need not be tied to a particular culture of a
particular patient and could be represented in micro-PROLOG as
two facts

    corynbacterium-non-diptheriae is-found-at-site (male urethra)
    mycoplasma is-found-at-site (male urethra)

along with the more general scheme

    X may-be-normal-in Y if
        Z is-sex-of Y and
        X is-isolated-from-site (x of Y) and
        X is-found-at-site (Z x)

The "fuzzy" rule-strength of Rule 6 might be replaced by a
measure of frequency such as

    mycoplasma is-found-at ((male urethra) sometimes)

Obviously the examples in this section were chosen to
illustrate the advantages of representing knowledge in micro-
PROLOG. In fact, other uses of micro-PROLOG in law, biology,
geology and biochemistry reaffirm its suitability for representing
information from a variety of sources.

11.4   A simple interactive shell

Generalising the is-reported program

In Section 8.3 a metalogical program was defined for asking
the user to confirm the presence or absence of symptoms which
might indicate faults in a bicycle. We shall use a revised form of
the "is-reported" program of that example for the interactive
subcomponent of our expert sytem shell. The relations "was-
present" and "was-absent", used to describe the user's confirmation
or denial of the presence of symptoms, are replaced by the more

general purpose relation names "was-confirmed" and "was-denied" respectively. The complete program for "is-reported" is now

```
x is-reported if x was-confirmed & /
x is-reported if
        not x was-denied &
        x is-told &
        (x was-confirmed) add
x is-reported if
        not x was-confirmed &
        not x was-denied &
        (x was-denied) add &
        FAIL


was-denied data-rel
was-confirmed data-rel
```

We have removed the "/" after is-told because we are going to use the program for generating as well as for confirming and we would like the user to be asked repeatedly for answers to questions such as

        john likes X?

until a "no" is given. The removal of this "/" necessitates the addition, in the third rule, of the extra test "not x was-confirmed" to avoid its use after a successful application of the second rule.

As an immediate application of the interactive "is-reported" program consider the following tiny medical knowledge base:

```
x should-take y if
        (x has complained of z) is-reported and
        y suppresses z and
        not y is-unsuitable-for x

x is-unsuitable-for y if
        x aggravates z and
        (y has condition z) is-reported

aspirin suppresses inflammation
aspirin suppresses pain
lomotil suppresses diarrhoea
```

```
aspirin aggravates peptic-ulcer
lomotil aggravates impaired-liver-function

aspirin is-a-drug
lomotil is-a-drug
```

The combination of shell and knowledge base are illustrated in the following example interaction (the user's answers and queries are **emphasised**).

```
which(x : john should-take x)
john has complained of X ? ans pain
john has condition peptic-ulcer ? no
aspirin
john has complained of X ? ans diarrhoea
john has condition impaired-liver-function ? no
lomotil
john has complained of X ? no
No (more) answers.
```

The answers supplied by the user are recorded as

```
(john has complained of pain) was-confirmed
(john has complained of diarrhoea) was-confirmed
(john has condition peptic-ulcer) was-denied
(john has condition impaired-liver-function) was-denied
```

The "is-reported" program apparently works well enough. However, if we now repeat the original query after John's symptoms and complaints have been reported we find

```
which(x : john should-take x)
aspirin
No (more) answers
```

The explanation for the incomplete set of solutions is the "/" condition used in the first rule for "is-reported", where only the first confirmed symptom is picked up. We can cure this undesirable behaviour by deleting the "/" in the first rule for "is-reported" and inserting a suitable test in the second rule. Now "is-reported" is defined as

```
x is-reported if x was-confirmed
x is-reported if
        not x was-confirmed &
        not x was-denied &
        x is-told &
        (x was-confirmed) add
x is-reported if
        not x was-confirmed &
        not was-denied &
        (X was-denied) add &
        FAIL
```

We will now get the same answers to our query about what John should take, irrespective of whether his symptoms and existing complaints have already been reported.

Controlling the interaction

The "/" appeared in the first rule of the original definition of "is-reported" because "is-reported" was used in Chapter 8 solely as a test and never to generate all reported information. In fact, this difference between the generating and testing use of "is-reported" also occurs in our medical knowledge base. The rules for "should-take" and "is-unsuitable-for"

```
x should-take y if
        (x has complained of z) is-reported and
        y suppresses z and
        not y is-unsuitable-for x

x is-unsuitable-for y if
        x aggravates z and
        (y has condition z) is-reported
```

use "is-reported" in different ways during the evaluation of the query

```
which(x : john should-take x)
```

Because of the order in which micro-PROLOG tackles rule conditions the "should-take" rule causes the user to be asked first to generate a patient symptom and then a suitable drug is sought. This is exactly the preferred behaviour. The alternative order would generate a possible symptom and potentially efficacious drug, using "suppresses", and then ask the user if the patient did indeed have that symptom. But the user would grow impatient if a large number of irrelevant symptoms were subsequently asked about. When drugs are tested for their unsuitability the user is asked if the patient has a particular medical condition which has been generated by the drug name in "aggravates". The behaviour we do not want is for the user to be asked to supply medical conditions from which the patient is known to suffer, in which case irrelevant conditions may be reported. On the other hand, a query such as

which(x : x is-a-drug and x is-unsuitable-for john)

will cause the user to be asked if the patient has a variety of medical conditions when the user would prefer to supply the known medical conditions which then generate the unsuitable drugs. Obviously, then, it is possible to exploit the control behaviour of micro-PROLOG to obtain the desired behaviour of an interactive program. But, as we have illustrated, particular behaviour for one situation is not always suitable in general. Such variations in desired control would be better left to a more intelligent interactive shell so that the knowledge representation is declarative in style and free from constraints of control. A more detailed discussion of this topic is beyond the scope and aims of this chapter.

11.5   A more sophisticated shell

The shell should know what to ask about

At the end of the last section we stressed the undesirability of manipulating the representation of the knowledge so as to obtain a particular behaviour of the program. In this section we discuss a related problem. So far, any information that is to be retrieved from the user is declared as such by the explicit appearance of

information is-reported

in the rule. Consider how much clearer and uncluttered the rules would be if such a control mechanism was described separately. For example, the rules in our little medical knowledge base could be defined by

x should-take y if	(A)
x has-complained-of z and	
y suppresses z and	
not y is-unsuitable-for x	

x should-take y if   (A)
    x has-complained-of z and
    y suppresses z and
    not y is-unsuitable-for x

x is-unsuitable-for y if
    x aggravates z and
    y has-condition z

But how should we declare that information about the relations "has-complained-of" and "has-condition" is to be obtained from the user? We could do this by adding to the knowledge base the assertions

has-complained-of is-askable   (B)
has-condition is-askable

If at some later date we decide to make "has-condition" not askable but defined by some set of rules we simply delete "has-condition is-askable" and add the new rules without changing the rest of the knowledge base. By declaring separately in the knowledge base those relations the user knows about, we improve the clarity, the modularity and the flexibility of the knowledge representation.

This more elegant approach needs query evaluators that know about "is-askable" relations and which automatically query the user instead of searching for rules whenever they encounter a condition for such a relation.

Interactive "IS" and "WHICH" queries

Consider the following definition of the SIMPLE is command:

```
X  is  if
       Y  Parse-of-ConjC  X  &
       Y  ?  &
       /  &
       YES  PP
X  is  if  NO  PP
```

The conjunction of conditions in the **is** query is first parsed to its standard micro-PROLOG syntax using the "Parse-of-ConjC" relation described in Section 9.3. Then, the list of conditions is evaluated by the "?" primitive which is described in Section 9.2. Because "?" is a micro-PROLOG primitive, we cannot change its definition. However, in Section 9.5, an almost equivalent relation called "confirmed" was defined. We extend its definition to cover negated conditions.

```
()  confirmed
((NOT  ?  X)|Y))  confirmed  if  /  &
      not  X  confirmed  &
      Y  confirmed
((x|y)|Y))  confirmed  if
      ((x|y)|Y1)  CL  &
      Y1  confirmed  &
      Y  confirmed
```

The "/" in the second rule saves including a test in the third rule that the relation "x" is not "NOT".

There are now two stages left to complete the definition of "IS", the interactive version of the **is** command. Firstly, we replace "?" by "confirmed" in the definition and then we extend "confirmed" to handle relations declared as "is-askable". "IS" becomes

```
X  IS  if
       Y  Parse-of-ConjC  X  &
       Y  confirmed  &  /  &
       YES  PP
X  IS  if  NO  PP
```

and the extra rule for "confirmed" is

```
((x|y)|Y) confirmed if
    x is-askable &
    Parse-of-SS ((x|y) z ()) &
    z is-reported &
    Y confirmed
```

Notice, that before an askable condition is asked about, it is converted back to the sentence syntax using the **Parse-of-SS** relation described in Chapter 9. The "WHICH" command can be similarly updated to cope with "is-askable" relations.

```
WHICH((X : | Y)) if
    Z Parse-of-ConjC Y &
    (forall Z confirmed then X PP)
```

Now, with the definition (A) and declarations (B) given above, together with the earlier definitions of "aggravates", "suppresses" and "is-a-drug", the query:

```
WHICH(x : John should-take x)
```

will result in a similar interaction to that given in Section 11.4.

11.6   "why" explanations

What is a "why" explanation?

When are "why" explanations needed? Typically, when the interactive shell generates a question which appears, to the user at any rate, to be not following the context of previous questions or even to appear totally irrelevant. As an example, consider the incomplete dialogue taken from the example interaction in Section 11.4, suitably altered to take into account the changes in the rules

```
WHICH(x : john should-take x)
john has-complained-of x? ans pain
john has-condition peptic-ulcer?
```

Some users may be mystified at being asked about "peptic ulcer" and, before answering the question, would prefer to be told **why** this particular question has arisen. We shall allow the user to enter "why" to demand a *why* explanation.

There have been a variety of formats used for "why" explanations, some quite elaborate. The simplest explanation should describe how the current question has come about given the original query made by the user. The format we shall employ shows how the rules in the knowledge base have been used in evaluating the original query. It will be a description of the history or chain of rules connecting the user's query and the shell's question. Before we go on to describe how it can be implemented we illustrate the proposed format.

```
WHICH(x : john should-take x)
john has-complained-of X? ans pain
john has-condition peptic-ulcer? why

aspirin is-unsuitable-for john if
        aspirin aggravates peptic-ulcer &
        john has-condition peptic-ulcer

john should-take aspirin if
        john has-complained-of pain &
        aspirin suppresses pain &
        not aspirin is-unsuitable-for john

john has-condition peptic-ulcer?
```

Generating a "why" trace

The concept we must add to our interactive shell to handle "why" explanations is that of "history". Before we can show the user the "history" of the use of rules in the knowledge base we must somehow generate and record it. The rule for "confirmed"

```
((x|y)|Y) confirmed if
        ((x|y)|Y1) CL &
        Y1 confirmed &
        Y confirmed
```

is where the knowledge base rules and facts are "picked up". Obviously, this is the place to record such use of the knowledge base. The record could be kept in "confirmed" by an extra argument which defines the "historical" trace as a list of the rules used. So we need to redefine "confirmed" with this extra argument. Firstly, an empty list of conditions does not use any rules.

() confirmed X

When a new rule is picked up by a use of **CL** we simply add a copy of the rule (in clause form) to the front of the "why" trace. Hence,

((NOT ? X)|Y) confirmed Z if / &
    not X confirmed Z &
    Y confirmed Z

and

((x|y)|Y) confirmed Z if
    ((x|y)|Y1) CL &
    Y1 confirmed (((x|y)|Y1) | Z) &
    Y confirmed Z

The rule for "confirmed" which deals with askable relations eventually generates questions for the user. These questions and the user's answers are then handled by "is-reported". Therefore, the "why" trace must be passed on to "is-reported" so that, when the user demands a "why" explanation, the trace is at hand and can be presented to the user. The revised version of this rule is

((x|y)|Y) confirmed Z if
    x is-askable &
    Parse-of-SS ((x|y) z ()) &
    z is-reported Z &
    Y confirmed Z

"IS" and "WHICH" must also be altered to take account of the extra argument in "confirmed". The call to "confirmed" is made with an empty "why" trace.

X IS if
    Y Parse-of-ConjC X &
    Y confirmed () & / &
    YES PP
X IS if NO PP

```
WHICH((X : |Y)) if
     Z Parse-of-ConjC Y &
     (forall Z confirmed () then X PP) &
     PP (No (more) answers)
```

"is-reported" must itself pass on the "why" trace x to is-told because the appearance of the shell's question to the user and the acceptance of the user's answer is organised in is-told. This is where we shall "trap" and process a request for a "why" explanation. "is-reported" has two arguments; the first is the condition to be asked about and the second is the "why" trace. In sentence syntax its definition now becomes

```
x is-reported y if x was-confirmed
x is-reported y if
     not x was-confirmed &
     not x was-denied &
     x IS-TOLD y &
     (x was-confirmed) add
x is-reported y if
     not x was-confirmed &
     not was-denied &
     (X was-denied) add &
     FAIL
```

We replace is-told by "IS-TOLD" because is-told belongs to the SIMPLE front-end module which we do not want to alter. The "IS-TOLD" we define can handle "yes", "no" and "why" answers from the user. It is left to the reader to extend it to handle "just", "ans" etc. "IS-TOLD" must pose a question, accept an answer and succeed if the answer is "yes". An answer "no" should fail and a "why" request should generate a "why" explanation and repeat the question/answer phase.

```
X IS-TOLD Y if
     X P &
     " ? " P &
     Z R &
     ANSWER (X Y Z)
```

```
ANSWER (X Y yes) if /
ANSWER (X Y no) if / & FAIL
ANSWER (X Y why) if / &
        Y are-displayed &
        X IS-TOLD Y
```

The " ? " is a quoted constant which contains spaces.

Displaying the "why" trace

We shall give a very simple definition of "are-displayed". The "why" trace is a list of clauses and a clause is a conclusion followed by a list of conditions given as atoms. Hence

```
() are-displayed
(X|Y) are-displayed if
        X is-displayed &
        Y are-displayed


X is-displayed if
        X "?REV-P?" Y &
        PP &
        P true-of Y &
        PP
```

The condition "P true-of Y" is used instead of "Y PP" because the former will display the sentence Y as a *sequence* *without* the outer brackets whereas the latter would display it as a list with outer brackets.

"is-displayed" uses a program "?REV-P?" which is almost identical to "Parse-of-S" in Section 9.3. The difference is that "?REV-P?" produces a sentence form of a clause with embedded control characters which affect the way the sentence is displayed by the P primitive. The query

```
is( ((is-happy X)(likes Y X)) "?REV-P?" Z) &
        P true-of Z &
        PP)
```
produces
```
X is-happy if
        Y likes X
```

It is unfortunate that the query

    is(((is-happy Y)(likes X Y)) "?REV-P?" Z &
            P true-of Z &
            PP)

produces exactly the same output. The explanation for this is the renaming of variables by the program **P** as explained in Section 8.4. On most occasions this will not cause any problems for the "why" explanation. However, its adverse effect is illustrated in the following example

    &.WHICH(x : john should-take x)
    john has-complained-of X ? why

    john should-take X if
            john has-complained-of Y and
            X suppresses Y and
            not X is-unsuitable-for john

11.7   "how" explanations

What is a "how" explanation?

A "why" explanation gives inside information on how the explanation of a query is currently progressing. A "how" explanation should describe how a conclusion could be or has been made using the facts and rules in the knowledge base. "how" explanations will inevitably be similar to "why" explanations since both allow the user to see a complete or partial description of how a query is solved. It seems quite natural to explain how a conclusion was drawn by showing how the major steps involved were themselves established. Therefore, we explain how a conclusion was made from a rule by explaining how the conditions in the rule were themselves proved.

When should "how" explanations be demanded by the user? Suppose the user asks the system to solve an "IS" query. If the answer is "YES" then the user might like to know how the query was solved. Similarly, the user might request an explanation of how a solution has been obtained to a "WHICH" query.

Before describing the implementation of "how" the format

we propose is illustrated by the proof of the result "john should-take aspirin" from Section 11.4:

> how(john should-take aspirin)

To show that john should-take aspirin I used the rule

> X should-take Y if
>   X has-complained-of Z and
>   Y suppresses Z and
>   not Y is-unsuitable-for X

> You told me john has-complained-of pain
> I can show aspirin suppresses pain
> aspirin is-unsuitable-for john fails.

Of course, the user might now like to ask

> how (aspirin suppresses pain)

or

> whynot (aspirin is-unsuitable-for john)

We defer the "whynot" command to the last part of the chapter.

The explanation includes the general form of the rule used as well as descriptions of how each condition in the rule was itself deduced. Therefore, we shall need to distinguish between the form of the rule before and after its variables are bound. But once the variables are bound in a rule how can we retrieve the unbound form of the rule? Fortunately, micro-PROLOG provides access to its internal indexing of clauses which makes it very much easier to identify particular clauses. The **CL** primitive, described in Section 9.5, also has a three argument form. The first argument, X say, is the clause and the second and third arguments are numbers which identify the position of X in the sequence of clauses defining the same relation defined by X. The condition

> CL (((suppresses|X)|Y) 2 Z)

makes Z the position of the clause that matches ((suppresses|X)|Y) with the search starting at the second clause. On the otherhand, the condition

> CL (((suppresses|X)|Y) 2 2)

makes X and Y respectively the argument list and the body of
the second clause for "suppresses". When we use a particular
clause to conclude something we can make a note of its index
and then retrieve a fresh copy of the clause using the relation
name and index.

Implementing a simple "how" explanation

"how" should first determine which rule was used to prove
the simple condition; then it should show the general form of the
rule and finally explain briefly how each condition of the rule
was itself determined.

> X how if
>   Parse-of-SS ((Y|Z) X ()) &
>   proved ((Y|Z) x y) &
>   X is-shown &
>   Y show-clause x &
>   y are-explained

"proved" has three arguments : the first is the atom form of
the condition; the second is the index of a rule that can be used
to prove the condition and the third is the body of conditions
taken from the pattern matched version of this rule. "proved" can
be defined as:

> proved (X Y Z) if
>   CL ((X|Z) 1 Y) &
>   Z confirmed ()

"is-shown" must simply display the condition that has been
proved:

> X is-shown if
>   P true-of ('To show|X) &
>   P(" " I used) &
>   PP

and "show-clause" must pick up a copy of the clause that was
used and display it

X show-clause Y if
        CL (((X|Z)|x) Y Y) &
        ((X|Z)|x) is-displayed

We shall explain the deduction of three types of conditions.
Those conditions deducible from rules, those facts provided by
the user and conditions which are negated. We shall not show
how to explain **forall** or **isall** conditions. The simplest way to
explain a body of conditions is by

() are-explained
(X|Y) are-explained if
        X is-explained &
        Y are-explained

To distinguish between conditions which are deducible,
askable etc. we must check the relation name. A negated
condition succeeds because the condition itself fails.

(NOT ? X) is-explained if
        X Parse-of-ConjC Y &
        P true-of Y & P(" " fails) &
        PP

Otherwise, conclusions are drawn from rules or confirmed by the
user.

(X|Y) is-explained if
        X dict &
        Parse-of-SS ((X|Y) Z ()) &
        P true-of (I can show|Z) &
        PP
(X|Y) is-explained if
        X is-askable &
        Parse-of-SS ((X|Y) Z ()) &
        P true-of (You told me|Z) &
        PP

Improving the "how" explanation

The "how" we have defined needs to be extended to handle
conjunctive conditions, conditions involving system primitives such
as **LESS** as well as built-in relations such as **isall** and **forall**. Other

improvements can be made to give the user more information about how rule conditions were established. For example, "explain" could differentiate between conditions deduced from rules and those deduced from assertions. The former could be reported as being "shown" and the latter as being "known". We can actually use this "how" explanation to determine **how** a conclusion might be drawn. But it cannot deal comprehensively with such queries. Similarly, we have not handled the "how" explanation of a conclusion that actually fails. In this case, "how" should notice that it cannot prove the condition and use "whynot", which is described in the following section, to show why it cannot be proved. For example, we might modify "how" by adding an extra rule:

```
X how if
      Parse-of-SS ((Y|Z) X ()) &
      proved ((Y|Z) x y) & / &
      X is-shown &
      Y show-clause x &
      y are-explained
X how if
      P(I cannot prove|X) &
      whynot(X)
```

An illustration of this is the following

```
&.how(toffee is-unsuitable-for peter)
I cannot prove toffee is-unsuitable-for peter
To show toffee is-unsuitable-for peter I could use

X is-unsuitable-for Y if
      X aggravates Z &
      Y has-condition Z

toffee aggravates X fails
&.
```

11.8   "whynot" explanations

What is a "whynot" explanation

In our "how" explanation a negated condition was said to be proved by the failure of the condition. It is inevitable that, after such an explanation, we would be interested in **why** the condition did **not** succeed. Similarly, a "whynot" explanation would be informative after the failure of an **is** query. Whereas we explained how single unnegated conditions were proved from rules, we shall now explain why **conjunctions** of conditions do not succeed. We shall take the simple minded view that a conjunction of conditions fails because of the failure of a single condition somewhere in the conjunction and that the previously solved conditions have only a single solution. In other words, when a condition fails there is no point in backtracking to look for alternative solutions to preceding conditions.

The explanation of "john should-take aspirin" included the message that "aspirin is-unsuitable-for john" failed. We can use this failed condition to illustrate a "whynot" explanation

&.whynot(aspirin is-unsuitable-for john)
To show aspirin is-unsuitable-for john I could use

X is-unsuitable-for Y if
    X aggravates Z &
    Y has-condition Z

aspirin aggravates peptic-ulcer
john has-condition peptic-ulcer fails

Implementing a simple "why not" explanation

The top level rule for "whynot" needs no explanation:

X whynot if
    Y Parse-of-ConjC X &
    not Y confirmed () &
    Y explain-failure X

"explain-failure" should treat differently the cases where there is a single condition and where there is more than one condition in the conjunction. The single condition case requires no search for the failed condition. We keep the sentence form of the conjunction alive as a second argument in "explain-failure" so that it can be displayed later in the explanation.

(X) explain-failure Y if
    X explain-failure-of-Cond Y
(X Y|Z) explain-failure x if
    (X Y|Z) explain-failure-of-ConjC

While searching for the failing condition it is worth indicating to the user those conditions which succeed. Hence

(X|Y) explain-failure-of-ConjC if
    X confirmed () & / &
    Parse-of-Cond(X x ())
    P true-of x &
    PP &
    Y explain-failure-of-ConjC
(X|Y) explain-failure-of-ConjC if
    Parse-of-Cond(X Z ())
    P true-of Z &
    P(" " fails) &
    PP

"Parse-of-Cond" is similar to "Parse-of-SS" except that it also handles negated conditions.

A negated condition fails because the condition succeeds. Therefore

(NOT ? X) explain-failure-of-Cond Y if
    X confirmed () &
    X Parse-of-ConjC Z &
    P true-of (I can show|Z) &
    PP

There may be rules whose conclusions match the failed condition, but whose body of conditions fail. First we test to see if such a rule exists and then we must explain the failure of each in turn. This will involve explaining the failure of the body of conditions in the rule.

(X|Y) explain-failure-of-Cond Z if
    ((X|Y) | x) CL & / &
    (X|Y) explain-failure-of-rules-for Z
(X|Y) explain-failure-of-rules-for Z if
    (forall CL(((X|Y)|x) 1 y) then
            P true-of (To show|Z) &
            P(" " I could use) &
            PP &
            X show-clause y &
            x explain-failure-of-ConjC)

Of course, the user may have denied some condition

(X|Y) explain-failure-of-Cond Z if
    X is-askable &
    (X|Y) was-denied &
    P true-of (You denied|Z) &
    PP

Improving the "whynot" explanation

The implementation we have described for our "whynot" explanation could be improved in a variety of ways. For example, what should happen if the user asks for a "whynot" explanation of a conjunction of conditions which do not actually fail? One answer would be to have "whynot" call "how" in a similar way to the call of "whynot" by "how" as illustrated at the end of Section 11.8. Another improvement might be to explain the failure of a conjunction more completely than by searching for the first failed condition. After all, much more complicated kinds of failure are possible.

Bibliography

The books "Expert Systems in the Micro-electronic Age" (Edinburgh University Press) and "Introductory Readings in Expert Systems" (Gordon and Breach Science Publishers) edited by Donald Michie contain a number of articles which are worth investigating, particularly for overviews of knowledge representation. A description of expert systems from the logic programming point of view is given in the forthcoming book

"Logic Programming for Expert Systems" by the author and Marek Sergot.

Some or all of the ideas presented here have been implemented (not necessarily as described) by the author in an expert system shell APES and by Marek Sergot in his Query-the-User system.

12. The Logic of two-person games

M.H. van Emden & K. L. Clark

12.1 Introduction

Let us play a game you have never played before: in the graph of Figure 1 select any circle and place a token on it; we take turns making a move by selecting any arrow out of the node occupied by the token and moving the token along it to the circle pointed at by the arrow. The game is over as soon as a player who has to move finds the token on a circle without an arrow going out of it. That player, because he cannot make a move, has lost.

This game is of course of only passing interest. But it has its basic mechanics in common with chess and other intellectually challenging two person games. Chess can also be modelled by a loop-free graph. The nodes of the graph are the states of the chess game. This state is not only determined by what we see on the board, but also by how many moves have gone by since something irreversible has happened, by the status of castling privileges, and by *en passant* status. The rules of chess are intended to be such that the game must terminate after a finite number of moves. This means that the graph of chess has no loops in it, just like the graph of figure 1. Of course, in the chess graph one usually starts in one particular node which is the start state of the game. The moves of chess forbid a player from making a move such that in the new position his King can be taken. This means that sometimes a player whose move it is cannot make an allowed move. That player has lost.

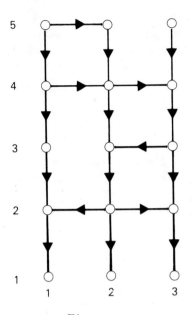

Figure 1
An example of a very small game graph

Let us now write a micro-PROLOG program that can play the game on the graph of Figure 1. By analogy with chess let us call the players Black and White. What is a good move for White? It is one such that, after it, there is no good move for Black. This is expressed by the micro-PROLOG sentence

> y good-w-move-from x if
>   y legal-move-from x & not z good-b-move-from y

The sentence is read as: the move to y from x is a good move for White if it is a legal move and if there is no good move for Black from y. We also need the mirror image sentence

> y good-b-move-from x if
>   y legal-move-from x & not z good-w-move-from y

This is all we need to say about the "good-move" relations. Notice that there is no good move for either player if there is no legal move. So, in the simplest case a good move for White is a move to a position from which there is no move for Black. More generally, a good move for White is a move to a position from which Black cannot make a good move, i.e. from which Black cannot make a move to a position from which there is not another good move for White. Conversely, a good move for Black is a move to a position from which White cannot make a move to a position that does not leave Black without another good move.

To get a complete program for the game it remains to define the "legal-move-from" relation. In figure 1 we have drawn a regular arrangement of nodes which invites a naming scheme using rows and columns. Another regular feature is that if a node has a downward neighbour, then it always has an arrow to it. Both these regularities will be used in our micro-PROLOG sentences for "legal-move-from". But we could have taken any graph provided that it has no loop in it. The complete program for the token move game is:

(x y) legal-move-from (z y) if 1 LESS z and SUM(x 1 z)
(5 2) legal-move-from (5 1)
(4 2) legal-move-from (4 1)
(4 3) legal-move-from (4 2)
(3 2) legal-move-from (3 3)
(2 1) legal-move-from (2 2)
(2 3) legal-move-from (2 2)

y good-w-move-from x if
        y legal-move-from x and
        not z good-b-move-from x

y good-b-move-from x if
        y legal-move-from x and
        not z good-w-move-from x

Let us call the last two rules of this program the Move Calculator I program.

To find out if White can win, starting in the top left-hand corner, against any play by Black, we can use the query

which(x : x good-w-move-from (5 1))

to ask for a good move for White from the node in row 5 and column 1. The evaluation of this query will explore the graph of the game. It will try all the legal moves for White until it finds a move to a node from which, no matter what subsequent counter moves are made by Black, there is always a good move response for White. In the end this good move response for White will be a move to a position from which there is no move for Black.

Most games have very large graphs, much too large to be represented by data bases consisting of unconditional sentences. However, the graphs are mathematical representations of the rules of the game. We can implicitly represent the game graph by expressing the rules of the game as micro-PROLOG rules.

Take for example the game of NIM. It is played with heaps of tokens, which are indistinguishable as far as the rules of the game are concerned. We represent a heap of n tokens in micro-PROLOG by a list of n 1's. The sets of heaps occurring in the game can then be represented by a list of such lists, for example

$$((1\ 1\ 1)\ (1\ 1)\ (1\ 1))$$

represents three heaps, having 3, 2, and 2 tokens respectively.To make a move from state x to state y we select an arbitrary nonempty heap, and take at least one token from it. This is expressed by the sentence

```
y legal-move-from x if
     APPEND(z1 (z2|z3) x) &
     z2 minus-some-is z4 &
     APPEND(z1 (z4|z3) y)
```

where z2 is some heap in the list of heaps x and z4 is the result of taking at least one token from z2, if this is possible. Minus-some can be just minus-one. Or it can be minus-some of the result of minus-one. These two alternatives are included in the following sentences:

```
x minus-some-is y if
     x minus-one-is y
x minus-some-is y if
     x minus-one-is z &
     z minus-some-is y
```

```
(1|x) minus-one-is x
```

We can also use **APPEND** for a more compact definition of "minus-some-is":

```
(1|x) minus-some-is z if APPEND(y z x)
```

The winner of this game is the player who takes the last token - the player who leaves his opponent with no move. By linking the Move Calculator I program with the above definition of "legal-move-from" we obtain a micro-PROLOG to play NIM.

We use the example of NIM only to give a concrete example of the principles of two person games. The analysis of what a good move is which is performed by Move Calculator I is only practicable for games with a few heaps each having only a few tokens. (In fact, for the game of NIM there is an alternative mathematical calculation that can be applied to a new game state to determine whether a move to that state is a good move.)

12.2 Game trees, forcing trees and the minmax principle

We now discuss a method for analysing more precisely what it means for a move to be "good". As a first step, this method requires us to consider a systematic arrangement of all possible lines of play from the current game position p. This arrangement usually takes the form of a tree structure called a *game tree*.

Figure 2 is an example of a game tree for NIM starting from a position with two heaps, having 1 and 3 tokens. This position is symbolized in the Figure by (1 3) and is shown as the root of the tree. As is usual for game trees, the tree is drawn inverted with the root at the top. In the tree every node has as its immediate descendants - its offspring nodes - all the nodes which are reachable in one legal move.

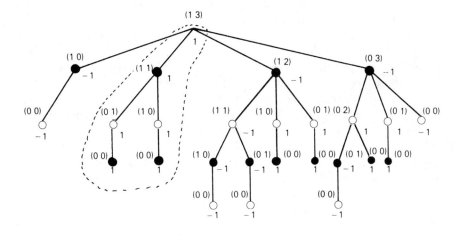

Figure 2
A game tree for NIM
The dotted outline shows a forcing tree. At an open circle it is White to move.

Each node in the tree has been labelled by a value of 1 or -1. If the value is 1, then the node is a good position for White; if it is -1, then it is a good position for Black. If a node with value 1 is a White to move position, it means that from that position there is at least one move for White to another good position for White. If it is a Black to move node every move (that Black can make) is to a another good position for White. The converse conditions apply to the -1 valued nodes.

In terms of this good/bad labelling of nodes we can recharacterise a good move for White as a move to a Black-to-move position which is good for White. Such a position is good for White only if every Black move is to a position which is still good for white, hence not good for Black. This accords with our original characteristion of a good move for White as a Move to a position from which there was no good move for Black.

Forcing Trees

Consider now the sub-tree of Figure 2 outlined with dots. This is a *forcing* tree for White from the root position. It is a subtree of the game tree with the following properties:
(1) all the nodes on it are good nodes for White,
(2) at every White-to-move node there is one offspring giving a good move for White from that node,
(3) at every Black-to-move node every legal-move offspring is present and from each such offspring there is a single branch to a new forcing tree for White.

The converse conditions apply to a forcing tree for Black. We can use a forcing tree from some game position p to play the game to a successful conclusion. The first move is to the single offspring node of the root p of the forcing tree. Then, no matter what move our opponent makes, there is a corresponding branch in the forcing tree. We follow that branch and continue to play with the forcing tree rooted at the new node.

What Move Calculator I does when evaluating the query

which(x : x good-w-move-from ((1) (1 1 1)))

is explore the game tree of Figure 2 from left to right until it finds this forcing tree. It then returns ((1) (1)) as the first position to which White should move. Ideally, since it has found the move only by finding the forcing tree, the forcing tree should then be used to continue the game. To obtain a program that does this we must give a micro-PROLOG definition of a forcing tree from a position p.

Let us represent a forcing tree from a position p as a list of lists of the form

(q (p1 F1) (p2 F2) .... (pk Fk))

where q is the good position to move to from p, p1 ... pk are all the legal positions to which the opponent might then move, and F1 ... Fk are all the forcing trees from these new positions. A forcing tree of one move to a winning position q will be the list comprising just the position q. The White forcing tree of Figure 2 is the structure

((1 3)	((0 1)	((0 0)))	((1 0)	((0 0))))
q	p1	F1	p2	F2

where the numerals are shorthand for the lists of 1's that we would use to represent each heap in micro-PROLOG.

The following definition of "forcing-tree-from" reflects the recursive structure of this list-of-lists representation. For extra readability the definition uses the **vars** comment facility of SIMPLE sentences that was described in Chapter 4 which enables us to use constants as variables.

> (q | L) forcing-tree-from p if
>   q legal-move-from p &
>   L isall ((p1 F1) : p1 legal-move-from q) &
>   L all-forcing-trees &
>   (q L p p1 F1) vars

> () all-forcing-trees
> ((p F) | L) all-forcing-trees if
>   F forcing-tree-from p &
>   L all-forcing-trees &
>   (p F L) vars

Note that if there are no legal moves from q then L will be the empty list of forcing trees and if there are no legal moves from p then there is no forcing tree from p.

When the program is used to find a forcing tree from a given position p it searches for a legal move position q, it then constucts a list of pairs comprising a response move and a variable standing for a forcing tree from the new position using the **isall** condition, finally it checks whether this list can be completed by giving every forcing tree variable a forcing tree value by a recursive use of "forcing-tree-from". If this can be done, it has found a forcing tree from p. This compact definition is another example of the power of having variables in the values found by the evaluation of a condition which will be given values by a later condition, the unique feature of logic programming that we mentioned in Chapter 3.

The following program defines a command relation "play" that tells micro-PROLOG to play a game as White from some position p. If micro-PROLOG can find a forcing tree from that position it plays the game using that tree prompting us for our moves. If it cannot find a forcing tree it pessimistically concedes the game.

x play if Z forcing-tree-from x & / & Z is-played
x play if PP(I concede the game)

(y | Z) is-played if
        PP(My move is to position y) &
        PP(Give new position for your move) &
        R(z) &
        (z Z1) ON Z &
        Z1 is-played

We leave it as an exercise for the reader to improve the program
so that it rejects any illegally entered moves and prompts for an
alternative move and it makes a move even if it cannot find a
forcing tree. That is, it makes some arbitrary move hoping its
opponent will make a mistake.

Minmax calculation of the 1, -1 values

A useful property of the 1, -1 evaluation of nodes is that
we can define the value that should be assigned to a node as a
numerical function of the values assigned to its offspring nodes.
Thus, if a node is a White-to-move position, then its value is the
maximum value of the values assigned to its offpring nodes. This
means that the White-to-move node will have value 1 if and only
if *at least one* of its offspring nodes has value 1. This exactly
corresponds to our our previous condition for when a White-to-
move node has value 1. A Black-to-move node is labelled with
the *minimum value* of the labels of its offspring nodes. This
means that the Black-to-move node will have value 1 if and only
if *every* offspring node has value 1. Again, this exactly corresponds
to the earlier condition for when a Black-to-move node has the
value 1. If a White-to-move node has no offspring it has the
value -1 because White has lost and a Black-to-move node with
no offspring node has value 1 because Black has lost.

The major advantage of this *minmax* characterisation of the
numerical values to be assigned to the non-terminal nodes of a
game tree is that it generalises to game trees that do not end in
definite winning positions for White or Black. Suppose that we
have a game tree from some position p representing some partial
forward play of say, two moves per player. At the end of each
branch let us suppose that we have a non-terminal state of the
game. These non-terminal states of the game usually cannot be

assigned 1 and -1 values representing definite good (winning)
positions for White or Black. However, we may be able to define
an *evaluation function* which assesses how good the position
looks for either player by assigning some numerical value between
1 and -1. The extremes of 1 and -1 will still be definite wins for
White and Black respectively. Numbers between 0 and 1 represent
more favourable positions for White, numbers between 0 and -1
more favourable positions for Black. The nearer to 1 the better
for White, the nearer to -1 the better for Black. Now, the value
of a White-to-move position which is not a terminal node of the
tree can still be computed as the maximum of the values of its
offspring nodes, because White can always move to the offsring
node with the highest value, this being White's best move.
Similarly, the value of a Black-to-move node is the minimum of
the values of the offspring nodes because Black can always move,
for a best move, to this least valued node.

Let us now turn to the problem of defining this more
general concept of the value of a position in micro-PROLOG.
First let us look at the problem of defining the relation

> val value-of-w-to-move p

which holds when val is the numerical value between 1 and -1 to
be assigned to White-to-move position p. Ultimately this will be
defined in terms of the "value-of-b-to-move" relation which has a
dual definition. There are two top-level defining sentences. One
for the case that p is terminal node of the game tree (but not
necessarily a terminal state of the game), the other for the case
when it is not a terminal node. In the first case the value of the
position p is its value as determined by some "terminal-value-for-
w-of" relation; in the second case it is the value of the position
p1 which is the best position for White to move to from p.

> val value-of-w-to-move p if
>   p terminal &
>   val terminal-value-for-w-of p &
>   (val p) vars
> val value-of-w-to-move p if
>   not p terminal &
>   (p1 val) best-w-move-from p &
>   (val p p1) vars

The "best-w-move-from" relation relates a position p to a
pair comprising the best move position p1 and its value val. The

White best-move node from a given position p is the node with the maximum value of all nodes representing legal moves from p.

(p1 val) best-w-move-from p if
    plist isall (q : q legal-move-from p) &
    (p1 val) max-of-all plist &
    (p1 val p q plist) vars

The "max-of-all" is a generalisation of the "Max-of" relation we defined in Chapter 7 and it can be given a similar tail recursive definition in terms of a more general relation

(p val) max-of-either (plist (p1 val1))

which holds when p is a position on plist with a maximum value val of all the positions on plist provided this maximum value is at least val1. Otherwise, (p val) is (p1 val1). The definition of "max-of-all" in terms of "max-of-either" is

(p val) max-of-all (p1 | plist) if
    val1 value-of-b-to-move p1 &
    (p val) max-of-either (plist (p1 val1)) &
    (p val p1 val1 plist) vars

and the tail recursive definition of "max-of-either" is

(p val) max-of-either (() (p val)) if (p val) vars
(p val) max-of-either ((p1|plist) (p2 val2)) if
    val1 value-of-b-to-move p1 &
    (p3 val3) better-of ((p1 val1) (p2 val2)) &
    (p val) max-of-either (plist (p3 val3)) &
    (p val p1 val1 p2 val2 p3 val3 plist) vars

(The definition is tail recursive despite the **vars** comment condition at the end of the recursive rule because this becomes a /* comment condition at the beginning of the rule when the sentence is compiled by SIMPLE.)

Notice that the value of each position in the list of positions to which White might move is found by using the dual relation "value-of-b-to-move". The definition of this relation is exactly the same as that of "value-of-w-to-move" except that it uses "min-of-all" instead of "max-of-all" and it uses "value-of-w-to-move" to find the value of each position in the list of positions for which it is finding the minimum value position. We leave it to the reader to find a more general definition of the value of a position in which the crucial "max-of-either", "min-of-either", "terminal-vale-for-w-of" and "terminal-value-for-b-of" relations are arguments of the relation relation. The relations "value-of-w-to-move" and "value-of-b-to-move" can then be defined in terms of this more general relation.

We have now constructed a generalisation of Move Calculator I which uses game values between -1 and 1 to assess how good a node is for Black or White. We shall call it Move Calculator II. It comprises the following rules:

```
val value-of-w-to-move p if
      p terminal &
      val terminal-value-for-w-of p &
      (val p) vars
val value-of-w-to-move p if
      not p terminal &
      (p1 val) best-w-move-from p &
      (val p p1) vars

(p1 val) best-w-move-from p if
      plist isall (q : q legal-move-from p) &
      (p1 val) max-of-all plist &
      (p1 val p q plist) vars

(p val) max-of-all (p1 | plist) if
      val1 value-of-b-to-move p1 &
      (p val) max-of-either (plist (p1 val1)) &
      (p val p1 val1 plist) vars

(p val) max-of-either (() (p val)) if
      (p val) vars
(p val) max-of-either ((p1|plist) (p2 val2)) if
      val1 value-of-b-to-move p1 &
      (p3 val3) better-of ((p1 val1) (p2 val2)) &
      (p val) max-of-either (plist (p3 val3)) &
      (p val p1 val1 p2 val2 p3 val3 plist) vars

(p1 val1) better-of ((p1 val1) (p2 val2)) if
      not val1 LESS val2 &
      (p1 val1 p2 val2) vars
(p2 val2) better-of ((p1 val1) (p2 val2)) if
      val1 LESS val2 &
      (p1 val1 p2 val2) vars
```

plus an analogous definition of "value-of-b-to-move"

Augmented with definitions of "terminal", "terminal-value-for-w-of", "terminal-value-for-b-of" and "legal-move-from" it can be used in a similar way to Move Calculator I to find good moves. For example, if we add

x terminal if not y legal-move-from x

-1 terminal-value-for-w-of (() ())
1 terminal-value-for-b-of (() ())

together with the legal-move definition for NIM we can find a good move for White with the query

which(x : x best-w-move-from ((1) (1 1 1)))

As with the similar query

which(x : x good-w-move-from ((1) (1 1 1)))

which uses Move Calculator I the evaluation will explore the game tree. However, since Move Calculator II finds the best move by using the minmax principle applied to all the offsprings of a node, it must search the whole of the game tree of Figure 2. Move Calculator I only needs to search the tree until it finds the forcing tree. However, Move Calculator II is the more general program. It can be used for finding best moves for games for which it is impossible to explore the game tree down to winning or losing positions and for such partial game trees the use of the minmax principle is essential. Move Calculator I can only stop its exploration at definite win/lose positions. Moveover, we can modify Move Calculator II in a subtle way so that it explores only as much of the game tree as is absolutely necessary in order to find a good move. To do this we must first generalise the relation "best-w-move-from" to the relation "good-enough-w-move-from" which can be used to find the first move to a position with a value that is higher than some given threshold *beta* if there is such a move. By appropriately initialising this beta threshold value and the corresponding *alpha* threshold for the analogous "good-enough-b-move-from" relation not all the game tree need be explored to find a good enough move. The pruning of the search of the game tree that the thresholds allow is called *Alpha-Beta* pruning.

12.3   Thresholds and Alpha-Beta Pruning

Consider the relation

(p1 val beta) good-enough-w-move-from p

which holds when p1 is a position with value val to which White
can move from p such that val is greater than or equal to beta
or p1 is the best move for White and val is less than beta. That
is, p1 is either good enough, or it is the best move possible. The
dual Black relation is

(p1 val alpha) good-enough-b-move-from p

which holds when p1 has value val which is less than or equal to
alpha (remember that larger negative values represent better
positions for Black) and p1 is therefore a good enough move for
Black or val is greater than alpha and p1 is the best move for
Black.

The alpha and beta represent thresholds. We should be able
to define the relations in such a way that a query such as

which(x : (x y 0.5) good-enough-w-move-from p)

where p is a game position in which we are interested, will find
the first position to which White can move with a game value y
at least 0.5, if such a move exists, without necessarily exploring
the whole of the game tree from position p.

The definitions of these "good-enough" relations will be
analogous to the definitions of the "best-move" relations. However
we shall need to generalise the "value-of" relations to "threshold-
value-of". In particular,

(val beta) threshold-value-of-w-to-move p

will now mean that val is the value of a good enough position
p1 to which White can move from p with a value at least beta
or that val is the value of the best move position from p. This
relation will be defined in terms of "good-enough-w-move-from",
just as "value-of-w-to-move" was defined in terms of "best-w-
move-from". The dual

(val alpha) threshold-value-of-b-to-move p

will mean that val is the value the position which represents the best Black move from p when this value is greater than alpha or it is the value of a position p1 which is a good enough move for Black with a value that is at most alpha. Notice that we can find the old value of a Black-to-move position as defined by the "value-of-b-to-move" relation by setting the alpha threshold to -1. Correspondingly, we can find the old value of a White-to-move position by setting the beta threshold to 1. The following is a definition of the "threshold-value-of-w-to-move" relation that closely follows the structure of the definition of the "value-of-w-to-move" relation. The "max-of" relations are generalised to "threshold-max-of" relations in order to handle the threshold value beta.

(p val beta) threshold-max-of-all plist

is now the relation which holds when p is the first position on plist with a value at least beta if there is such a position, otherwise it is the position with the best value. It is the evaluation of this relation and its dual

(p val alpha) threshold-min-of-all plist

that prunes the search of the game tree for suitably set threshold values.

The following program we shall call Move Calculator III.

```
(val beta) threshold-value-of-w-to-move p if
      p terminal &
      val terminal-value-for-w-of p &
      (val beta p) vars
(val beta) threshold-value-of-w-to-move p if
      not p terminal &
      (p1 val beta) good-enough-w-move-from p &
      (val beta p p1) vars

(p1 val beta) good-enough-w-move-from p if
      plist isall (q : q legal-move-from p) &
      (p1 val beta) threshold-max-of-all plist &
      (p1 val beta q plist) vars
```

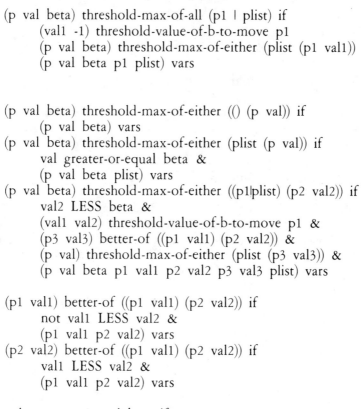

(p val beta) threshold-max-of-all (p1 | plist) if
    (val1 -1) threshold-value-of-b-to-move p1
    (p val beta) threshold-max-of-either (plist (p1 val1))
    (p val beta p1 plist) vars

(p val beta) threshold-max-of-either (() (p val)) if
    (p val beta) vars
(p val beta) threshold-max-of-either (plist (p val)) if
    val greater-or-equal beta &
    (p val beta plist) vars
(p val beta) threshold-max-of-either ((p1|plist) (p2 val2)) if
    val2 LESS beta &
    (val1 val2) threshold-value-of-b-to-move p1 &
    (p3 val3) better-of ((p1 val1) (p2 val2)) &
    (p val) threshold-max-of-either (plist (p3 val3)) &
    (p val beta p1 val1 p2 val2 p3 val3 plist) vars

(p1 val1) better-of ((p1 val1) (p2 val2)) if
    not val1 LESS val2 &
    (p1 val1 p2 val2) vars
(p2 val2) better-of ((p1 val1) (p2 val2)) if
    val1 LESS val2 &
    (p1 val1 p2 val2) vars

val greater-or-equal beta if
    not beta LESS val &
    (val beta) vars

plus an analogous definition of "threshold-value-of-b-to-move"

Notice that there is now an extra rule for "threshold-max-of-either" which allows for early termination of the tail recursive evaluation as soon as a position which meets the threshold limit is found. Also notice the thresholds of the two conditions for the relation "threshold-value-of-b-to-move". In the definition of "threshold-max-of-all", where the relation is used to find the actual value of the first Black to move position on the list of positions to which White can move, it is set to -1. This ensures that val1 will be the proper value of this position for Black in that it will be the value of the position which is Black's best move. However, in the definition of "threshold-max-of-either" the threshold is given as val2, which is the current best value of any position to which White might move. In general this value will be greater than -1. Let us see why, for this condition, we do not need to set the threshold to -1.

Consider the condition

(val1 val2) threshold-value-of-b-to-move p1   (A)

If the value of p1 is greater than or equal to val2 because there is no good enough position to which Black can move with a value less than val2 then this condition is equivalent to the old

val1 value-of-b-to-move p1   (B)

condition of Move Calculator II. The value val1 of the new position p1, since it is greater than or equal to the old current maximum val2, will become the new current maximum value for the evaluation of the recursive "threshold-max-of-either" condition of the the rule. However, if there is a position to which Black can move from p1 with a value less than val2 then the value val1 found by the evaluation of (B) will be less than or equal to that found by the evaluation of (A), but both values will be less than the value val2 of the current maximum. This is because the evaluation of (B) will find the least value of a position to which Black can move (this being the best move for Black) which must be less than or equal to the threshold limited value of val1 found by (A), which is just the value of a good enough move for Black. In this case, although (A) is not equivalent to (B), it returns an appoximation to the value of val1 that would be given by (B) which confirms that this value is less than the value val2 of the current best move for White. The current maximum value val2 will therefore be passed on to the recursive condition of the rule just as it would be if (B) were used instead of (A). Viewing the definition logically rather then behaviourally, we can use val2 as a threshold because the conjunction of conditions

(val1 val2) threshold-value-of-b-to-move p1 &
(p3 val3) better-of ((p1 val1) (p2 val2))

defines the same val3 value as does the conjunction

val1 value-of-b-to-move p1 &
(p3 val3) better-of ((p1 val1) (p2 val2))

It is this clever setting of the threshold to the current maximum that results in a drastic reduction of the search of the game tree.

The two queries

which(x y : (x y) best-move-for-w-from P)

which(x y : (x y 1) good-enough-move-for-w-from P)

where P is some White-to-move position, will give the same
position and value answers but in general the evaluation of the
second query will expore far less of the game tree.

Behaviour of Move Calculator III

This reduction of the extent of the game tree searched by
Move calculator III is illustrated by the game tree of Figure 3.
The tree illustrates a typical situation where Move Calculator II
does unnecessary work. In finding the value of the Black-to-move
root node and the best move for Black Move Calculator II will
explore the tree from left to right. Suppose it has just determined
that the game value at P is 0.5. That means that at the root the
value is *at most* 0.5: Q or R might yield a value lower than 0.5.
However, as soon as the value 0.7 of QP is known, the the value
of Q is *at least* 0.7 since Q is a White-to-move node. So Q
cannot be a better position for Black than P irrespective of the
values of QQ or QR. Move Calculator II will none the less find
their values. Move Calculator III will not find their values. The
value 0.5 of P will be used as the threshold for the finding of
the value of Q and the move to QP will be considered a good
enough move for White because it has a value greater than the
threshold.

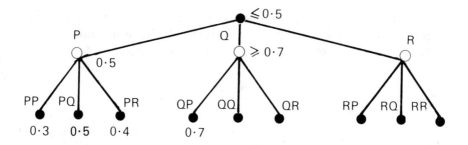

Figure 3

12.4   Concluding remarks

We have demonstrated a basic technique for programming computers to play games. The significance of the technique (or the lack of it) must primarily be understood in relation to chess. Chess is a competitive sport, a science, and a fascinating intellectual challenge. Programming a computer to play chess yields insight into human thinking. Let us first consider how minmax can be applied here.

To run the minmax algorithm requires a relatively modest amount of memory because only the information associated with a path from the root needs to be stored at any given moment. But there are so many paths that the algorithm typically takes too much computing time. We saw two ways of reducing the amount of computational work: Alpha-Beta pruning and the use of evaluation functions. The first method saves by shortening some of the paths. It does not affect the accuracy of the result. But the saving is modest. The second method saves by shortening all paths. One can save almost as much as one likes by making the paths short enough. But then the cost in terms of accuracy can be considerable.

Programs for playing the entire game of chess rely, apart from evaluation functions and Alpha-Beta pruning, also on restriction of moves and on stored openings. Let us say that these programs are of *Shannon type*, as all of these stratagems have already been proposed in 1950 by Claude Shannon ["Programming a computer to play chess", Philosophical Magazine, vol. 41, pp. 356-375]. Move restriction is very effective because in most situations many legal moves are downright idiotic and can be identified as such by simple rules, without having to go into minmax at all.

Shannon-type programs for chess have an interesting history. The earliest were built around 1960 and performed miserably, even though running on the largest and fastest computers available. Human chess players got used to not taking them seriously until about 1980 when, to the surprise of many, the best of these programs had achieved almost a national master's level. The basic paradigm was exactly the one outlined by Shannon; the change was brought about mainly by the increased power of computer hardware (just one additional level in the game tree makes a big difference, both in power of play and in hardware requirements). Improved programming techniques also had to do with it, but these did not include anything that a chess player who is not also a programmer would recognize as having to do with chess.

In a sense these strong chess-playing programs still play miserably: there is no discernible plan or theme; they are utterley opportunistic. However, they make no blunders. Their performance shows that even expert human players make a fair number of blunders and that their human expert opponents do rather poorly at detecting them. And a strong chess-playing program never fails to take advantage of a blunder.

Let us assume that a human chess expert determines his moves by some kind of information processing rather than by magic. The basic capabilities of the human brain as an information processor are known to be several orders of magnitude smaller than those of large computers. This holds for speed as well as for the amount of memory available to a human for a single problem. (The total amount of human memory seems to be quite large.) Keeping these limitations in mind, the performance of human chess experts is rather impressive. What is it that allows them to do so well? Are there useful programming techniques to be learned, allowing saving in memory or processing time?

To say that the human experts use knowledge and that the programs do not is to beg the question; at least as long as definitions of knowledge are not precise enough to clearly imply that the humans have it and that the programs do not. But without such a definition of knowledge we can at least test for a difference in nature between a program performing a mental skill and a human expert at that skill. We can ask:

* Can a human *monitor* the performance of the computer program?

* Can a nonexpert human *learn* from reading the listing of the computer program (plus database)?

When a chess-playing program is of Shannon type, the answer to both of these questions is negative. This outcome of the test, though not directly contributing to a definition "knowledge", at least points out a fundamental difference in nature between the *modus operandi* of the program and the human expert.

For a chess program to be knowledge-based both the questions have to be answered affirmatively. Chess endgames have been used for early experiments in knowledge-based programming ["Advances in Computer Chess" vol. I (1977), vol. II (1980), vol. III (1982), edited by M.R.B. Clark, Edinburgh University Press]. It is only here that logic programming, as a distinctive technique, comes into its own. An example is described in ["Chess-endgame advice" by M.H. van Emden; in "Machine Intelligence 10", edited by D. Michie and J. Hayes, Ellis Horwood 1982]. Knowledge-based programming has the potential of making software in general easier to write, to understand, and to modify. The serious problems in these respects are caused to a considerable degree by knowledge being cryptically coded in machine-oriented formalisms. Ensuring that computer programs can be monitored during execution is currently hardly recognized as a problem (see, however, "New face of AI" by D. Michie; AISB Quarterly, vol. 29, pp 14-19), but this will change, as full automation of critical functions such as control of nuclear reactors and air traffic is seriously contemplated.

13.   micro-PROLOG for Problem Solving

R.A. Kowalski & M.J. Sergot

Introduction

Artificial Intelligence is concerned with making machines perform tasks, normally considered to require intelligence. Although one way to proceed is by attempting to simulate human reasoning, it is not the only way. In this chapter we shall consider how to make machines perform certain 'hard' tasks, but without claiming that the methods used resemble those of human beings.

Traditionally, an important area of Artificial Intelligence research has been problem solving. There is a sense, of course, in which all intelligence involves problem solving. But in this chapter we shall look specifically at some of the classic problem solving techniques of Artificial Intelligence. In particular we shall look at problem solving by **searching** for a solution. We shall investigate the river-crossing and water-containers problems in some detail and devote particular attention to loop detection.

To some extent, this chapter can be regarded as bridging the gap between the specification of problems as investigated in Chapter 3 of "Logic For Problem-Solving" by R.A.Kowalski and the implementation of effective problem-solvers in micro-PROLOG.

13.1   Problem solving by search

As a concrete example consider the *river-crossing problem*:

A farmer, a wolf, a goat, and a cabbage are all on the north bank of a river. There is a boat in which the farmer can row across. He can take at most one passenger with him, regarding the cabbage as one of the passengers. Unfortunately, if ever the wolf and the goat are left on a bank without the farmer present, the wolf will eat the goat. Similarly, the goat will eat the cabbage unless the farmer is there to prevent it. How can the farmer get them all across, without any of them being eaten ?

Simple puzzles of this kind are actually very useful. We can concentrate on how to search for solutions, without worrying too much about problems of representing the 'world'.

In abstract terms, the type of problem we want to solve can be characterized by:

given some initial state, a goal state, and a set of allowed operations or moves which transform one state into another, find a way of getting from the initial state to the goal state.

In the river-crossing example, the initial state is the one in which 'everyone' is on the north bank of the river. The goal state is the one in which everyone is on the south bank. There are two types of legal move, subject to the constraint that nothing is eaten: one in which the farmer rows over on his own, the other where the farmer takes across one of his three 'companions'.

In the broadest terms, there are three aspects to solving problems by search. We need some way of representing the states of the 'world'; we need to describe the problem in the chosen representation; and we need to specify how to search for solutions. In this chapter we shall examine the last two questions only. The first belongs to the field of Knowledge Representation, which is an important area of research in its own right, for "real world' problems in particular. For simple puzzles, the representation problem is less critical, although an ingenious choice can sometimes make the problem solution very easy. A classical example of this is Amarel's study of representations in the missionary and cannibals problem [see "Further Reading"].

In any case, for the river-crossing problem, there is an obvious, if special-purpose, choice. There are only four individuals. Each of them can be on one of two banks in a particular state. So let

(x y1 y2 y3)

represent the 'state of the world' in which

```
the farmer   is on bank   x
the wolf     is on bank   y1
the goat     is on bank   y2
the cabbage is on bank    y3
```

Initially, with everyone on the north side of the river, the state is

(N N N N)

The goal state is

(S S S S)

   Now we need to give a description of the problem. First, remember that there is a constraint on what states are allowed. We must eliminate those states in which the wolf can eat the goat, or the goat can eat the cabbage.
   Let

Illegal (x y1 y2 y3)

hold when one of the individuals can be eaten in the state (x y1 y2 y3). This can be defined by:

Illegal (x y y z) if x opp y

[the wolf and goat are together, and the farmer is on the opposite bank]

Illegal (x y z z) if x opp z

[the goat and cabbage are together, away from the farmer]. The assertions

N opp S
S opp N

tell us enough about the 'geography' of this world.
   To describe the problem, we specify the possible states of the problem 'world'. Let

State (x y1 y2 y3)

hold when the state represented by (x y1 y2 y3) is a possible state. We know that the initial state must be possible, so

    State (N N N N)

We can describe the other states by specifying the effect of the two types of move.

The farmer can row over on his own, as long as the resulting state is not illegal:

    State (x2 y1 y2 y3) if
        x2 opp x1 and
        not Illegal (x2 y1 y2 y3) and
        State (x1 y1 y2 y3)

The farmer can take one of three passengers, but only if the passenger is on the same side of the river as he is. We still need the additional condition that the resulting state is not illegal, of course.

farmer takes wolf:
    State (x x y z) if x opp X and
        not Illegal (x x y z) and
        State (X X y z)

farmer takes goat:
    State (x y x z) if x opp X and
        not Illegal (x y x z) and
        State (X y X z)

farmer takes cabbage:
    State (x y z x) if x opp X and
        not Illegal (x y z x) and
        State (X y z X)

The fact that we need four rules to describe the two types of move is a feature of the representation and not of the problem itself. In a 'situation calculus' representation as discussed in Chapter 6 of "Logic for Problem Solving" by R.A.Kowalski, there would be a more direct relationship between the rules in the representation and the semantics of the problem domain. Although the situation calculus representation is more flexible and general-purpose, it is also more complicated and it would distract our attention from the problems of search which are the subject of this chapter.

The State relation as defined here describes all the allowed states in the river-crossing problem. It constitutes a *specification* of the problem: we can check whether the goal state is one of the allowed states by posing the appropriate query; we could also, if we had access to a trace of the computation, extract from it the sequence of moves which gets the farmer and all his passengers to the other side of the river.

Unfortunately, this specification does not work as a micro-PROLOG program for **solving** the problem. When executed by micro-PROLOG, the query which checks whether the goal state (S S S S) is possible,

is (State (S S S S))

goes into a loop which never terminates. The farmer rows the goat back and forth across the river without end. Re-ordering the rules for State does not help.

To see why this should be so, and to suggest how the problem specification could be changed to behave better as a problem solving program, it is useful to view the State relation as defining a *graph* of allowed river-crossing states. In effect, the State definition is an implicit rule-based description of a graph of connected states, similar to the graphs of games treated in Chapter 12. The nodes in the graph are the allowed states; the arcs in the graph correspond to the legal moves. For the river-crossing problem, the graph looks like this:

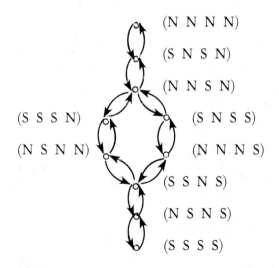

Notice that the goal state (S S S S) is in the graph. It's just as well, for otherwise the problem would be insoluble.

The difficulty with micro-PROLOG's problem solving behaviour arises because the graph of connected states has loops (and lots of them at that). micro-PROLOG's backtracking strategy unfortunately leads it round these loops. We need an alternative formulation of graphs, and a definition of paths through them, which is more sophisticated. We want to ensure that, used procedurally, this path finding definition behaves effectively even in graphs with loops. The next section presents the details.

It is useful to contrast the graphs of problems treated in this chapter with the graphs of games and activities as examined in the Chapters 10 and 12. The graphs in critical path analysis and two person games are loop-free. Whereas micro-PROLOG successfully executes their specifications, no matter how inefficiently, it does not successfully execute ours. A similar phenomenon arises with expert systems applications. micro-PROLOG's built-in backtracking is generally adequate for rule sets which do not generate loops. It is quite inadequate for rule sets which do.

13.2   An alternative formulation of path finding

Problem solving of the type with which we are concerned in this chapter reduces to finding a path of connected states in a graph. The difficulty lies not in the detailed structure of the states, but rather in managing the loops which are usually present in the graph. It is useful therefore to make the appropriate abstraction, ignoring the structure of the states, and considering only the form of the graph. In this section, we shall be examining the problem of path finding in graphs, independently of what the graph itself may represent.

As a concrete example consider this simple graph:

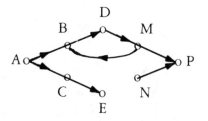

A rule-based description of the graph, analogous to the

specification of the river-crossing problem we had earlier, is given by the rules:

	State (A)
State (B) if State (A)	State (M) if State (D)
State (C) if State (A)	State (B) if State (M)
State (D) if State (B)	State (P) if State (M)
State (E) if State (C)	State (P) if State (N)

We have seen the problem with this formulation of graphs already. Since the graph has a loop, micro-PROLOG's backtracking execution strategy itself goes round the loop repeatedly without termination. We need an alternative description of graphs, which gives us more control over the path finding process. In fact, such a description is obtained when rules like

State (B) if State (A)

are replaced by rules of the form

A to B

In this alternative formulation, the example graph illustrated above would be described by the facts:

A to B	D to M
A to C	M to P
B to D	M to B
C to E	N to P

We could define the notion of paths in this formulation by including the rule

x to y if x to z and z to y

This works well in theory, but it too gives rise to loops in practice. (In fact this definition will loop even for graphs without loops!) We can give a description of path finding which behaves better, by using different predicates for immediate connections and for indirect connections. We can define, for example,

x connects-to y if x to y
x connects-to y if x to z and z connects-to y

so that the query

> is (A connects-to P)

checks whether a path exists from A to P. In solving it micro-PROLOG works forwards from the initial state A towards the goal state P.

We can also construct the actual path by including an extra parameter. Let

> Path (x y z)

hold when z is a path from x to y. Paths can be represented conveniently as lists, so:

> Path (x x (x))
> Path (x y (x|X)) if
>   x to z and
>   Path (z y X)

Notice that this definition again finds paths by searching forwards from the initial state towards the goal state when executed by micro-PROLOG.

For practical problem solving however, it is often desirable to avoid finding paths with loops in them. We can modify the definition of Path by including an extra condition to check for loops:

> Path (x x (x))
> Path (x y (x|X)) if
>   x to z and
>   Path (z y X) and
>   not x ON X

Here, the relation ON is the list membership relation defined earlier in the book. Since paths are represented as lists, the condition

> not x ON X

eliminates loops by eliminating those paths in which the new state to be included is already present in the path.

Unfortunately, this modified definition still does not work as a micro-PROLOG program. Although it does rule out paths with loops in them, it does not rule out going into a loop while trying to find a solution. Problems with looping occur because the path being constructed cannot be accessed for loop checking until it has been constructed in full. Yet this construction is exactly the part of the program which loops.

It is possible to avoid this difficulty by recording explicitly the loop-free path constructed so far. This can be represented by a relation

Extend (X Y z)

which holds when X, the loop-free path constructed so far, can be extended to a loop-free path Y which ends at goal state z.

Extend (X X z) if X ends-at z
Extend (X Y z) if
     X1 is-a-one-step-extension-of X and
     Loop-free (X1) and
     and Extend (X1 Y z)

The first rule of the Extend definition states simply that any loop-free path which already ends at the goal state is an acceptable solution. Read procedurally, the second rule makes a one-step loop-free extension to the loop-free partial path constructed so far, and then tries again.

This definition constructs paths and avoids going into loops when searching forwards from a given initial state. We can find the loop-free paths from A to P by extending the trivial loop-free path (A):

which (x : Extend ((A) x P))

We can also find all the loop-free paths beginning at A by asking:

which (x : Extend ((A) x y))

The definitions of 'one-step-extension' and 'Loop-free' are simplified if paths are represented in reverse order. So the path

(M D B A)

is a loop-free extension of the path

(D B A)

It is easy to define a one-step extension to a partial path:

(x|X) is-a-one-step-extension-of X if
    X ends-at y and y to x

Here, 'ends-at' accesses the last state in the path so far. Because paths are represented in reverse order, the appropriate definition is simply

(x|X) ends-at x

Since we have insisted that the path constructed so far is loop-free, the auxiliary definition

Loop-free ((x|X)) if not (x ON X)

is enough to do loop detection on the newly extended path.

Notice that, strictly speaking, we have defined a more general relation:

Extend (X Y z)

holds when path Y, ending in z, extends path X without introducing any new loops not already on X.

Understood procedurally, the Extend relation searches for paths by extending a given partial loop-free path forwards from the initial state towards the goal state. One path at a time is constructed, with micro-PROLOG backtracking to try a new alternative only when a 'dead end' is encountered or when a solution path is successfully completed. As we shall see in later sections, this behaviour corresponds to a *depth-first search strategy*.

But there are other ways to find paths through a graph. In later sections we shall develop a general path finding program. For the moment, however, notice that an alternative path finding strategy is obtained if, instead of searching forwards from the initial state, we search backwards, from the goal state towards the initial state. In fact, it is very easy to generalize the Extend definition slightly to allow for this alternative. We need only modify 'one-step-extension', replacing the 'to' relation there by an auxiliary, and as yet unspecified, lower level relation 'TO':

(x|X) is-a-one-step-extension-of X if
      X ends-at y and
      y TO x

Everything else remains unchanged. We can recover the **forwards** search strategy by specifying simply

      x TO y if x to y

We get the alternative **backwards** strategy by choosing instead

      x TO y if y to x

So now we can find, for example, all loop-free paths from A to P, searching **forwards** from the initial state A to the goal state P, by asking

      which (x : Extend ((A) x P))

and providing the appropriate TO definition

      x TO y if x to y

      We can find the same paths by searching **backwards** from goal state P to initial state A, by asking

      which (x : Extend ((P) x A))

and supplying instead the TO definition for backwards search

      x TO y if y to x

A solution to the river-crossing problem

      In order to solve the river-crossing problem using the "Extend" relation we need to reformulate the problem description as a graph in terms of the 'to' relation.

farmer rows over on his own:
      (x y z Z) to (X y z Z) if x opp X and
            not Illegal (X y z Z) and
            not Illegal (x y z Z)

farmer takes wolf:
        (x x y z) to (X X y z) if x opp X and
                not Illegal (X X y z) and
                not Illegal (x x y z)

farmer takes goat:
        (x y x z) to (X y X z) if x opp X and
                not Illegal (X y X z) and
                not Illegal (x y x z)

farmer takes cabbage:
        (x y z x) to (X y z X) if x opp X and
                not Illegal (X y z X) and
                not Illegal (x y z x)

Notice that, if we want the flexibility of searching for paths both forwards from the initial state and backwards from the goal state, then we have to include an extra, and potentially redundant, 'not Illegal' condition in each rule. This ensures that **both** the states involved are allowed ones.

Solving the problem now reduces to finding loop-free paths between the initial state (N N N N) and the goal state (S S S S). If we wish to search forwards from the initial state, we supply the appropriate definition of 'TO'

        x TO y if x to y

and ask for all loop-free paths ending at (S S S S) which can be constructed by extending the loop-free path ((N N N N)):

        which (x : Extend(((N N N N)) x (S S S S))

To solve the same problem by backward search we give the appropriate TO variant

        x TO y if y to x

and ask instead for loop-free extensions of the path ((S S S S)):

        which (x : Extend(((S S S S)) x (N N N N))

In both cases we get the same two loop-free paths as solutions to the river-crossing problem.

The water-containers problem

Another example to which we will refer later is the *water-containers problem*:

> There are two containers. One has a capacity of 7 litres, the other a capacity of 5 litres. Initially, both are empty. At any time, either container can be filled with water from some external source, or be emptied by pouring out its contents. Water can also be transferred from one container to the other, until the first is empty, or until the second is full. Find a sequence of these actions which leaves exactly 4 litres of water in the larger container. The volume of water left in the smaller container does not matter.

There is an obvious special-purpose choice for representing states. Let

$$(x \ y)$$

name the state in which x litres of water are in the large container and y litres are in the small one. As before, we need to describe the graph of allowed states for this problem. This involves specifying in the 'to' relation all the legal moves which we are given:

fill large container:
   (x y) to (7 y)

fill small container:
   (x y) to (x 5)

empty large container:
   (x y) to (0 y)

empty small container:
   (x y) to (x 0)

transfer until large container empty:
   (x y) to (0 z) if
        SUM (x y z) and
        z lesseq 5

transfer until small container empty:
    (x y) to (z 0) if
            SUM (x y z) and
            z lesseq 7

transfer until large container full:
    (x y) to (7 z) if
            SUM (x y X) and
            7 LESS X and
            SUM (7 z X)

transfer until small container full:
    (x y) to (z 5) if
            SUM (x y X) and
            5 LESS X and
            SUM (z 5 X)

Solving the problem by forward search reduces to finding all loop-free paths ending at a goal state of the form (4 x) and extending the trivial loop-free path ((0 0)). This is done by posing the query

    which (x : Extend(((0 0)) x (4 y)))

and supplying the forward search version of TO:

    x TO y if x to y

Notice that the water-containers problem is much harder to solve by searching backwards from a goal state than it is by searching forward from an initial one. In fact, although a backward search solution is theoretically possible, it would not be attempted in practice, because there are too many choices for x and y when solving goals like

    SUM (x y 7)

This difficulty is reflected in micro-PROLOG's behaviour: the implementation of SUM gives "Too many variables" error in these circumstances.

13.3   Alternative search strategies

The path finding behaviour of the Extend relation incorporates depth-first search when executed by micro-PROLOG. That is, one path at a time is developed in full before backtracking causes other alternatives to be tried. As we mentioned earlier however, there are other strategies which are useful when searching for paths.

Typical search strategies, other than depth-first search, involve developing more than one path at a time. In order to define a general purpose path finding program, we need to record explicitly, not just one partial path, but the set of all partial paths currently being explored. At each stage of the path finding process one of these paths is selected for extension. How we decide which of the candidate paths to extend is determined by the specific search strategy we adopt. A *search strategy* is just some systematic method for exploring a graph.

What we have described is clearly a generalization of the Extend relation. So let

Expand (X y z)

hold when X is the set of partial paths constructed so far, and path y is an extension of one of them which ends at state z. For forward search, z is the goal state. For backward search it is the initial state.

The definition of Expand is straightforward:

Expand (X y z) if y ON X and y ends-at z
Expand (X y z) if
    Select (x X X1) and
    Y isall (x1 : x1 is-a-one-step-extension-of x) and
    Insert (Y X1 Z) and
    Expand (Z y z)

The first rule states that any of the paths constructed so far, which ends at the state we are interested in, is an acceptable solution. The second rule, read procedurally, selects one of the candidate paths, finds all of its one-step extensions, inserts them into the set of partial paths, and then tries the process again. Notice that if the selected path has no extension then it is simply eliminated from the set of partial paths under consideration.

We choose the usual method of representing sets as lists.

Select (x Y Z)

holds when element x is selected from the list Y leaving the list Z.

Insert (X Y Z)

holds when list X is inserted into list Y to give list Z.

Different search strategies are obtained by giving different definitions of Select and Insert. We shall consider what are the appropriate choices for the most common types of search strategies. For the moment though, notice that we have defined general purpose path finding without including loop detection at this stage. Loop detection is not always necessary. In fact, we shall choose to specify different search strategies using the Select relation alone. Variations in Insert will be reserved for incorporating loop detection when it is required. Details of this will be presented in the next section.

Before discussing specific search strategies, it is worth reformulating the Expand definition to make it more self-contained. This simply involves expanding out the 'one-step-extension-of' relation we had earlier:

Expand (X y z) if y ON X and y ends-at z
Expand (X y z) if
        Select(X1 X Y) and
        X1 ends-at x1 and
        X2 isall ((x2|X1) : x1 TO x2) and
        Insert (X2 Y Z) and
        Expand (Z y z)

Notice that keeping the TO relation in the definition still gives the flexibility of choosing forward search

x TO y if x to y

or backward search

x TO y if y to x

as required.

Depth-first search

We have defined Expand so that different choices for Select will determine different search strategies. In particular, we can recover the depth-first strategy in a straightforward way by treating the list of paths as a *stack*, inserting new paths at the front of the list and selecting them from front. Specifically

Select (x (x|X) X)
Insert (X Y Z) if Append (X Y Z)

gives the required behaviour. A new alternative will not be tried until the current front path has been completely explored. If this reaches a dead-end it is automatically deleted from the set of paths so far, and the new front path provides the next alternative to be tried.

It is important to note a disturbing property of depth-first search in the case of graphs with loops. Exploration of a new path is never begun until the current path under development has been completely exhausted. As a consequence, depth-first search is **unsafe** in the absence of loop detection. The search can continue working down a looping and therefore infinitely long path which does not lead to the goal state, without ever finding solutions which may exist on neighbouring paths. Since micro-PROLOG itself works depth-first without loop checking, this explains the problems we had earlier with naive path finding definitions in graphs with loops.

Breadth-first search

Depth-first search explores one path at a time. Paths which are $n+1$ states long are preferred for extension to those which have n states in them. Breadth-first search is in complete contrast. All paths n states long are extended in preference to any which have $n+1$ states. All paths are thus developed in step. As a consequence, breadth-first search is *safe*. It guarantees that solution paths will be found if they exist, even if the graph being searched has loops and no loop detection is incorporated. An interesting incidental property of breadth-first search, moreover, is that it always finds first the shortest solution path.

We can arrange for the search strategy to be breadth-first

simply by treating the list of paths as a *queue* and appropriately modifying the Select relation. Any new paths generated are inserted at the front of the list but paths for extension are selected from the end. We can use Append to access the last element of a list, so

> Select (x y z) if Append(z (x) y)
> Insert (x y z) if Append(x y z)   [as before]

does the trick.

Alternatively, of course, we could have specified a slightly different but still breadth-first strategy by inserting at the end and selecting from the front:

> Select (x (x|y) y)
> Insert (x y z) if Append (y x z)

Although this latter choice is arguably simpler, the first alternative has the advantage that varying the Select relation alone determines different search strategies. We will reserve variations in Insert to incorporate loop detection, discussed in the next section.

General search strategies

In summary, we have considered what are the appropriate Select and Insert definitions for depth-first and breadth-first search. More elaborate strategies can be obtained by giving more elaborate definitions for these relations. A fuller and more detailed account of search strategies developed in Artificial Intelligence is provided in Nilsson's book "Problem Solving Methods in Artificial Intelligence".

More generally, a search strategy can be directed by *evaluation functions*. Every partial path constructed so far is assigned a value (by estimating, for example, how close it is likely to be to a solution). Now, at every stage of the search, that path is selected for extension which has the highest value associated with it. Such evaluation functions can be accommodated by appropriately defining the Select and Insert relations. Details are left to the reader.

As an illustration of the power of evaluation functions, consider a modified water-containers problem in which the aim is to find a sequence of moves which solves the original problem with the minimum amount of water transferred, say. A search strategy directed by evaluation functions can be used to solve the problem, by recording with every partial path the amount of water transferred so far. The evaluation function assigns the highest value to the partial path which involves transferring the least amount of water.

13.4   Incorporating loop detection

For practical problem solving the incorporation of some form of loop detection is often essential. Indeed, as we have seen, the absence of loop detection can be disastrous in the context of depth-first search. And even though breadth-first search is safe when there are loops present in the problem graph, loop detection reduces the number of partial paths which need to be maintained at any time.

The general purpose Expand program has been written so that loop detection can be incorporated by a suitable elaboration of the lower level Insert relation alone. So far, without loop detection, the Insert relation is defined simply as:

Insert (X Y Z) if Append (X Y Z)

That is, every one of the newly generated paths is included in the set of partial paths constructed so far, whether it contains loops or not.

However we can reformulate the Insert relation so that only loop-free paths are inserted.

Insert (() x x)
Insert ((x|X) Y Z) if
      Has-loop (x) and
      Insert (X Y Z)
Insert ((x|X) Y (x|Z)) if
      not Has-loop (x) and
      Insert (X Y Z)

If we begin the path finding process with a set of partial paths which are initially loop-free, it is very easy to check whether a new path extended by a single node has a loop. Simply

Has-loop ((x|X)) if x ON X

Any search procedure which incorporates loop detection is

necessarily *incomplete*, in the sense that it overlooks possible solutions (all those which have loops). This incompleteness is not a problem in practice, though, because the effect of loop detection is only to eliminate redundant solutions.

The Insert definition given above guarantees that every solution path found by Expand will be loop-free. We can incorporate a more drastic type of loop detection, however, by incorporating two checks before a newly generated path is inserted into the set of partial paths:

(1) each new path must itself be loop-free, as above
(2) each new loop-free path is included only if its end state is not already present in **any** of the partial paths constructed so far.

The corresponding Insert relation is a further elaboration of the one given above.

> Insert (() x x)
> Insert ((x|X) Y Z) if
>   Has-loop (x) and
>   Insert (X Y Z)
> Insert ((x|X) Y Z) if
>   not Has-loop (x) and
>   Merge (x Y Y1) and
>   Insert (X Y1 Z)

It is the Merge relation which checks whether the new end state is already present:

> Merge (x Y Y) if x already-in Y
> Merge (x Y (x|Y)) if not (x already-in Y)
>
> (x|y) already-in Y if z ON Y and x ON z

This scheme has the advantage that it maintains a more compact set of partial paths. It has the possible disadvantage however that acceptable loop-free solutions may be eliminated. To see why, consider a breadth-first search for a path from A to E in this simple graph:

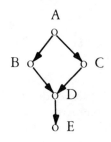

One of the acceptable loop-free solutions

(E D B A) or (E D C A)

would be eliminated at some stage in the path-finding process, because the state D would be present already in the other partial path constructed.

Clearly any search procedure with this drastic loop detection scheme is incomplete with respect to finding all solution paths. But again, there is no state in the graph which cannot be reached when this form of loop detection is included. Thus, if only a single solution path is required, there is no damaging loss of solutions. In other cases, however, where the problem graph may be very large and include many loops, a search including the drastic loop detection scheme may still be the most appropriate in spite of its incompleteness. The possible disadvantage of missing acceptable solutions may be outweighed by the saving in space for a smaller set of candidate paths to be maintained.

In summary, we have defined a relation "Expand" which simulates general search strategies by depth-first search alone (i.e. using micro-PROLOG). By choosing different variants of the lower level relation "Select" we can simulate different search strategies. By choosing different variants of the lower level relation "Insert" we can incorporate different loop detection schemes. And by choosing different variants of the lower level relation "TO" we can specify different directions for the path finding.

We have therefore the possibility of implementing any desired search scheme by a suitable combination of the lower level relations. In order to exploit this flexibility, the Expand relation and variants of its lower level routines can all be stored in separate micro-PROLOG files (or modules). Now by loading an appropriate combination of files, any desired search scheme can be obtained.

13.5   Brute search vs expertise

We have looked at the two simplest types of search strategy, depth-first and breadth-first, in some detail. Many further elaborations can be devised and implemented along the same lines. Indeed at one time many researchers in Artificial Intelligence seemed to believe that the problem of constructing an intelligent general purpose problem solver reduced to the problem of devising a sophisticated and ingenious enough search strategy. The success of expert systems (see Chapter 11) suggests a quite different approach to problem solving however.

By way of illustration, consider the well-known puzzle of Rubik's cube. In theory it would be possible to choose some representation of the cube's configuration (states) and specify the legal operations and rotations which transform one configuration into another (problem graph description). Now the problem of solving Rubik's cube reduces to finding a path in this graph. Of course, due to the sheer number of possible configurations, this method of solving the problem is quite impractical. Expert Rubik cube solvers use a completely different technique. Their problem solving is guided by a number of high level sub-goals (get all the corners in position, complete one face, etc.), relying on a repertoire of complicated moves each of which has some known overall effect. Expert systems have shown how this type of expertise can be captured in rule form.

To illustrate this distinction further, recall the water-containers problem. We gave a formulation earlier which found a solution by search. We can also give an alternative formulation in the expert system style.

The problem we have is to capture an experienced water-container solver's expertise in rule form. Such an expert might rely on the following rules of thumb:

whenever the big container is empty, fill it up;
whenever the small container is full, empty it;
in all other cases, transfer as much water as possible from the large container to the small one.

We can code this expertise as micro-PROLOG rules, so that

Solve(x y z)

holds when path z is a solution to the problem of getting from state x to state y:

Solve (x x (x))

when the big container is empty, fill it up:
Solve ((0 x) Y ((0 x)|Z)) if Solve ((7 x) Y Z)

when the small container is full, empty it:
Solve ((x 5) Y ((x 5)|Z)) if Solve ((x 0) Y Z)

otherwise transfer water:
Solve ((x y) Y ((x y)|Z)) if
        not (x EQ 0) and
        not (y EQ 5) and
        Transfer (x y x1 y1) and
        Solve ((x1 y1) Y Z)

The Transfer relation describes the details of transferring water from the large container to the small one:

Transfer (x y 0 z) if
        SUM(x y z) and
        z lesseq 5
Transfer (x y z 5) if
        SUM(x y X) and
        X LESS 5 and
        SUM (z 5 X)

Now to find solutions to the water-containers problem using the expert's method, simply ask

which (x : Solves ((0 0) (4 y) x))

Clearly, any solutions this expert obtains will be *correct*. All the moves he makes are legal ones, even if he ignores some that are available to him (he never empties the big container for example). It is harder to decide whether his solution method is *complete* however. In fact, in this example, the expert's method will always find a solution if the problem can be solved at all. The proof of this statement is left to the reader. The point is that establishing correctness and completeness causes real problems for expert systems in practice.

Blind search and coded expertise are two constrasting

methods for solving problems. We might expect that, in general, it is best to adopt a combination of the two.

Further reading

R.A.Kowalski, Logic for Problem Solving, Elsevier-North Holland, 1979.
N.J. Nilsson, Problem Solving Methods in Artificial Intelligence, McGraw-Hill, 1971.
S. Amarel, On machine representations of problems of reasoning about actions - The missionaries and cannibals problem. Machine Intelligence III, Edinburgh University Press, 1966.

Answers to Exercises

Chapter 1

Exercises 1-1

1. a. &.list mother-of
       Elizabeth1 mother-of Henry
       Katherine mother-of Mary
       Jane mother-of Edward
       Anne mother-of Elizabeth2
       &.delete mother-of 2
       &.add 2 (Catherine mother-of Mary)
       &.list female
       Elizabeth1 female
       Katherine female
       Mary female
       Elizabeth2 female
       Anne female
       Jane female
       &.delete female 2
       &.add 2 (Catherine female)
       &.
    b. &.add 1 (Henry-Snr father-of Arthur)
       &.add 1 (Arthur male)

2. You should enter the following sentences using **add** or
accept:

    Washington-DC capital-of USA
    Ottawa capital-of Canada
    London capital-of United-Kingdom

Paris capital-of France
Rome capital-of Italy
Lagos capital-of Nigeria
USA country-in North-America
Canada country-in North-America
United-Kingdom country-in Europe
France country-in Europe
Italy country-in Europe
Nigeria country-in Africa

3.   Enter the following sentences using **add** or **accept**:

Tom-Sawyer written-by Mark-Twain
For-Whom-The-Bell-Tolls written-by Ernest-Hemingway
Oliver-Twist written-by Charles-Dickens
Great-Expectations written-by Charles-Dickens
Romeo-And-Juliet written-by William-Shakespeare
Death-Of-A-Salesman written-by Arther-Miller
Macbeth written-by William-Shakespeare
Tom-Sawyer type Novel
For-Whom-The-Bell-Tolls type Novel
Romeo-and-Juliet type Play
Death-Of-A-Salesman type Play
Oliver-Twist type Novel
Great-Expectations type Novel
Macbeth type Play
Charles-Dickens writer
William-Shakespeare writer
Arther-Miller writer
Mark-Twain writer
Ernest-Hemingway writer

4.   Use the following sentences:

wheel part-of bicycle
pedals part-of bicycle
frame part-of bicycle
brake-system part-of bicycle
lighting-system part-of bicycle
chain part-of bicycle
handle-bars part-of bicycle
saddle part-of bicycle
brake-cable part-of brake-system
brake-block part-of brake-system

dynamo part-of lighting-system
lights part-of lighting-system
electric-flex part-of lighting-system
hub part-of wheel
gear-cogs part-of wheel
spoke part-of wheel

Exercises 1-2

1. a. NO. *Is Jane the mother of Elizabeth2?*
    b. YES. *Is Henry-Snr a father (of someone)?*
    c. Henry
         No (more) answers
       Who are the children of Henry-Snr?
    d. YES. *Is there a daughter of Katherine?*
    e. Edward
         No (more) answers
       Who are the sons of Henry?
    f. Henry-Snr Mary
         Henry-Snr Elizabeth2
         Henry-Snr Edward
         No (more) answers

    Which are all the paternal grandfather, grandchild pairs?

2. a. is(Katherine mother-of Edward)
    b. which(x : x father-of y)
    c. is(Jane mother-of x and Henry-Snr father-of x)
    d. which(x : Henry father-of x and
                       Katherine mother-of x)

3. a. is(Rome capital-of France)
    b. is(Washington-DC capital-of x and x country-in Europe)
    c. all(x : x capital-of y and y country-in Europe)
    d. is(x capital-of Italy)
    e. which(x : x country-in North-America and y capital-of x)
    f. which(x : y country-in x and z capital-of y)

4. a. NO. *Is Oliver Twist written by Charles Dickens?*
    b. YES. *Is there a novel written by Mark Twain?*

    c. Romeo-And-Juliet William-Shakespeare
       Macbeth William-Shakespeare
       Death-Of-A-Salesman Arther-Miller
       No (more) answers

    Which are all the plays and their authors?
    d. Oliver-Twist
       Great-Expectations
       No (more) answers

    Which are the novels written by Charles Dickens?
    e. Mark-Twain
       Ernest-Hemingway
       Charles-Dickens
       Charles-Dickens
       William-Shakespeare
       Arther-Miller
       William-Shakespeare
       No (more) answers

    Who are the people who have written something?

Charles-Dickens and William-Shakespeare appear twice because both of them are recorded as having written two things. In answering the query

    which(x : y written-by x)

micro-PROLOG finds all the sentences of the form "y written-by x" and for each one it finds it gives us the 'x'.

5.   a. all(x : x part-of bicycle)
    b. is(dynamo part-of bicycle)
    c. is(spoke part-of y)
    d. which(x : dynamo part-of x & x part-of bicycle)
    e. which(x : x part-of braking-system)

Exercises 1-3

1.   a. YES
    b. 22
       No (more) answers

c. 17
   No (more) answers
d. YES
e. YES
f. 63
   No (more) answers
g. NO
h. 3 2
   No (more) answers

2. a. which(x : SUM(9 7 x))
    b. which(x : TIMES(y 7 65) & y INT x)
    c. which(x : SUM(29 53 y) and TIMES(x 2 y))
    d. is(TIMES(x 5 93) & x INT)
    e. is(TIMES(17 3 x) and x LESS 50)

Exercises 1-4

1. a. which(x : x location (y z) and London location (X Y)
                  and X LESS y)
    b. which(x : x location (y z) and Rome location (X Y)
                  and Y LESS z)
    c. is(x country-in Europe and y capital-of x and
                  y location (z X) and Rome location (Y Z) and
                  London location (x1 y1) and
                  Y LESS z and
                  z LESS x1)
    d. which(x : x country-in Europe and y capital-of x and
                  y location (z X) and London location(Y Z) and
                  X LESS Z)
    e. which(x y : x country-in y and z capital-of x and
                  z location (X Y) and Rome location (Z x1) and
                  X LESS Z and x1 LESS Y)

2. a. which(x1 : Apple costs y & Wallet contains z &
                  TIMES(x y z) & x INT x1)
    b. is(Bread costs x & Cheese costs y &
                  Wallet contains z & SUM(x y X) & X LESS z)
    c. which(x : Wallet contains y & Cheese costs z &
                  Apple costs X & SUM(z X Y) & SUM(x Y y))
    d. which(x : Apple costs y & Bread costs z &
                  TIMES(y 5 X) & TIMES(z 3 Y) &
                  SUM(X Y Z) &
                  Wallet contains z & SUM(x z Z))

3.   a. is(Oliver-Twist published 1850)
      b. which(x : x published 1623)
      c. which(x : Tom-Sawyer published x)
      d. is(Oliver-Twist published x &
           Great-Expectations published x)
      e. is(Macbeth published x and Romeo-And-Juliet published y
               and x LESS y)
      f. which(x : x published y &
           For-Whom-The-Bell-Tolls published z &
           y LESS z)
      g. is(x published y and y LESS 1600)

Chapter 2

Exercises 2-1

1.   a. x maternal-grandmother-of y if x mother-of z &
               z mother-of y
      b. x father-of-son y if x father-of y & y male
      c. x mother-of-daughter y if x mother-of y & y female

2.   a. x city-in Europe if x capital-of y & y country-in Europe
      b. x North-of London if x location (y z) &
               London location (X Y) & X LESS y
      c. x West-of y if x location (z X) & y location (Y Z) &
               Z LESS X
      d. all(x : x city-in Europe)
      e. is(x North-of London)
      f. which(x : x North-of London & x West-of Rome)

3.   a. x fiction if x type Novel
           x fiction if x type Play
      b. x classic if x written-by William-Shakespeare
           x classic if x written-by Charles-Dickens
      c. x cont-literature if x published y and 1900 LESS y
      d. which(x : x classic)
      e. which(x : y published Z & Z LESS 1900 &
               y written-by x)
      f. which(x : x fiction & x cont-literature)

Exercises 2-2

1. a. x grandfather-of y if x father-of z
                    and z parent-of y
    b. x grandmother-of y if x mother-of z
                    and z parent-of y
    c. x child-of y if y parent-of x
    d. x grandchildof y if y grandparent-of x

2. a. Henry-Snr
        Henry
        Henry
        Henry
        Elizabeth1
        Katherine
        Jane
        Anne
        No (more) answers

Notice that we get "Henry" three times. This is because Henry
has three children recorded in the data base.

    b. Mary
        more? (y/n) **y**
        Elizabeth2
        more? (y/n) **y**
        Edward
        more? (y/n) **y**
        No (more) answers
    c. YES

3. a. which(x : y father-of Edward & x mother-of y)
    b. which(x : y grandchild-of Henry-Snr & x mother-of y)
    c. is(x child-of Katherine & x male)
    d. which(x : y child-of Henry & y male &
                    x mother-of y)

Exercises 2-3

1. a. Edward is male grandchild of Henry-Snr
        Edward is male grandchild of Elizabeth1
        No (more) answers

     b. Katherine is a wife of Henry
        more?(y/n) **y**
        Anne is a wife of Henry
        more?(y/n) **y**
        Jane is a wife of Henry
        more?(y/n) **y**
        No (more) answers
     c. Henry
        Jane
        Henry-Snr
        Elizabeth1
        No (more) answers
     d. Henry
        Mary
        Elizabeth2
        Edward
        No (more) answers
     e. NO
     f. Mary
        Elizabeth2
        No (more) answers

2.   a. x greater-than y if y LESS x
    b. x greateq x
       x greateq y if y LESS x
    c. z divisible-by x if TIMES(x y z) and y INT

3.   a. x Nineteenth-Century-Author if y written-by x and
                y published z and
                1800 lesseq z and z LESS 1900
    b. x Contemporary-Playwright if
                y written-by x & y type Play &
                y published z and 1900 lesseq z
    c. x available-at y if x published z and z LESS y
    d. which(x : x available-at 1899)
    e. which(x : x written-by y and
                y Nineteenth-Century-Author and
                x available-at 1980)

4.   a. x indirect-part-of y if x part-of y
       x indirect-part-of y if z part-of y &
              x indirect-part-of z

b. x indirectly-contains y if y part-of x
    x indirectly-contains y if y part-of Z &
        x indirectly-contains Z
c. all(x : x indirect-part-of bicycle)
d. all(x : x indirectly-contains spokes)

Exercises 2-4

1. (x x) GCD x
   (x y) GCD z if
          x LESS y & SUM(x y1 y) &
          (x y1) GCD z
   (x y) GCD z if
          y LESS x & SUM(y x1 x) &
          (x1 y) GCD z

2. y between (x y) if x LESS y as the last rule

3. x even if TIMES(y 2 x)
   x even-num-in (y z) if
      x between (y z) & x even
  all(x : x even-num-in (1 100))

4. all(x y : x between (1 13) & TIMES(x y 12) & y INT)

5. x divisor-of y if x between (2 y) & TIMES(x z y) & z INT

Chapter 3

Exercises 3-1

1. a. (wheel frame pedals saddle handle-bars lighting-system
         brake-system)
     (hub spokes gear-cogs)
     (brake-cable brake-block)
     (dynamo lights electric-flex)
     No (more) answers
  b. NO

    c. bicycle
       wheel
       brake-system
       lighting-system
       No (more) answers
    d. NO.

2.   (Oliver Twist) written-by (Charles Dickens)
     (Great Expecations) written-by (Charles Dickens)
     (Macbeth) written-by (William Shakespeare)
                  .
                  .
                  .

     (Macbeth) type Play
           .
           .
           .

     (Charles Dickens) writer
           .
           .
           .

Exercises 3-2

1.   x childless-wife if (y x) parents-of ()

2.   a. Jane
       No (more) answers
    b. No (more) answers
    c. YES
    d. Henry
       Henry
       Bill
       Paul
       Samuel
       No (more) answers
    e. Henry father Sally mother Margaret child Bob child
       Paul father Jill mother John child Janet child
       No (more) answers
    f. (John Janet)
       No (more) answers

3.   a. Dickens
        No (more) answers
     b. YES
     c. (Tom Sawyer) Twain
        No (more) answers
     d. (William Shakespeare) was a great playwright
        No (more) answers
     e. Tom
        Oliver
        Great
        No (more) answers

Exercises 3-3

1.   a. x=A; y=B; z=C; Z=(D E)
     b. x=A; y=B; z=C; Z=(D)
     c. x=A; y=B; z=C; Z=()
     d. No match
     e. No match
     f. No match

2.   a. (x (y z) x1)
     b. ((x y|z)|Y)

3.   x=(C A B); y=(A B)

4.   a. (x y) indirect-part-of z if (x y) part-of z
             (x y) indirect-part of z if
                 (x1 y1) part-of z &
                 (x y2) indirect-part-of x1 &
                 TIMES(y1 y2 y)
         z indirectly-contains (x y) if (x y) part-of z
         z indirectly-contains (x y) if
                 (x y1) part-of z1 &
                 z indirectly-contains (z1 y2) &
                 TIMES(y1 y2 y)

Exercises 3-4

1.   a. (English French)
        No (more) answers
     b. English
        English
        No (more) answers

     c. English
       Welsh
       Gaelic
       No (more) answers
     d. YES
     e. x British-language if y spoken-in United-Kingdom and
          z spoken-in Canada and
          x belongs-to y and x belongs-to z
     f. x Minor-language if (y|z) spoken-in X and x belongs-to z

2.   a. O
       B
       B
       No (more) answers
    b. YES

3.   a. x parent-of-children y if z parents-of y &
             x belongs-to z
    b. x child-of y if z parents-of X and
           x belongs-to X and y belongs-to z

Exercises 3-5

1.   .x mother-of-children-number y if
        x mother-of children z and z has-length y
    which(x : Jill mother-of-children-number x)

2.   a. which(x : y parents-of z
           & z has-length 5 & x belongs-to y)
    b. which(x : 5 length-of X and
           y parents-of X and x belongs-to y)

3.   (2 X Y)
    (X 2 Y)
    (X Y 2)
    No (more) answers

Exercises 3-6

1.   a. which(x : (Arthur Robert) have-descendant-chain x)
      (Peter)
      No (more) answers

b. which(x : (Jane Robert) have-descendant-chain y &
        y has-length x)
   2
   No (more) answers
c. which(x y : (x y) have-descendant-chain (z))
   John Peter
   Arthur Robert
   Mary Robert
   No (more) answers

2.   x is-a-great-grandparent-of y if
         (x y) have-descendant-chain (z1 z2)

Exercises 3-7

1.   which(x : y isall(z : Peter parent-of z and z male) and
        y has-length x)

2.   a. which(x : x isall(y : y family Smith))
    b. which(x : y isall (z : z family Jones) &
          y has-length x)

3.   x last-of (x)
    x last-of (y1 y2|z) if x last-of (y2|z)

4.   (x y) adjacent-on (x y|z)
    (x y) adjacent-on (z|X) if (x y) adjacent-on X

5.   x max-of (x)
    x max-of (y Z|X) if x1 max-of (Z|X) &
        x greater-of (x1 y)

6.   (a b)
    ()
    (c (d e) f)
    g
    a
    b
    c
    (d e)
    f
    d
    e
    No (more) answers

x somewhere-on (x|X)
x somewhere-on (y|X) if x somewhere-on X
x somewhere-on ((y|Y)|X) if x somewhere-on (y|Y)

Chapter 4

Exercises 4-1

1.   x odd if x INT & not x even

2.   a. the
        quick
        fox
        No (more) answers
     b. (E F)
        No (more) answers

3.   a. x a-man-with-no-sons if x male &
                    not(x father-of y & y male)
     b. x a-mother-with-no-daughters if x mother-of y &
                    not(x mother-of z & z female)

4.   a. x Overdue if
                    Issue(y x z X Y) &
                    not Return (y x z Z) &
                    x1 date &
                    x1 after Y
     b. (x y z) after (X Y Z) if Z LESS z
        (x y z) after (X Y z) if Y LESS y
        (x y z) after (X y z) if X LESS x
     c. x Banned if Issue(x y z X Y) and y Overdue

5.   x prime if x INT & not x has-divisor
     which(x : x between (2 15) & x prime)

6.   x atomic-part if not y part-of x
     which(x : x indirect-part-of bicycle & x atomic part)

Exercises 4-2

1.   x union-of (y z) if x isall(X : X member-of-either (y z))

2.   x subset-of y if
              X intersection-of (x y) &
              () difference-between (x X)

3.   X set-union-of (Y Z) if
              X1 union-of (Y Z) &
              X2 intersection-of (Y Z) &
              X difference-between (X1 X2)

4.   x flattens-to y if y isall (z : z individual-on x)
Flattened list preserves the order of elements if the last rule for
"individual-on" becomes the first rule

Exercises 4-3

1.   a. x novelist if
              x writer &
              (forall y written-by x then y type Novel)

     b. x modern-author if
              x writer &
              (forall Z written-by x & Z published y then
                    1900 lesseq y & y LESS 2000)

2.   a. x positive-nums if
              (forall y belongs-to x then 0 LESS y)

     b. x all-male if
              (forall y belongs-to x then y male)

3.   a. disjoint(X Y) if
              not(x belongs-to X & x belongs-to Y)
     b. disjoint(X Y) if
              () isall (x : x belongs-to X & x belongs-to Y)
     c. disjoint(X Y) if
              (forall x belongs-to X then not x belongs-to Y)

4.   x prime if (forall y between (2 x) then not y divides x)

Exercises 4-4

1.   x union-of (y z) if
                x isall (X : (either X belongs-to y or X belongs-to z))

2.   x last-of y if
                (either y EQ (x) or y EQ (z|Z) & x last-of Z)

3.   (x y) adjacent-on z if
                (either z EQ (x y|Z) or
                z EQ (x1 y1|Z) and (x y) adjacent-on (y1|Z))

Exercises 4-5

1.   1 factorial 1
      x factorial y if
                1 LESS x &
                x1 = (x - 1) &
                x1 factorial y1 &
                y = (y1*x)

      function factorial

      a. #(factorial (6/3))
      b. #(factorial (mod 27 4))

2.   a. (X LESS Y) #
                (*(x 7 X1) &
                X1 factorial X &
                *(y 9 Y1) & +(3 Y1 Y))
      b. (x EQ z) # (-(y 1 y1) &
                rem(56 y1 y2) & y2 factorial x)

3.   () length 0
      (x|y) length z if y length z1 & z = (z1 + 1)
      () sum 0
      (x|y) sum z if
                y sum z1 &
                z = (z1 + x)
      function length
      function sum

a. #(length (2 4 6 -8 23 9))
b. #((sum (2 4 6 -8 23 9))/(length (2 4 6 -8 23 9)))
c. x average y if
$$y \; = \; ((sum \; x)/(length \; x))$$
function average

4.   a. all(x : y mark & x = (y/60 * 100))
      b. which(z : x isall (y : y mark) &
              z = ((average x)/60 * 100))

Exercises 4-6

1.   which(sum y average z : (X a list) is-told &
              y = (sum X) &
              z = (average X))

2.   all(product of X and Y is Z :
              (give X Y and product Z) is-told & Z = (X * Y))

3.   x male if (x male) is-told
      x female if (x female) is-told

a. You will only be asked YES/NO questions about the recorded children of Tom.
b. You will be asked to volunteer names of all the males which are then checked using the "father-of" condition.

Chapter 5

Exercises 5-1

1.   (J U M B O)
      No (more) answers

2.   () (J O H N)
      (J) (O H N)
      (J O) (H N)
      (J O H) (N)
      (J O H N) ()
      No (more) answers

3. (C Y) (I L)
    No (more) answers

4. (D A M S O N) 6
    No (more) answers

5. () X X more? (y/n).y
    (X) Y (X|Y) more? (y/n).y
    (X Y) Z (X Y|Z) more? (y/n).y
    (X Y Z) x (X Y Z|x) more? (y/n).n

6. which(x : append(x x (2 3 4 2 3 4)))
    (2 3 4)
    No(more) answers

7. which((the|y) :
    append(x (the|y) (the man closed the door of the house))
    (the man closed the door of the house)
    (the door of the house)
    (the house)
    No(more) answers

8. which((y|z) : y belongs-to (a the) &
      append(x (y|z) (Sam threw a ball into the lake))
    (a ball into the lake)
    (the lake)
    No(more) answers

9. which(y : append(x (y) (2 3 4)))
    4
    No(more) answers

10. () ordered
    (y) ordered
    (y y|x) ordered if
         (y|x) ordered
    (y z|x) ordered if
         y LESS z &
         (z|x) ordered

11. remove-all(x () ())
     remove-all(x (x|X) Y) if
            remove-all (x X Y)
     remove-all(x (y|X) (y|Y)) if
            not x EQ y &
            remove-all(x X Y)

12. () compacts-to ()
     (x|X) compacts-to (x|Z) if
            remove-all(x X Y) &
            Y compacts-to Z

Exercises 5-2

1.   a. (J K L M)
            No (more) answers
     b. (F)
            (F R)
            (F R E)
            (F R E D)
            (F R E D A)
            (R)
            (R E)
            (R E D)
            (R E D A)
            (E)
            (E D)
            (E D A)
            (D)
            (D A)
            (A)
            No (more) answers
     c. (C I R E)
            No (more) answers

2.   y last-of z if append(x (y) z)

3.   y belongs-to z if append(x (y|Y) z)

4.   x power-list (()|y) if y isall(z : z segment-of x)

5.   x palindrome if x reverse-of x

6.   (x y) adjacent-on Z if append(X (x y|X1) Z)

7.   delete(x (x|X) X)
      delete(x (y|X) (y|Y)) if delete(x X Y)

8.   a. split-on(x X X1 X2) if
                      append(X1 X2 X) &
                      X1 has-length x
      b. split-on(x X X1 X2) if
                      x length-of X1 &
                      append(X1 X2 X)
      c. split-on(0 X () X)
              split-on(y (x|X) (x|X1) X2) if
                      0 LESS y &
                      SUM(y1 1 y) &
                      split-on(y1 X X1 X2)

a. is the least efficient since it uses "appends-to" to generate
canditate splittings that are then checked for the right length.
b. is more efficient. There is no search but "length-of" and
"appends-to" are both recursively defined so there is a double
recursion in the use of b.
c. only involves one recursion. It is the most efficient although
perhaps the least 'obvious' definition of the relation.

Exercises 5-3

1.   () quick-sort ()
       (x) quick-sort (x)
       (x1 x2|X) quick-sort y if
              partition((x2|X) x1 y1 y2) and
              y1 quick-sort Y1 and
              y2 quick-sort Y2 and
              append(Y1 (x1|Y2) y)

2.   partition(() X () ())
       partition((x|y) X (x|y1) y2) if
              x LESS X and
              partition(y X y1 y2)
       partition((x|y) X y1 (x|y2)) if
              not x LESS X and
              partition(y X y1 y2)

3.   (0 ()) merge-sort ()
    (1 (x)) merge-sort (x)
    (y X) merge-sort Z if
        1 LESS y &
        merge-split((y X) Y1 Y2) &
        Y1 merge-sort Z1 &
        Y2 merge-sort Z2 &
        merge(Z1 Z2 Z)

    merge-split((y x) (y1 x1) (y2 x2)) if
        y1 = (div y 2) &
        y2 = (y - y1) &
        split-on(y1 x x1 x2)

plus the old rules for "merge" and "split-on".

To sort using this program, we use a query such as

    which(x : (6 (4 3 6 100 -5 3)) merge-sort x)

in which the length of the list to be sorted is also given.

Chapter 6

Exercises 6-1

1.   a. (S (NP (DT the)
             (NE (A sad)
                (N boy)))
         (VP (V likes)
           (NP (DE a)
             (NE (A happy) (N girl)))))
    b. (S (NP (DT the) (N boy))
        (VP (V kicked)
           (NP (DT the) (N ball))))
    c. (S (NP (DT a) (NE (A lonely) (N man)))
        (VP (V wandered)
           (NP (DT the) (N hills))))
    d. (S (NP (DT a) (N piper))
        (VP (V plays) (NP (DT a) (N tune))))

2.   The extension needed is:

    x is-verb-expression (VE y z) if
        APPEND(x1 x2 x) and
        x1 is-adverb y and
        x2 is-verb-expression z

    (x and) is-adverb (AD x) if
        x dictionary ADVERB
    (x) is-adverb (AD x) if
        x dictionary ADVERB

    slowly dictionary ADVERB
    deliberately dictionary ADVERB

3.   x is-noun-phrase (NP X Y) if
        APPEND((x1) (x2|x3) x) &
        (x1) is-determiner X &
        (x2|x3) is-noun-expression Y

    (x) is-noun-expression (N x) if
        x dictionary NOUN
    x is-noun-expression (NE X Y) if
        APPEND((x1) x2 x) &
        (x1) is-adjective X &
        x2 is-nound-expression Y

Note that we can remove the "APPEND" condition in the "is-noun-phrase" rule and in the second rule for "is-noun-expression" altogether, e.g.

    (x1|x2) is-noun-expression (NE X Y) if
        (x1) is-adjective X &
        x2 is-noun-expression Y

Exercises 6-2

1.   (x1 x2) is-verb-phrase (VP X Y) if
        (x1 x3) is-verb-expression X &
        (x3 x2) is-noun-phrase Y

    (x1 x2) is-verb-expression (VE X Y) if
        (x1 x3) is-adverb X &
        (x3 x2) is-verb-expression Y

         ((x|y) y) is-adverb x if
                   x dictionary ADVERB

Exercises 6-3

1.   () D-quick-sort (z z)
       (x|X) D-quick-sort (Z1 Z2) if
                 partition(X x Y1 Y2) &
                 Y1 D-quick-sort (Z1 (x|Z3)) &
                 Y2 D-quick-sort (Z3 Z2)

      x quick-sort y if
                   x D-quick-sort (y ())

2.   (x1 x2) is-verb-phrase ((VP X Y) case Z) if
                 (x1 x3) is-verb-expression (X case Z) &
                 (x3 x2) is-noun-phrase (Y case Z1)

      (x1 x2) is-verb-expression (VE X Y) case Z) if
                 (x1 x3) is-adverb X &
                 (x3 x2) is-verb-expression (Y case Z)
      (x1 x2) is-verb-expression (X case Z) if
                 (x1 x2) is-verb (X case z)

      ((X|y) y) is-verb ((V X) case Z) if
           X dictionary (V Z)
              etc..

Chapter 7

Exercises 7-1

       a. all(x : John likes y & female!(y) & mother!(y x))
       b. which(y : written by!(Oliver-Twist x) &
                   y written-by x & published!(y z) & z LESS 1860)
There is no need to make the **LESS** a single solution condition
since it is a micro-PROLOG primitive.

Exercises 7-2

1.   x min-of (y|z) if
              x Min-of (z y)

      y Min-of (() y)
      z Min-of ((y1|Z) y) if
              smaller-of!(y2 y1 y) &
              z Min-of (Z y2)

2.   () sort ()
      x sort (y|z) if
              y min-of x &
              delete(y x x1) & / &
              x1 sort z

3.   tail-fact(x 1 x)
      tail-fact(x y z) if
              tail-fact#((x*y) (y - 1) z)
      x factorial y if
              tail-fact(1 y x)

4.   partition(() x () ())
      partition((x|y) X y1 y2) if
              (either x LESS X & y1 EQ (x|Y1) & y2 EQ Y2
              or not x LESS X & y1 EQ Y1 & y2 EQ (x|Y2)) &
              / & partition(y X Y1 Y2)

Chapter 8

Exercises 8-1

1.   all(x : employee true-of x)

2.   which((x Jonesly) : employee true-of (x Jonesly))

Exercises 8-2

1.   () ordered y
      (x) ordered y
      (x1 x2|x) ordered y if
              y true-of (x1 x2) &
              (x2|x) ordered y

2.   maplist(X () ())
         maplist(X (x|x1) (y|y1)) if
                X true-of (x y) &
                maplist(X x1 y1)

      a. which(x : maplist(double (3 -5 9 5) x))
             x double y if TIMES(x 2 y)
      b. which(x : maplist(father-of x (Tom Bill Mary)))
      c. is(maplist (parent-of (John Jill Frank) (Jim Mary Sally)))

3.   a. which(x : reduce(TIMES (3 6 -5 8) x))
      b. which(x : reduce(add1 (0 2 4 -5 7 78) x))

      add1(x y z) if
          SUM(x 1 z)
Notice that a 0 has been added to the front of the list.

Exercises 8-3

1.   x length-is y if
             x VAR &
             y has-length x
      x length-is y if
             not x VAR &
             x length-of y

Exercises 8-4

1.   a. x male-test if
                    x male
             x male-test if
                    not x male &
                    not x female &
             x ask-about

      x ask-about if
             (x male) is-told & / &
             (x male) add

```
    x ask-about if
        (x female) add & FAIL
  b. "ask-about" needs to be defined as:

    x ask-about if
        (x male) is-told & / &
        (x male) add
    x ask-about if
        (x female) is-told &
        (x female) add &
        FAIL
```

Exercises 8-5

1.   which(x : is-told Sum-is x)
or which(x : y isall(z : z is-told) & y sum x)

2.   all(x : x mother-of y & not x female & (x female) add)

Exercises 8-6

```
1.    x answered-with yes
      x answered-with no if FAIL
      x answered-with just if
          x has-given-values

2.    x Edit if
              x list & P(sentence number) &
              y R &
              y respond-edit x

      no respond-edit y
      x respond-edit y if x INT &
              y edit x &
              x Edit

3.        end List
          x List if x list &
                  y R &
                  y List
```

4.   New-Super if P(&) & R(x) &
            (either x command y & y get-args z &
                  (either x true-of z or PP(?))
            or PP(Invalid command)) & /
            & New-Super

      0 get-args ()
      x get-args (X|Y) if
            X R &
            get-args#((x - 1) Y)

Chapter 9

Exercises 9-1

1.   ((has-length () 0))
      ((has-length (x|y) z)
            (has-length y z1)
            (SUM z1 1 z))

2.   ((capital-of Washington-DC USA))
      ((capital-of Ottawa Canada))
      ((capital of London United-Kingdom))
      ((capital-of Paris France))
      ((capital-of Rome Italy))
      ((capital-of Lagos Nigeria))
      ((country-in USA North-America))
      ((country-in Canada North-America))
      ((country-in United-Kingdom Europe))
      ((country-in France Europe))
      ((country-in Italy Europe))
      ((country-in Nigeria Africa))
      ((location Washington-DC (38 -77)))
            etc..

3.   ((delcl x)
            (CON x)
            (R y)
            (DELCL y x))
      ((delcl x)
            (LST x)
            (DELCL x))

Exercises 9-2

1. ((pair () () ()))
    ((pair (x|x1) (y|y1) ((x y)|z))
            (pair x1 y1 z))

2. ((dot x y z)
            (pair x y Z)
            (maplist sum-pair Z Z1)
            (reduce SUM Z1 z))
    ((sum-pair (x y) z)
            (SUM x y z))

3. ((has-val x x)
            (NUM x))
    ((has-val (x y z) Y)
            (has-val x X)
            (has-val z Z)
            (y X Z Y))

Exercises 9-3

    ((ONE (x|y))
            (? y)
            (P x "more(y/n)?")
            (R z)
            (IF (EQ z "n")
                    ()
                    (FAIL)))
    ((ONE (x|y))
            (PP No (more) answers))

Exercises 9-4

    ((confirmed X)
        (select x X Y)
        (CL (x|Z))
        (confirmed Z)
        (confirmed Y))
    ((Select x y z)
            (sort y (x|z) fewer-clauses) /)
    ((fewer-clauses x y)
            (number-of-clauses x x1)

       (number-of-clauses y y1)
       (LESS x1 y1))

Note that we could define "number-of-clauses" using the program:

    ((number-of-clauses x y)
       (isall z (CL (x|X)))
       (length-of z y))

Index